Luke's Gospel

from

The Learning BIBLE™

CONTEMPORARY ENGLISH VERSION

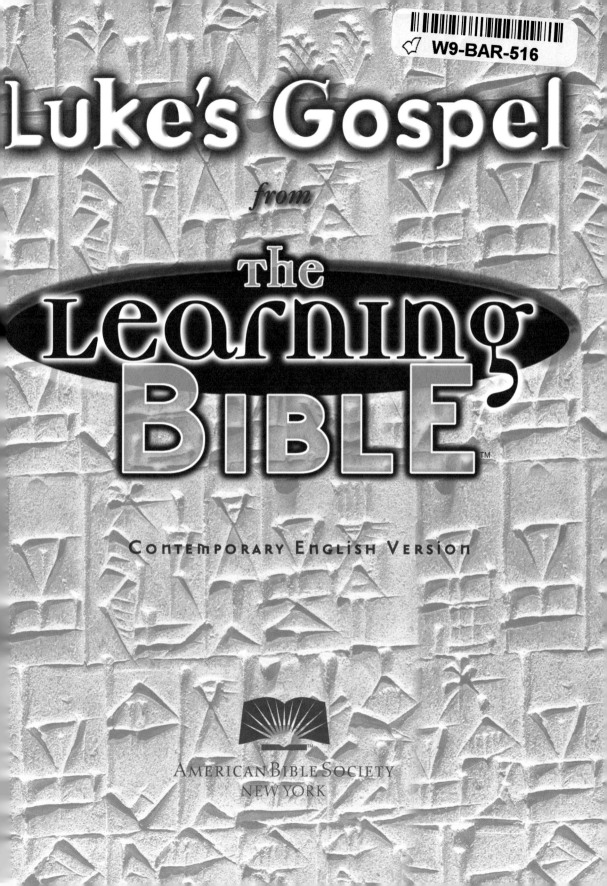

AMERICAN BIBLE SOCIETY
NEW YORK

Luke's Gospel

Contemporary English Version

Credits that appear on pages 211, 212 are hereby made a part of this copyright page.

The Scripture translation used in this publication is the *Contemporary English Version*, copyright © 1995, American Bible Society. All rights reserved.

1-58516-480-1
Printed in Mexico
Eng. Port. CEV560P-110179
ABS-6/00-10,000—RRD1

CONTENTS

Alphabetical Listing of Abbreviations

ACTS	Acts	JAMES	Jas	NEHEMIAH	Neh
AMOS	Amos	JEREMIAH	Jer	NUMBERS	Num
1 CHRONICLES	1 Chr	JOB	Job	OBADIAH	Obad
2 CHRONICLES	2 Chr	JOEL	Joel	1 PETER	1 Pet
COLOSSIANS	Col	JOHN	John	2 PETER	2 Pet
1 CORINTHIANS	1 Cor	1 JOHN	1 John	PHILEMON	Phlm
2 CORINTHIANS	2 Cor	2 JOHN	2 John	PHILIPPIANS	Phil
DANIEL	Dan	3 JOHN	3 John	PROVERBS	Prov
DEUTERONOMY	Deut	JONAH	Jonah	PSALMS	Ps
ECCLESIASTES	Eccl	JOSHUA	Josh	REVELATION	Rev
EPHESIANS	Eph	JUDE	Jude	ROMANS	Rom
ESTHER	Esth	JUDGES	Judg	RUTH	Ruth
EXODUS	Exod	1 KINGS	1 Kgs	1 SAMUEL	1 Sam
EZEKIEL	Ezek	2 KINGS	2 Kgs	2 SAMUEL	2 Sam
EZRA	Ezra	LAMENTATIONS	Lam	SONG OF SONGS	Song
GALATIANS	Gal	LEVITICUS	Lev	1 THESSALONIANS	1 Thes
GENESIS	Gen	LUKE	Luke	2 THESSALONIANS	2 Thes
HABAKKUK	Hab	MALACHI	Mal	1 TIMOTHY	1 Tim
HAGGAI	Hag	MARK	Mark	2 TIMOTHY	2 Tim
HEBREWS	Heb	MATTHEW	Matt	TITUS	Titus
HOSEA	Hos	MICAH	Mic	ZECHARIAH	Zech
ISAIAH	Isa	NAHUM	Nah	ZEPHANIAH	Zeph

WELCOME TO THE CONTEMPORARY ENGLISH VERSION

Languages are spoken before they are written. And far more communication is done through the spoken word than through the written word. In fact, more people *hear* the Bible read than read it for themselves. Traditional translations of the Bible count on the *reader's* ability to understand a *written* text. But the *Contemporary English Version* differs from all other English Bibles—past and present—in that it takes into consideration the needs of the *hearer,* as well as those of the reader, who may not be familiar with traditional biblical language.

The *Contemporary English Version* has been described as a "user-friendly" and a "mission-driven" translation that can be *read aloud* without stumbling, *heard* without misunderstanding, and *listened to* with enjoyment and appreciation, because the language is contemporary and the style is lucid and lyrical.

The *Contemporary English Version* invites you to *read,* to *hear,* to *understand,* and to *share.*

The Word of God now as never before!

HOW TO USE THE
LEARNING BIBLE

The *Learning Bible* is an easy and colorful way to discover God's Word. Whether you began reading the Bible as a child or whether you are taking on this challenge now for the first time, the *Learning Bible* will help you get the most out of the time you set aside for this important educational and spiritual experience. This short article will introduce you to the many features and tools that are built into the *Learning Bible*. Take a moment to locate them in the text and become familiar with how they work. Each feature is designed to help you in one of three ways: (1) Point you in the right direction; (2) Get you the information you need; and (3) Help you connect with the Bible's message.

Getting You Pointed in the Right Direction

When church members have been surveyed and asked why they don't read the Bible on their own more often, the most frequent replies are "I don't know where to begin" and "I began at the beginning with GENESIS, but couldn't get through LEVITICUS." The Bible is a difficult book to read and even a modern translation can be hard to understand, because the events and customs it describes happened "long ago and far away" (some as far back as 1000 B.C.). Because the Bible is a collection of many books, it doesn't matter which book of the Bible you read first. Some people like to begin with GENESIS. Others want to learn about Jesus right away, and select one of the Gospels. Wherever you begin, the *Learning Bible* has a number of tools to help you find your footing and head you in the right direction on the path of discovery.

Introductions and Outlines

Each book of the Bible starts with an Introduction, which gives information about who may have written the book and when it may have been written. It also introduces the book's important themes and provides you with clues to understanding its structure, including an outline of the book's contents.

In addition, the *Learning Bible* has Introductions to the Old and New Testaments and to groups of books within each Testament. These Introductions will give you a quick overview of the books contained in these sections and can help you decide which ones you'll want to read first.

Section Headings and Summary Introductions

The Bible text, which runs in the wide columns on either side of the book's "gutter," is divided by headings that have been added to make it easy for the reader to follow the action or the framework of a book. The large purple Section Headings are followed by short summaries of key events or teachings that will be covered in the Scripture text to follow. Some of these large sections may be further divided by blue-green headings that are printed in all capital letters. Note that both types of headings are taken directly from the outlines in the books' Introductions. The smaller, black headings that divide the Bible text sometimes are followed immediately by "parallel text references" in parentheses. A parallel text is a Scripture passage that is very similar to the one that follows on the page. These appear frequently in the Gospels, but appear in other books as well. For guidance on how to look up these parallel text references, see the explanation in "How To Look Up a Scripture Reference" (shaded box below).

Getting You the Information You Need

The *Learning Bible* is designed so that you won't have to leave your chair in order to get the information you need to understand what's going on in the Bible. Definitions of words and explanations of concepts and customs that may be unfamiliar are on the page near the Scripture text they refer to. Or, you can find them in clearly identified sections positioned throughout the *Learning Bible*.

The Contemporary English Version Translation

The translators of the *Contemporary English Version (CEV)* did many things to make the Bible easy to read and understand. For instance, special care was taken to make sure that figures of speech and customs that ancient people would have understood, but which modern people cannot, have been phrased in ways that are clear and to the point. For more about the CEV translation, see the Preface called "The Contemporary English Version" on p. v.

Notes

The *Learning Bible* provides six different categories of notes, which appear in the narrow outside columns on each page. Each of these categories is marked with its own colored symbol:

Geography

People and Nations

Objects, Plants, and Animals

History and Culture

Ideas and Concepts

Cross references

HOW TO LOOK UP A SCRIPTURE REFERENCE

Here's a helpful hint for those who are unfamiliar with looking up Bible passages. Like many books, the Bible is divided into units (here called "books" of the Bible); and each book is divided into chapters. However, unlike most books, chapters are divided into much smaller units called "verses" (usually consisting of a sentence or two). Both chapters and verses are numbered. This provides a very convenient and useful system for identifying specific verses in the Bible. References to Bible passages will be listed in the following way.

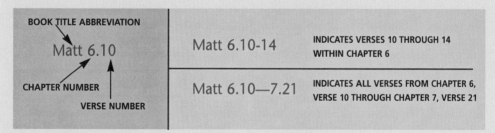

BOOK TITLE ABBREVIATION		
Matt 6.10	Matt 6.10-14	INDICATES VERSES 10 THROUGH 14 WITHIN CHAPTER 6
CHAPTER NUMBER / VERSE NUMBER	Matt 6.10—7.21	INDICATES ALL VERSES FROM CHAPTER 6, VERSE 10 THROUGH CHAPTER 7, VERSE 21

The more you look up Scripture references, the sooner you will become familiar with the abbreviations used and this system of notation. In the meantime, the "Alphabetical Listing with Abbreviations" located immediately after the "Contents" page will help you become familiar with any abbreviations you don't recognize.

Mini-Articles and Background Articles

Some important topics call for more information than can be given in a simple note in the margin. The *Learning Bible* has over one hundred mini-articles on such topics positioned at various places in the text. Like the marginal notes, they are keyed with one of the five color symbols to let you know if it is an article about Geography, People, an Object, History and Culture, or an Idea and Concept. The *Learning Bible* also includes fifteen longer background articles that give an overview of important topics. These are collected in three separate sections: (1) Articles on the Bible and how it came to be, (2) Articles on the ancient world and the religion of Israel, and (3) Articles on the world in the time of Jesus. A complete list of these articles is given on the contents page.

Cross References

Sometimes the author of one book of the Bible quotes another book of the Bible or makes a statement that is very similar to what another biblical author has written. Where this has happened, the *Learning Bible* lists a cross reference. Cross references are shown in one of three ways: (1) Listed within a note, footnote, or article; (2) included in a list of parallel text references under a Scripture text heading (see p. vii); or (3) listed without text or comment after the orange symbol at the bottom of the narrow column on any page.

Footnotes

The *CEV* Bible was translated into English from ancient Greek and Hebrew manuscripts. These manuscripts are very old and were copied out by hand. Consequently, they do not always agree with one another word for word. When these differences occur, translators need to decide which manuscript to use in the translation. After making their decision, they often list other possible renderings in a footnote. They also use footnotes to identify when the original language text is unclear and to explain other decisions they had to make.

Charts and Bible Timeline

The *Learning Bible* provides throughout the book a number of charts that summarize detailed information and display it in a way that is easy for the reader to look up.

Maps

The events described in the Bible occurred over a period of thousands of years and in places as far apart as Mesopotamia, Ethiopia, Greece, and Rome. To help the reader keep track of the way the "Bible Lands" changed from one era to the next, the *Learning Bible* provides a number of reference maps. Large, full-color, topographical maps keyed to specific periods of history are gathered together in the Mini-Atlas at the back of this volume. These provide a good overview of the Holy Land and include most of the place names you will encounter when reading the Bible. From time to time, one of the articles or marginal notes will direct you to one of these maps. In addition, there are a number of small spot maps positioned at various points within the text for quick reference or to provide specific information not found in the Mini-Atlas maps.

Illustrations and Photographs

The *Learning Bible* also provides illustrations, diagrams, and photographs to help you understand life in Bible times and to get a view of the way the Holy Land looks today.

Helping You Connect with the Bible's Message

Most people who read the Bible are looking for more than information about ancient people and customs. They believe (or hope) it contains truth, comfort, and spiritual insight that will provide them with guidance for their daily lives. The *Learning Bible* has a number of features that will help you understand and appreciate the impact God's Word has had and continues to have.

Art from Around the World

The events and stories in the Bible have touched people's hearts and lives throughout the world for many centuries. The *Learning Bible* includes reproductions of paintings, drawings, sculpture, and other powerful works of art from many cultures.

Questions about Each Book of the Bible

Sections of "Reflection Questions" are provided at various points within the Scripture books. These questions are intended to help you review the content of the book, discover what it means, and see how it relates to your life today. You can answer these questions silently to yourself, keep a "devotional journal" of your responses, or use the questions as a discussion guide for group Bible study.

Memory Verses

Many people find comfort and strength from memorizing Scripture verses. A number of important and inspirational verses have been highlighted in the top outside corners of the pages. These are by no means the *only* verses worth memorizing, but they do represent the kinds of messages that you'll discover each time you read the Bible.

It's never too soon to begin discovering God's Word for yourself . . . or to rediscover it, if you set it aside because you found it too difficult to understand. The *Learning Bible* gives you the help you need to make Bible reading a consistent part of your life. Start reading it today!

Your teachings are wonderful,
and I respect them all.
Understanding your word
brings light to the minds
of ordinary people.
I honestly want to know
everything you teach.
Psalm 119.129-131

BACKGROUND ARTICLES

·

INTRODUCTION TO
THE GOSPELS AND ACTS

·

LUKE

The Bible is like a small library that contains many books written by many authors. The word "Bible" comes from the Greek word biblia, meaning "books." It took well over 1000 years for all of these books to be written down, and it was many more years before the list of books now known as the Bible came together in one large book.

Passing Stories Along

Before anything in the Bible was written down, people told stories about God and God's relationship with the people we now read about in the Bible. This stage of passing on stories by word of mouth is known as the "oral tradition." This stage of relating stories by word of mouth lasted for many years as families passed along the stories of their ancestors to each new generation. In the case of the Jewish Scriptures (Old Testament), some stories were told for centuries before they were written down in a final form.

Long before the Bible was ever written, its stories, teachings, lists of ancestors, and poems were passed along from one generation to the next by word of mouth in storytelling gatherings. This is known as "the oral tradition."

Writing Down the Bible Stories

Eventually, as human societies in the Near East began to develop forms of writing that were easy to learn and use (around 1800 B.C.), people began to write down the stories, songs (psalms), and prophecies that would one day become a part of the Bible. These were written on papyrus, a paper-like material made from reeds, or on vellum, which was made from dried animal skins. (See the mini-article called "Scrolls," p. 186). But all the books found in the Old Testament were not written down at one time. This process took centuries. While some books were being written and collected, others were still being passed on in storytelling fashion. Since these stories were sometimes written in a piecemeal fashion, and since sometimes more than one version of a story was collected, parts of the Bible can be confusing to modern readers. For example, compare Genesis 1.1-24 to Genesis 2.5—3.24, and 1 Samuel 16.14-23 to 1 Samuel 17.55-58.

The very first manuscripts of the books that make up the Old and New Testaments have never been found, and most likely wore out from continued use or were destroyed centuries ago. However, copies of these manuscripts were made by hand and became valued possessions of synagogues, churches, and monasteries. Before these copies wore out, new copies were made, and then eventually copies were made from these copies—and so on, from one generation to the next. Some very old copies of both the Old and New Testament writings have been preserved, and they are now stored in museums and libraries around the world in places like Jerusalem, London, Paris, Dublin, New York, Chicago, Philadelphia, and Ann Arbor, Michigan.

Once the stories of the Bible began to be written down, it became necessary to make new copies before the old ones wore out from repeated use and became unreadable. Sometimes several scribes made copies while another scribe read the text aloud.

Collecting the Jewish Scriptures

It is not possible to know exactly when all the books of the Jewish Scriptures were finally collected. Some of the writings in the Jewish Scriptures may go back as far as 1300 B.C., but the process of bringing the books together may not have begun until around 400 B.C. This collecting of books continued while new books were being written as late as the second century B.C. The process of deciding which books would be part of the official Jewish Scriptures went on until almost A.D. 100. This work was often done by Jewish rabbis (teachers).

Preparing the Bible for a Changing World

It was during this time that the Jewish Scriptures were translated into Greek. This translation is called the Septuagint, which means "seventy," and is often identified by the Roman numeral for seventy (LXX). The legend of how the Septuagint came to be, and how it got its name is told in a document called the *Letter of Aristeas.* The legend says that seventy-two scholars began translating the Jewish Scriptures from Hebrew, all at the same time. The *Letter* goes on to say that they all finished at the same time, in seventy-two days, and that all seventy-two scholars discovered that their translations were exactly the same! All the seventy-some numbers in this story gave the translation its name. This Greek version of the Bible was used by Jewish people scattered throughout the Roman world, because most of them spoke Greek instead of Hebrew. The oldest copies of the Septuagint date from the second century B.C., more than one hundred years before Jesus was born. The Septuagint was also the main version of the Jewish Scriptures used by early Christians.

It is not exactly clear how it was decided which books should be considered holy enough to be included in the Jewish Scriptures. We do know that around A.D. 100, a group of Jewish scholars met at Jamnia, a center of Jewish learning west of Jerusalem. During this time, the scholars debated which books should be in the Jewish Scriptures. Probably these scholars' discussions were a large part of the Jewish community's decision that thirty-nine books should be on the holy list (canon). Seven books, sometimes called the Deuterocanonical books (meaning "second list"), were not included on the list. Today, most Protestant churches follow the original list of thirty-nine books and call it the Old Testament. The Roman Catholic, Anglican (Episcopal), and Eastern Orthodox churches include the Deuterocanonical books in their Old Testament. For more about this, see the article called "What Books Belong to the Bible?," p. 7.

The Stories of Christ and His First Followers

Jesus and most of his followers were Jewish, and so they used and quoted the Jewish Scriptures. After Jesus died and was raised to life around A.D. 30, the stories about Jesus, as well as his sayings, were passed on by word of mouth. It wasn't until about A.D. 65 that these stories and sayings began to be gathered and written down in books known as the Gospels, which make up about half of what Christians call the New Testament. The earliest writings of the New Testament, however, are probably some of the letters that the apostle Paul wrote to groups of Jesus' followers who were scattered throughout the Roman Empire. The first of these letters, probably 1 THESSALONIANS, may have been written as early as A.D. 50. Other New Testament writings were written in the late first century or early second century A.D.

The New Testament books were written in Greek, an international language during this period of the Roman Empire. They were often passed on and read as single books or letters. For nearly three hundred years (A.D. 100-400), the early church leaders and councils argued about which New Testament writings should be considered holy and treated with the same respect given to the Jewish Scriptures. In A.D. 367, Athanasius, the bishop of Alexandria, wrote a letter that listed the twenty-seven books he said Christians should consider authoritative. His list included the books already in widest use in the Christian churches, and the writings he named are the same twenty-seven books that today we call the New Testament.

Translating the Bible

When the New Testament books were written, the Greek language was understood all over the Mediterranean world. But by the late second century A.D., local languages were becoming popular again, especially in local churches. Translations of the Bible were then made into Latin, the language of Rome; Coptic, a language of Egypt; and Syriac, a language of Syria. In A.D. 383, Pope Damasus I assigned a scholar priest named Jerome to create an official translation of the Bible into Latin. It took Jerome about twenty-seven years to translate the whole Bible. His translation came to be known as

A page from the Aleppo Codex, perhaps the most accurate text of the Hebrew Scriptures.

A page from the Septuagint, the Greek translation of the Jewish Scriptures.

John 18.31-33, the earliest surviving fragment of the New Testament.

the Vulgate and served as the standard version of the Bible in Western Europe for the next thousand years. By the Middle Ages, only scholars could read and understand Latin. But by the time Johannes Guttenberg invented the modern printing press (around 1456), the use of vernacular (local or national) languages was becoming acceptable and widespread in official, educational, and religious settings. And as more people began to learn to read, there was a new demand for the Bible in vernacular languages. And so translators like Martin Luther, William Tyndale, Cassiodoro de Reina, and Giovanni Diodati began to translate the Bible into the languages that people spoke in their everyday lives.

The process of Bible translating continues today, and it has been helped by some recent discoveries. For example, many ancient Greek manuscripts of the New Testament have been found in the last 150 years. In 1947, some very old manuscripts of the Jewish Scriptures were found in caves at Qumran, Murabba'at, and other locations just west of the Dead Sea in Israel, and have become known as the Dead Sea Scrolls. These manuscripts, which date from between the third century B.C. and the first century A.D., have helped modern scholars to better understand the wording of certain texts and to make decisions about how to best translate specific verses or words. See the photograph on p. 127.

The Bible is a very old book that has come to us because many men and women have worked hard copying and studying manuscripts, examining important artifacts and ancient ruins, and translating ancient texts into modern languages. Their dedication has helped keep the story of God's people alive.

The Bible as Christians know it today did not begin as one large volume—with Old and New Testaments. It came into being as part of a selection process called "canonization." The Greek word for "canon" can mean many things, such as "measuring rod" or "ruler." At first, the early church leaders used "canon" to mean a "standard," and later a "list" or "catalog" of authoritative writings. There were many books circulating among the churches throughout the Roman world that were read and studied by the early church. It was important for the church leaders at that time to go through a process of deciding which books were holy and had authority for God's people. This process did not happen overnight. In some cases, it took hundreds of years from the time they were written to decide which of the many writings that were being read should be part of Holy Scripture, that is, the Bible.

The Hebrew Scriptures and the Old Testament

The books in the Old Testament section of the *Learning Bible* are translations of the Hebrew Scriptures still used by the Jewish people in their worship services today. These books were written by many different authors over a period of hundreds of years. The Introductions to the individual books of the Old Testament in the *Learning Bible* offer some suggestions about where and when these books may have been written, so this article will not try to deal with this issue.

It can be said that the Old Testament developed in stages and its books were collected in groups. Before the process of collecting books and putting them in some kind of order took place, individual manuscripts were hand-copied and passed among groups. The earliest literature of the Jewish people may date as far back as

BOOKS OF THE HEBREW SCRIPTURES, OR "TANAK"

TORAH (The Law)	NEVI'IM (The Prophets)	KETHUVIM (The Writings)
GENESIS	JOSHUA	PSALMS
EXODUS	JUDGES	JOB
	SAMUEL (1 & 2 Sam)	
LEVITICUS	KINGS (1 & 2 Kgs)	PROVERBS
	ISAIAH	
NUMBERS	JEREMIAH	RUTH
DEUTERONOMY	EZEKIEL	SONG OF SONGS
	BOOK OF THE TWELVE	
	Hosea	ECCLESIASTES
	Joel	
	Amos	LAMENTATIONS
	Obadiah	
	Jonah	ESTHER
	Micah	
	Nahum	DANIEL
	Habakkuk	EZRA-NEHEMIAH
	Zephaniah	
	Haggai	CHRONICLES (1 & 2 Chr)
	Zechariah	
	Malachi	

THE OLD TESTAMENT IN CHRISTIAN BIBLES

The Old Testament in Christian Bibles contains all of the books included in the Jewish Scriptures. Some Christian traditions, however, also include books that are not part of the Hebrew Bible. Most of these books were included in the Septuagint, a Greek translation of the Hebrew Bible that was used by the apostles and the early Christians.

The Protestant Old Testament contains only the books found in the Hebrew Bible, but arranges them in a different order. The Catholic Old Testament contains all of these books

PROTESTANT	CATHOLIC	ORTHODOX
GENESIS	GENESIS	GENESIS
EXODUS	EXODUS	EXODUS
LEVITICUS	LEVITICUS	LEVITICUS
NUMBERS	NUMBERS	NUMBERS
DEUTERONOMY	DEUTERONOMY	DEUTERONOMY
JOSHUA	JOSHUA	JOSHUA
JUDGES	JUDGES	JUDGES
RUTH	RUTH	RUTH
1 SAMUEL	1 SAMUEL	1 KINGDOMS (1 SAM)
2 SAMUEL	2 SAMUEL	2 KINGDOMS (2 SAM)
1 KINGS	1 KINGS	3 KINGDOMS (1 KGS)
2 KINGS	2 KINGS	4 KINGDOMS (2 KGS)
1 CHRONICLES	1 CHRONICLES	1 CHRONICLES
2 CHRONICLES	2 CHRONICLES	2 CHRONICLES
EZRA	EZRA	*1 ESDRAS*
NEHEMIAH	NEHEMIAH	*2 ESDRAS (EZRA + NEH)*
ESTHER	*TOBIT*	*ESTHER (with additions)*[1]
JOB	*JUDITH*	*JUDITH*
PSALMS	*ESTHER (with additions)*[1]	*TOBIT*
PROVERBS	*1 MACCABEES*	*1 MACCABEES*
ECCLESIASTES	*2 MACCABEES*	*2 MACCABEES*
SONG OF SONGS	JOB	*3 MACCABEES*
ISAIAH	PSALMS	PSALMS (plus *Ps 151*)
JEREMIAH	PROVERBS	*PRAYER OF MANASSEH*
LAMENTATIONS	ECCLESIASTES	JOB
EZEKIEL	SONG OF SONGS	PROVERBS
DANIEL	*WISDOM OF SOLOMON*	ECCLESIASTES

Books listed in the Catholic and Orthodox columns that are printed in *red italics* are part of the traditional Protestant Apocrypha. Books that are printed in *black italics* are traditionally included only in Orthodox Bibles.

[1]ESTHER in Catholic and Orthodox Bibles includes six additional passages that are found in the Septuagint version of ESTHER.

plus the other books that were part of the Septuagint. The Orthodox Old Testament includes all of these books, plus *3* and *4 Maccabees, Prayer of Manasseh, Psalm 151*, and *1 Esdras* which are included in the Orthodox Bible because they appear in some versions of the Septuagint. The list below shows the order in which these books usually appear in Bibles printed for each of these Christian communities.

PROTESTANT	CATHOLIC	ORTHODOX
HOSEA	*SIRACH*[2]	SONG OF SONGS
JOEL	ISAIAH	*WISDOM OF SOLOMON*
AMOS	JEREMIAH	*SIRACH*[2]
OBADIAH	LAMENTATIONS	HOSEA
JONAH	*BARUCH* (with Letter of Jeremiah)	AMOS
MICAH		MICAH
NAHUM	EZEKIEL	JOEL
HABAKKUK	*DANIEL (with additions)*[3]	OBADIAH
ZEPHANIAH	HOSEA	JONAH
HAGGAI	JOEL	NAHUM
ZECHARIAH	AMOS	HABAKKUK
MALACHI	OBADIAH	ZEPHANIAH
	JONAH	HAGGAI
	MICAH	ZECHARIAH
	NAHUM	MALACHI
	HABAKKUK	ISAIAH
	ZEPHANIAH	JEREMIAH
	HAGGAI	*BARUCH*
	ZECHARIAH	LAMENTATIONS
	MALACHI	*LETTER OF JEREMIAH*
		EZEKIEL
		DANIEL (with additions)[2]
		4 MACCABEES (in Appendix)

[2]*SIRACH* is also known as *Ecclesiasticus*.

[3]DANIEL in Catholic and Orthodox Bibles includes additional sections sometimes printed with the titles: "Prayer of Azariah and the Song of the Three Young Men," "Susanna," and "Bel and the Dragon."

the time of Moses or earlier (about 1300 B.C.), while other literature found in the Old Testament (for instance DANIEL) may have been written as late as the second century B.C. That would mean that the literature collected into the Old Testament was written over a period of 1000 years or more!

While the writing of Hebrew manuscripts was taking place, the process of collecting and editing was also going on. One important collection of books was called "The Law," which included the first five books of the Bible. "The Law" is also called by its Hebrew name, *Torah*, and by the name *Pentateuch,* which is the Greek term for a five-volume book. Another collection was called "The Prophets." In the Jewish Bible, this collection includes certain books that Christians would call "history books." The last major group of books to be collected was simply called "The Writings." They contain books of poetry and wise sayings, and books that Christians would consider prophetic or historical in nature. Because different religious traditions arrange these books differently, a chart has been provided for easy reference.

It is not known exactly how or when the books of the Old Testament were selected and approved for inclusion in the Hebrew Scriptures, but it is certain that the books of the *Torah* were accepted as authoritative almost from the time they were written. There is also some evidence that the list of authoritative books was not finalized until after A.D. 100. Only the books on this final list were considered to be Scripture by the Jewish people.

The chart on p. 7 shows the three main sections of the Hebrew Scriptures: The Law, The Prophets, and The Writings. If you compare this list to the chart on p. 8, you'll notice that all of these books are included in the Old Testaments of Christian Bibles, though they are grouped differently and placed in a slightly different order. The Hebrew word for Bible is *Tanak* (sometimes spelled *Tanakh*). This is an acronym, or a

word made from the first letters of the Hebrew words for each of the three main sections: *Torah, Nevi'im,* and *Kethuvim.*

If you further examine the chart on p. 8, you'll notice that some Christian traditions include other books in their Old Testaments as well. These additional writings are known as "Apocryphal" or "Deuterocanonical" books. The term "apocrypha" comes from a Greek word meaning "hidden," and today suggests books that have been "set aside" or given secondary status. The term "deuterocanonical," a word that Catholics prefer to use when referring to many of these same books, means books that came into the canon at a later (secondary) date, in order to distinguish them from the Hebrew Scriptures discussed above. In the 1600s, some Protestant Christians began to use only the Jewish list of Old Testament books, while the Roman Catholic and Eastern Orthodox Christians continued to use some or all of the Apocryphal/Deuterocanonical books as well. Some of these books are discussed in the following section on Greek versions of the Jewish Scriptures.

Greek Versions of the Jewish Scriptures

In the third century B.C. Jewish scholars in Alexandria, Egypt, translated the Hebrew Scriptures into Greek, since many Jewish people lived in Greek-speaking areas of the Mediterranean world, and spoke Greek on an everyday basis. This Greek version of the Jewish Scriptures is known as the Septuagint (commonly abbreviated LXX). For an explanation of this name, see the article called "How the Bible Came to Us," p. 3.

Some of the Jewish scholars in Egypt did not agree about what books should be included in the official list of Scriptures, even though a canon was being agreed upon by another group of Jewish scholars in Palestine. For example, some of the Egyptian scholars would allow only documents written in Hebrew or Aramaic (a Semitic language similar to Hebrew). Other

Alexandria on the Nile Delta was one of the most important cultural centers in the Mediterranean world in the first century A.D. Its library had over four hundred thousand volumes and would have been used frequently by the large Jewish community that lived there. The Septuagint, a Greek translation of the Hebrew Bible, was made by Jewish scholars in Alexandria.

Greek-speaking Jews included documents originally written in Greek (some of them from as late as the first century A.D.). These Greek writings included:

Historical writings: *1 Esdras* (a Greek version of EZRA in the Hebrew Bible, with some additions); *Judith; Tobit; 1–4 Maccabees*; and

Poetic and prophetic writings, wisdom, and tales: *Sirach* (sometimes called *Ecclesiasticus*); *Wisdom of Solomon; Baruch; Letter of Jeremiah; Susanna; Prayer of Azariah and the Song of the Three Young Men;* and *Bel and the Dragon.*

Though most of these titles may not sound familiar to many Christians today, many of the early Christians seem to have accepted them as part of their Scriptures. Aside from these documents, there were also additions to the Greek translation of the Hebrew book of ESTHER that was made in the second and first centuries B.C. And, some of the tales listed above were added

to the Greek translation of DANIEL (see the notes in the chart on p. 8).

The Roman Catholic Bible still includes many of these books, along with the fuller versions of the books of ESTHER and DANIEL. The Greek Orthodox Bible includes many of these books, plus a few others, such as the *Prayer of Manasseh* and an extra psalm (151). Although most Protestant Bibles now follow the list called "Hebrew Scriptures" shown in the chart on p. 7, and exclude the "extra" books, some editions include them but place them between the Old and New Testaments or at the end of the Bible.

The New Testament

Jesus and his disciples spoke Aramaic and used the Hebrew version of the Jewish Scriptures, but the apostle Paul and many other early Christians spoke Greek and used the Greek version of the Jewish Scriptures (Septuagint). Of the many Old Testament passages quoted or referred to in the New Testament, most are taken from the Septuagint. Though a small number of Christians, by the third and fourth centuries, thought that the Jewish Scriptures should not be part of the Christian Bible, most believed, as did the writers of the New Testament, that the Jewish Scriptures were the Word of God. They considered these writings to be holy and authoritative, and to be suitable for instructing Christians about God and faith (see Mark 7.13; Rom 3.2; 2 Tim 3.16; Heb 1.1). After all, they would have argued, Jesus said that he did not come to do away with the Law and the Prophets, but to give them their full meaning (Matt 5.17-19).

The twenty-seven books that are included in the present New Testament were written by a number of different authors, the earliest ones being written as early as A.D. 50 and none being written any later than the early part of the second century. Exact dating is not possible, but certain books give clues about when they may have been written. The letters of Paul are probably the oldest writings included in the New Testament.

MATTHEW, MARK, LUKE, and JOHN (the Gospels) were probably written between A.D. 60, ten years before the temple was destroyed in Jerusalem, and A.D. 100. Most scholars agree that MARK was probably the first Gospel written, since MATTHEW and LUKE seem to take many of their details and the order of events directly from MARK. Some of the other letters and REVELATION were probably some of the last books to be written, since they seem to give a picture of the situations Christians faced at the end of the first century and in the early part of the second century A.D. See the introduction to each New Testament book for an explanation of when they might have been written.

The books included in the present New Testament were not the only letters or Gospels written by Christians during the first and second centuries. It took many years of debate between church leaders and scholars to finally settle on an accepted list (canon) of New Testament books. Various church leaders proposed different lists in the three hundred years that followed the writing of the New Testament books, but the list proposed in A.D. 367 by Athanasius, a bishop of Alexandria, is the accepted list that nearly all Christian traditions accept today.

How did the church leaders decide which books should become part of the accepted list? There were probably three "tests" they used to make their decision. First of all, a book had to have some connection with one of the early apostles. This meant that either the apostle was judged to be the writer of the book, or the material was thought to capture the key teachings of that apostle. Second, the book or letter had to be in agreement with the Jewish Scriptures and other accepted New Testament writings. The third test had to do with usage. Was the book or letter accepted and being used by a majority of Christians? If so, the case for including it as part of the New Testament was stronger.

The Protestant, Roman Catholic, and Eastern Orthodox churches all generally consider the twenty-seven books of the New Testament to be "canonical" and usually list them in the same order in their Bibles.

Most books fall into one particular category of literature or another. An instruction booklet for making something uses technical language; a novel will probably use some kind of fictional narrative; a book of poetry may use rhymed or non-rhymed verse; and a book of history uses factual narrative writing. The type of book almost always determines the literary form used. The Bible is bound as one large book, but it is really made up of many different books using many different kinds of literature. This makes the Bible both challenging and exciting to read.

When studying the books of the Bible, it is important to look not only at the information a book contains but also at the literary form that the author has used. The kind of literature used can give clues about what the author was trying to say. For example, look at 1 Samuel 1.1-28 and compare it to 1 Samuel 2.1-10. These passages from the same book use two different kinds of writing. The first section is more like prose, or story, while the second section is a prayer or song in poetic form. Noticing the change from prose to poetry can give a reader more to think about regarding the text.

A brief example from the New Testament is the story of Jesus' birth. Luke 2.1-21 tells of the events of Jesus' birth and gives many details regarding the birth itself. In contrast, JOHN does not use a story to tell about Jesus' birth. Instead, it begins with a poem (1.1-14), which refers to Jesus as "the Word" and "the true light" that became "a human being." How do these different kinds of literature influence the way we think about who Jesus is? Why has the writer of each of these Gospels emphasized different aspects of Jesus' birth and identity? Looking at how a writer chooses to share information can open the way for new ways of understanding what the Bible has to say.

The Bible includes a great number of types of literature. Some forms of literature describe an entire book. In the Bible the most important of these forms are laws and rules, history, poetry and songs, wisdom sayings and proverbs, Gospels, letters, and apocalyptic writings. Other forms of literature describe sections within a book. The most important of these forms are prose narrative, prayers, parables, prophecies (oracles), and long family lists (genealogies).

Literary Forms for Whole Books

Laws and rules. Many ancient Near Eastern cultures developed law codes. One of the most famous was the Code developed by the Babylonian leader named Hammurabi (ruled from about 1792 to 1750 B.C.). The first five books of the Jewish Scriptures (Old Testament) make up the section known as the *Law,* or *Torah.* Not all of the literature in these five books includes laws, but much does. These laws include both laws that forbid things ("Do not...") and laws that encourage things ("Do..."), and were given to the people of Israel in order to help them worship correctly and treat one another with respect and care. The most well-known law literature in the Bible is the Ten Commandments (Exod 20.1-17; Deut 5.6-21). Other examples are found in Exodus 21.1—23.19; Leviticus 1.1—7.36; Numbers 6.1-21; 35.16-34; Deuteronomy 14.3—17.7; James 4.11,12.

History. In the Old Testament, history writings tell the story of Israel's history from the settlement of Canaan in 1250 B.C. to the fall of Jerusalem in 587 B.C. These books describe the activities of such important figures as the prophets Elijah and Elisha, and the kings of Israel and Judah, including King David and King Solomon. These books also include information about the events of the two Israelite kingdoms after the split in 931 B.C. Examples of history books in the Old Testament are JOSHUA and 1 and 2 KINGS. In the New Testament, ACTS tells the history of the early church.

Poetry and songs. This is a large category that includes different forms. Poetry is

LES
PSEAVMES DE DAVID.
PSEAVME I. C. M.
Pseaume de doctrine. Beatus vir qui non abiit in consilio.

This French New Testament, printed in 1664, includes psalms marked with musical notation for singing. Although little is known about the exact way the psalms of the Bible were originally performed, the beautiful poetry of PSALMS has never ceased to inspire Jews and Christians to put them to music and to perform them as part of their worship.

used especially in PSALMS, JOB, and the SONG OF SONGS. But poetry can be found in many books of the Bible. Some poems in the Bible are examples of old hymns or songs. Many of the psalms were meant for use in worship and prayer. The speeches of the prophets include poetic forms of language. Translating Hebrew poetry into English is not simple, and sometimes special techniques that are effective in the original language cannot be meaningfully carried over into English. One important feature of Hebrew poetry is the repeating of a .single idea in two similar but different ways. This is called "parallelism" and an example is Psalm 22.9,10. Other examples of poetry in the Old Testament include: Exodus 15.1-18; Job 22.21-30; Psalm 23; Isaiah 5.1-7; and Jonah 2.2-9. Poetry is also used in the New Testament. Some examples are Luke 1.46-55; Philippians 2.6-11; and Revelation 15.3,4.

Wisdom sayings and proverbs. The large division of the Old Testament called "Wisdom and Worship" literature includes poetry, psalms, stories, and more. Here, wisdom sayings and proverbs have a unique style which makes them read like common sense reflections about the world, God, and the place of human beings. Wisdom sayings fill a book like PROVERBS, but they can also be found in other books. Books like ECCLESIASTES and JOB offer wisdom along with the kinds of philosophic reflections listed above. Wisdom writings usually do not give much direct information about Israel's history. Instead, they raise questions about moral issues, and ask hard questions about life. Some of these Wisdom writings are attributed to Solomon because he was known as Israel's wisest king, but were probably written after his time and credited to him as a way of honoring him. In addition to the books already mentioned, Psalm 1 and Psalm 37 are good examples of wisdom literature. Wisdom sayings are also an important part of the New Testament. Examples can be found in Jesus' "Sermon on the Mount" (Matt 5–7) and in James 3.2-8; and 4.13-17.

Gospels. MATTHEW, MARK, LUKE, and JOHN are the four books of the New Testament which tell about the life and teachings of Jesus. These books are called "Gospels." The word "gospel" comes from the Old English word *godspel,* which is a strict translation of the Greek word *euangelion*, meaning "good news." For more about this important and unique kind of literature see the Introduction to the Gospels and ACTS, p. 22.

Letters. A number of books in the New Testament are letters written by the apostle Paul or others. These letters are written in the formal Greek letter-writing style of the first century A.D. The person writing a letter is identified first (Rom 1.1-6). This is followed by the name of the persons being written to, and a greeting (Rom 1.7). The largest section of a letter is the "body" (Rom 1.16—15.35). In most of Paul's letters, a prayer of thanksgiving follows the greeting (Rom 1.8-15),

Paul traveled to many parts of the Roman Empire preaching the Good News about Jesus Christ. As he moved from place to place he wrote to many of the churches he helped set up in different cities to give them encouragement and advice. These letters, an important part of the New Testament, are the only documents we have from this great "Apostle to the Gentiles."

and a final greeting and blessing closes the letter (Rom 16.1-27). Within each letter a number of different kinds of literature can be found, including prayers, instructions, teaching, wisdom, warnings, hymns or songs, and personal news.

Some writings in the New Testament that have also been called "letters" deal with more general questions that would be of concern to Christian communities almost anywhere. HEBREWS is an example of this type. Brief letters to the Seven Churches of Asia Minor appear in Revelation 2,3. The Bible books that are letters or written in the style of letters can be found after ACTS and before REVELATION.

Apocalyptic writings. "Apocalyptic" comes from the Greek word *apokalypsis*, meaning "a revealing or an unveiling." This type of literature is sometimes called prophecy (see p. 16 for more about prophecies).

Like prophecy, apocalyptic writings deal with future events, but apocalyptic writings have certain other features that make them unique. For instance, apocalyptic literature contains visions from God, people appearing in the shape of animals or beasts, colors and numbers that have secret meanings, and predictions about a coming Day of the LORD. They were usually written during times of trouble and speak of a time when God will bring in a new creation, and everyone who has been faithful will live with God forever. DANIEL and REVELATION are two books most commonly identified as apocalyptic literature.

Literary Forms for Sections in Books

Prose narrative. Prose is a term that describes many forms of narrative and descriptive literature. Prose is often used when telling stories about people and historical events. It can include dialogue. Most of the Bible is written in prose. A very common form of prose in the Bible is the story. Some stories are short and are told in a few chapters within a book like the stories of Noah (Gen 6–10) and Joseph (Gen 37.1—47.26). Other stories take up a whole book, like RUTH, or ESTHER. As described earlier, the Gospels tell the story of Jesus' life, death, and resurrection. But the Gospels contain other stories as well, such as the story of John the Baptist (Matt 3.1-17; 11.1-19; 14.1-12). ACTS tells many stories about Peter, Paul, and other followers of Jesus who preached the good news about Jesus Christ.

Prayers. Prayers appear in the Bible in both prose and poetry. What makes "prayer" a unique category of literature is that it expresses direct communication between people and their God. PSALMS contains many prayers that are written in poetic form. Some psalm prayers were written for group worship when all the people came together to ask for God's help (Ps 79; 80), to give thanks to God at the time of harvest (Ps 126), or to celebrate the crowning of a new king (Ps 21). Other psalm prayers are more personal. They were used as individual prayers expressing sadness, asking for help, giving thanks, or asking for forgiveness, (see Ps 12; 51; 120; 138). Prayers can be found throughout the Bible. (Some examples are Gen 18.27,28; Exod 17.4; Judg 5.2-31; 1 Sam 2.1-10; 1 Kgs 3.6-9; Jon 2.2-9; Luke 11.2-4; 22.42; John 17.1-26; Rom 16.25-27; and Heb 13.21.) Perhaps the most famous prayer in the Bible is the one Jesus taught his disciples (Matt 6.9-13).

Prophecies. Prophecies, or prophetic speeches, make up a large portion of the Old Testament. Many prophetic speeches (also called oracles) begin with the phrase "The LORD has said" or "The LORD God says." This phrase makes it clear that the message given by the prophets is not their own, but comes from God. Prophetic speeches often look like Hebrew poetry and even use some of the features of poetry, such as parallelism. The books of prophecy in the Old Testament often combine a story giving information

Jesus' parables have been a rich source of inspiration for artists over the centuries. This nineteenth century engraving shows the different kinds of soil Jesus described in his parable of the Sower (Luke 8.4-15).

about the prophet and his work along with his prophetic messages from God. Vivid examples of prophecies in the Old Testament include Isa 1.2-31; 10.24-27; Jer 2; Ezek 36.22-32; Amos 5.4-27; and Zech 9.1-17. The New Testament includes examples of prophetic speeches as well, especially when telling the stories of John the Baptist and Jesus (Matt 3.1-12; 24.1-31). See also 2 Pet 3.8-13.

Parables. Parables are stories about familiar, everyday things that were told in order to teach an important truth about God and life in God's kingdom. The Gospels show that Jesus used parables frequently when talking to his disciples and to the crowd who came to hear him speak. Parables can be very short (Matt 13.44-48 is made up of three very short parables); or they can be somewhat longer, involving several characters or images (Luke 10.30-37; 15.11-32).

Long family lists (genealogies). A number of long family lists appear in the Bible. They trace the family background of important figures in Israel's history and show how people are related to one another. One particularly important list found at the beginning of MATTHEW traces Jesus' family line back to King David (Matt 1.1-17). The author of MATTHEW included this genealogy in his Gospel to show that Jesus was descended from King David and that he was the Messiah that the prophets said would come to save the people. Although it is not always clear why a list of a person's ancestors is given in the Bible, it is clear that for the people of Israel, and other people in the ancient Near East, family connections were important. Some other genealogies and lists of names are found in Genesis 5.1-32; 1 Chronicles 1–8; Ezra 8.2-14.

Translation is the process of communicating a message into a language that is different from the one in which the message was originally written. The message may be in a song, a poem, a story, directions, a telephone message, or a sermon. But if a person is not able to understand that message because it is written or told in an unfamiliar language, the message must be translated. Without the process of translation, that message will never be effectively communicated to a new audience (group of listeners). The message may be heard, but it will not be understood. This is especially important when the Bible is the message to be communicated.

The Bible is made up of several individual books that were written and told long ago in various languages quite unfamiliar to us today. These books came together over a period of more than a thousand years to form what we know as the Bible. None of these books was originally written in English (or Spanish or most other languages used throughout the world today). They were written in ancient Hebrew and Aramaic (for the Hebrew Scriptures/Old Testament) and in Greek (for the New Testament). Without Bible translation, people today would have to learn these three languages in order to read and understand the words of the Bible!

The Beginnings of Bible Translation

The work of translating the Bible began around 250 B.C. when a group of Jewish scholars translated the Hebrew Scriptures into Greek because many Jewish people were living in places where Greek was the everyday language. This translation is known as the Septuagint. The purpose of the Septuagint was clear: to communicate the Hebrew Scriptures in the language familiar to most of the Jewish people in these particular places.

Since that first Bible translation, the words of both the Hebrew Scriptures and the New Testament have been translated into hundreds of languages. These languages include ancient languages (like Coptic, Arabic, Latin, and Syriac), as well as more recent, modern languages (like Portuguese, Russian, Navajo, Danish, Spanish, and English). The purpose behind all these Bible translations is exactly the same as that behind the Septuagint: to put the words of the Bible into a language that people will understand.

How Is Bible Translation Done?

Until recently, most Bible translations were done according to an approach called "formal equivalence" (or "word-for-word translation"). The goal of the formal equivalence approach is to communicate both the words and the grammatical structure (the "form") of the original language (or source language) into the other language (or receptor language). Such an approach would suggest that the translation is truly accurate and precise. What sometimes happens, however, is that the translation looks and sounds unnatural in the receptor language because it does not follow the rules of grammar and sentence structure of that language.

In the 1960s, a new way of thinking about Bible translation developed based on recent theories in communication that focused more on the needs of the audience than on the form of the message. The result was another approach for Bible translation. This new approach is called "functional equivalence" translation and emphasizes the need to translate the *meaning* of the words in whole thought units (like phrases, sentences, and paragraphs), rather than translating the individual words themselves. This approach is more concerned about the "function" of the words which carry meaning than about their "form."

Whether using a formal equivalence approach or a functional equivalence approach, Bible translators are always concerned to use the best Hebrew and Greek manuscripts available for their work. Translators base their translations on "critical editions" (or standard editions) of the Hebrew Scriptures and the New Testament, which offer careful assessments of all available ancient biblical manuscripts. These critical editions ensure that the translations are based on the most accurate and reliable manuscripts available.

Translating the Bible into English

The story of the translation of the Bible into English is long and complex. The chart of the English Bible on p. 19 helps to sort through many of the difficulties in understanding this history. It is important to remember, though, that each of these English Bible translations set out to make versions of the Bible that were reliable and understandable to various audiences.

One of the most important Bible translators was the Englishman William Tyndale (1484-1536), often called "The Father of the English Bible." Tyndale wanted to make the Scriptures understandable to all people. But due to the political and religious tensions that existed throughout Europe during the Reformation (14th-17th centuries), he was unable to get permission to do his translation in England. So he went to Germany, where he published his New Testament in February, 1526. Though he experienced a great deal of opposition, he continued his work of translating the Old Testament from Hebrew, and he published the Pentateuch (GENESIS through DEUTERONOMY) in 1530. In 1536, Tyndale was found guilty of heresy, and in October of that same year, he was strangled and burned at the stake.

Tyndale's work and influence can still be seen in what is surely the most significant English Bible translation ever done, the King James Version of the Bible, published in 1611. The King James Version (also called the Authorized Version) was prepared at the request of King James I of England at a time when several sectarian versions of the English Bible were in use (most notably the Geneva Bible, favored by Puritans, and the Bishops' and Great Bibles used by the official Church of England; see the chart). Although there was resistance to the King James Version at first (since many people felt a loyalty to their own sectarian translations), it eventually won wide acceptance and became the standard English version of the Bible in the English-speaking world for three centuries. The style of the King James Version is at times unfamiliar to us today because of its very literal dependence on Hebrew and Greek sources (clearly, a "formal" equivalence approach). Still, it remains one of the most widely used English translations of the Bible today.

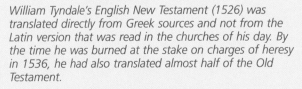

William Tyndale's English New Testament (1526) was translated directly from Greek sources and not from the Latin version that was read in the churches of his day. By the time he was burned at the stake on charges of heresy in 1536, he had also translated almost half of the Old Testament.

The Bible in English

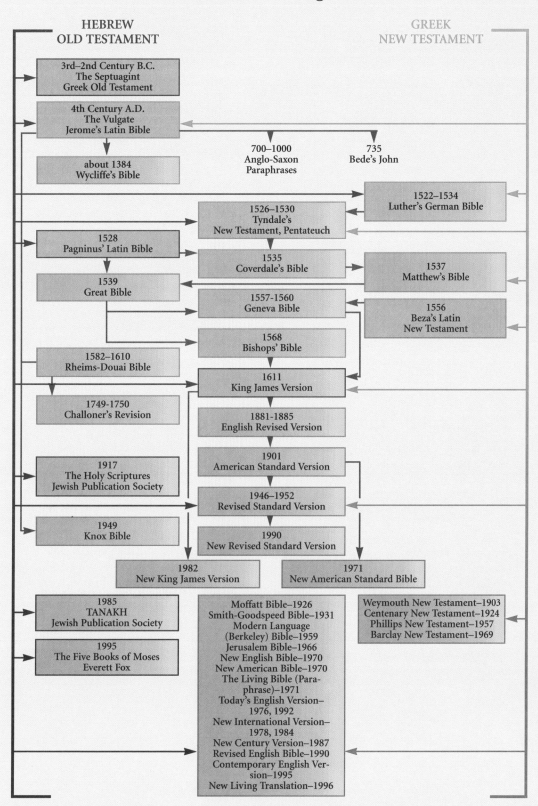

HEBREW
OLD TESTAMENT

GREEK
NEW TESTAMENT

3rd–2nd Century B.C.
The Septuagint
Greek Old Testament

4th Century A.D.
The Vulgate
Jerome's Latin Bible

about 1384
Wycliffe's Bible

700–1000
Anglo-Saxon
Paraphrases

735
Bede's John

1522–1534
Luther's German Bible

1526–1530
Tyndale's
New Testament, Pentateuch

1528
Pagninus' Latin Bible

1535
Coverdale's Bible

1537
Matthew's Bible

1539
Great Bible

1557-1560
Geneva Bible

1556
Beza's Latin
New Testament

1582–1610
Rheims-Douai Bible

1568
Bishops' Bible

1611
King James Version

1749-1750
Challoner's Revision

1881-1885
English Revised Version

1917
The Holy Scriptures
Jewish Publication Society

1901
American Standard Version

1946–1952
Revised Standard Version

1949
Knox Bible

1990
New Revised Standard Version

1982
New King James Version

1971
New American Standard Bible

1985
TANAKH
Jewish Publication Society

1995
The Five Books of Moses
Everett Fox

Moffatt Bible–1926
Smith-Goodspeed Bible–1931
Modern Language
(Berkeley) Bible–1959
Jerusalem Bible–1966
New English Bible–1970
New American Bible–1970
The Living Bible (Para-
phrase)–1971
Today's English Version–
1976, 1992
New International Version–
1978, 1984
New Century Version–1987
Revised English Bible–1990
Contemporary English Ver-
sion–1995
New Living Translation–1996

Weymouth New Testament–1903
Centenary New Testament–1924
Phillips New Testament–1957
Barclay New Testament–1969

Why So Many English Bible Translations?

Since the publication of the King James Version, there have been dozens of English Bible translations. Many of them are based on the formal equivalence approach to Bible translation (like the New Revised Standard Version and the *Tanakh*), and others use the functional equivalence approach (like the Contemporary English Version and the New Living Translation). With so many different English Bible translations done over the past several hundred years, including quite a number of new ones published in the recent past, the Bible reader today must wonder why there are so many of them.

First, languages constantly change. New words are always being added and others take on different or added meanings. For example, only recently have we begun using the word "internet" as part of every-day speech. And when we hear the word "cool" in a conversation today, it is not always referring to the weather! These two words are examples of how the English language has recently changed.

Second, Bible scholars are always learning new things about ancient Israel and the Near East that can help us better understand the historical and cultural context out from which the Bible emerged. For example, we understand much more clearly today the way the various social classes interacted in the ancient world, as well as the more intimate workings of families, clans, and tribes in ancient Israel. Such discoveries sometimes affect how we understand the words and stories of the Bible. In addition, archaeologists continue to find documents and libraries that help translators understand the ancient Hebrew and Greek languages better, and so help them translate the Bible more accurately. For example, the King James Version translates 1 Samuel 17.22 like this: "And David left his carriage in the hand of the keeper of the carriage, and ran into the army." The translators had difficulty with one of the Hebrew words in the manuscripts they used, and translated "his carriage" and "keeper of the carriage" based on the context of the narrative. As translators learned more about the Hebrew language and its vocabulary, however, they understood that the verse did not talk about David's "carriage," but about the "carried things" or "baggage" that he had with him for the soldiers in the army. And so, the translators of the Revised Standard Version (published in 1952) were able to translate the same verse more accurately: "And David left the things in charge of the keeper of the baggage, and ran to the ranks."

Among recent archaeological discoveries that help translators understand Hebrew and Greek better are the famous Dead Sea Scrolls. This very important discovery consists of a huge collection of manuscripts (including important copies of the Scriptures themselves) which shed light on ancient Israel, the Hebrew language, the beginnings of the early Church, and the way the Scriptures were organized and used by ancient communities.

With so many translations of the Bible available today in English and other languages, it is important to remember that no matter who does a Bible translation or which basic approach is used, the purpose is to make the Bible reliable and understandable to those who want to read and hear its message of justice, hope, and love. Without the skill, sacrifice, and efforts of Bible translators, the message of the Bible might have been lost to us forever.

THE GOSPELS AND ACTS

THE FOUR GOSPELS (MATTHEW, MARK, LUKE, and JOHN) present various accounts of the life and teachings of Jesus Christ. ACTS gives a detailed report of what happened to some of Jesus' early followers as they carried the message about Jesus from Jerusalem to the other areas of the Roman Empire.

The word "Gospel" comes from an Old English word that means "good news." The Greek word that is translated as "gospel" or "good news" is *euangelion* (see Mark 1.1). The English words "evangelist" and "evangelism" also come from this word. An evangelist is one who tells good news.

The Gospels were probably written down in their present form between thirty and sixty years after Jesus' crucifixion. Since Jesus himself left no writings, the Gospels record stories and eyewitness descriptions that had been passed on by word of mouth for a number of years. At first, Jesus' followers were so eager to tell the message about him that they didn't think it was necessary to write down what he had said and done. But as Jesus' first followers and eyewitnesses grew older and died, it became more important to have a written record of what Jesus did and taught, and to describe his death and how God brought him back to life.

Although other "gospels" about Jesus were written and circulated, the only ones accepted as reliable by the whole church were MATTHEW, MARK, LUKE, and JOHN. It is not certain who actually wrote these Gospels, since the names of the authors are never given in the books themselves. Most likely they were written by early followers of Christ who heard about Jesus from one or more of Jesus' first disciples. For more about how these four Gospels became part of the New Testament, see the article called "What Books Belong in the Bible?," p. 7.

Many sources were used to write the Gospels. These sources probably included various collections of Jesus' sayings and stories that were available to the Gospel writers. For example, a number of Jesus' sayings are similar in MATTHEW and LUKE, so they may have been working with the same source. Both of them also appear to have used MARK for their basic outlines. But MATTHEW and LUKE also used different sources to describe the events surrounding Jesus' birth, since MARK has nothing to say about Jesus' childhood. MATTHEW, MARK, and LUKE have so much material in common and follow the same basic outline, that they are sometimes referred to as the "Synoptic" Gospels (from the Greek word *synopsis*, which means "seeing together").

The three Synoptic Gospels are more like each other than any of them is like JOHN. While MATTHEW, MARK, and LUKE focus on Jesus' public teaching and miracle working in Galilee, JOHN contains information about Jesus' early work in Judea. JOHN also contains some of Jesus' sayings that are not found in the other Gospels. These include the so-called "I am" sayings, such as "I am the bread that gives life!" (John 6.35) and "I am the light for the world!" (John 8.12). The order of events in JOHN does not follow the order shared by the Synoptic Gospels. And JOHN does not include any of Jesus' stories (parables) that are found in the other three Gospels. For more about what makes each of these accounts of Jesus' life and ministry unique, see the Introductions to each Gospel.

Although the identity of the author of ACTS is not known, scholars agree that it was written by the same person who wrote LUKE. Besides being addressed to someone known as Theophilus (Luke 1.1-4; Acts 1.1), these books share a written style of Greek that is more formal than the Greek used in the other Gospels or in any other book of the New Testament. A number of common themes also tie these two books together as the work of one author. These themes are listed in the Introductions to the individual books of LUKE and ACTS.

LUKE

"Timing is everything," so the saying goes.
Read Luke to find about how God chose Jesus
and sent him to earth when the time was right.

Holy Spirit: The Holy Spirit is very important in both LUKE and ACTS as God's power at work in the world. The Holy Spirit does miraculous things like causing the virgin Mary to become pregnant. The Holy Spirit leads people (Luke 4.1, 14; Acts 8.29, 39) and gives them special power, such as the ability to preach about Jesus (Acts 2.1-11). The Holy Spirit gave the first apostles courage to preach and helped the church grow and become stronger (Acts 9.31). See also the mini-article called "Holy Spirit," p. 169.

Elijah: Elijah was a prophet in Israel more than 800 years before Jesus was born. His name means, "My god is Yahweh." Yahweh was the Hebrew name for Israel's God. Elijah was known for his power to work miracles and for his strong desire for people to worship only Yahweh. Later prophets expected God to send Elijah back to earth to warn people of God's judgment (Mal 3.1-4; 4.5,6). Some people thought John the Baptist was Elijah come back again (see Mark 6.14,15). For more, see the mini-article called "Elijah," p. 162.

WHAT MAKES LUKE SPECIAL?

LUKE is the first part of a two-volume work that includes ACTS. This is clear from the introductions to both books (see Luke 1.1-4 and Acts 1.1-5). These books together tell about the life of Jesus from his birth until he was taken to heaven (LUKE). Then they report how the early followers of Jesus continued to spread the teachings of Jesus and tell about his life (ACTS).

WHY WAS LUKE WRITTEN?

The author of LUKE says that he has "made a careful study of everything and then decided to write and tell you exactly what took place" (1.3) concerning Jesus. The book is dedicated to Theophilus, a friend or supporter.

WHAT'S THE STORY BEHIND THE SCENE?

LUKE was likely created from at least three different sources: (1) the book of MARK; (2) a collection of Jesus' sayings, which MATTHEW also used; and (3) a collection of stories not included in any other Gospel. Luke probably wrote this Gospel some time after A.D. 70, the year the Romans destroyed Jerusalem and the temple while putting down a Jewish revolt. Luke 19.43,44 appears to give details of this event. LUKE's stories about the birth of Jesus are more detailed than those of any other New Testament book. And some familiar stories told by Jesus are found only in LUKE: "The Good Samaritan" (10.25-37), "One Sheep" (15.1-7), and "Two Sons" (15.11-32). LUKE is the only Gospel that tells how Jesus visited the home of the hated tax collector named Zacchaeus (19.1-10) and promised life in paradise to a dying criminal (23.39-43).

LUKE, like the book of ACTS, often mentions God's Holy Spirit (1.15, 35; 4.1, 14, 18; 10.21; 11.13). LUKE also shows how important prayer was to Jesus (3.21; 6.12; 9.18; and 23.34,46). From LUKE we learn of three stories that Jesus used in teaching about prayer (11.5-9; 18.1-8, 9-14).

Jesus' concern for the poor is an important theme in LUKE. The good news is preached to them (4.18; 7.22); they receive God's blessings (6.20); they are invited to a great banquet (14.13,21); the poor beggar named Lazarus is taken to heaven by angels (16.20,22); and Jesus commands his disciples to sell what they have and give the money to the poor (12.33).

Traditionally, the writer of LUKE and ACTS has been identified as the companion and co-worker of Paul (Phlm 24; Col 4.14).

He wrote in the style of the Greek and Roman historians and biographers of his day. Many think that he was not Jewish and lived outside of Judea, and that he was writing for a Gentile audience (see the mini-article called "Gentiles," p. 166). This is supported by a key theme in LUKE: God sent Jesus to be the Savior of all people, both Jews and Gentiles.

HOW IS LUKE CONSTRUCTED?

Note in the following outline how LUKE is organized around important events in Jesus' life and the places where these events happen.

1.1 *the story of what God has done among us:* In this brief introduction (1.1-4), the author of LUKE shows that he is aware that others have tried to tell the story about Jesus' miracles and teachings and about how Jesus died and was raised to life. Such stories are called "Gospels," an Old English word that is a translation of the Greek word *euangelion*, meaning "good news." For more, see the Introduction to the Gospels and Acts, p. 22.

Preparing the Way for Jesus

The writer of LUKE begins by explaining why he has written this Gospel. Then the focus shifts to events surrounding Jesus' birth. One important event is the birth of John the Baptist who, as an adult, preaches a message that is intended to get people ready to receive Jesus. The last part of this section tells about John baptizing Jesus and how the devil tests Jesus in the wilderness.

INTRODUCTION:
WHY LUKE WROTE THIS BOOK

1 Many people have tried to tell the story of what God has done among us. ²They wrote what we had been told by the ones who were there in the beginning and saw what happened. ³So I made a

1.3 *Theophilus:* The name means "friend of God" in Greek. Some think this name stands for anyone who is a friend or follower of Jesus. Others think Theophilus was a Roman official or someone of importance who paid for the writing and copying of LUKE.

1.5 *Herod was king of Judea:* Also known as Herod the Great, he was made governor of Galilee when the Romans occupied Palestine. He became king in 37 B.C. and died shortly after Jesus was born (Matt 2.19). Even though he was an Idumean and not actually Jewish, he tried to become popular with the Jewish people by rebuilding the temple in Jerusalem.

1.5 *Zechariah . . . Elizabeth:* Both Zechariah and his wife Elizabeth were from priestly families. King David divided the male descendants of Aaron the first high priest, into twenty-four divisions of priests. Each division took a turn serving in the temple. Abijah was head of the eighth division (1 Chr 24.10). See also 1 Samuel 1 and the mini-article called "Israel's Priest," p. 171.

1.9 *custom . . . to burn incense:* One of the jobs of the priests was to put fresh incense on an altar in the temple after the morning and evening sacrifices were made. Incense was made of frankincense, other gums and spices, and salt.

1.13 *John:* John the Baptist. The name John means "The Lord is kind." See the mini-article called "John the Baptist," p. 174.

1.15 *never drink wine or beer:* In ancient Israel, a group called the Nazirites made a vow never to drink alcoholic drinks (Num 6.1-4). Some people think that John was a Nazirite.

1.19 *Gabriel:* This angel first appears in DANIEL as a messenger who brings Daniel the wisdom to understand a vision (Dan 8.16; 9.21).

careful study[a] of everything and then decided to write and tell you exactly what took place. Honorable Theophilus, [4]I have done this to let you know the truth about what you have heard.

TWO MIRACULOUS BIRTHS

Angels announce the birth of both John and Jesus. Elizabeth, John's mother, and Mary, the mother of Jesus, both become pregnant in miraculous ways. This section includes Mary's famous song of praise and events surrounding the births of John and Jesus.

An Angel Tells about the Birth of John

[5]When Herod was king of Judea, there was a priest by the name of Zechariah from the priestly group of Abijah. His wife Elizabeth was from the family of Aaron. [6]Both of them were good people and pleased the Lord God by obeying all that he had commanded. [7]But they did not have children. Elizabeth could not have any, and both Zechariah and Elizabeth were already old.

[8]One day Zechariah's group of priests were on duty, and he was serving God as a priest. [9]According to the custom of the priests, he had been chosen to go into the Lord's temple that day and to burn incense, [10]while the people stood outside praying.

[11]All at once an angel from the Lord appeared to Zechariah at the right side of the altar. [12]Zechariah was confused and afraid when he saw the angel. [13]But the angel told him:

Don't be afraid, Zechariah! God has heard your prayers. Your wife Elizabeth will have a son, and you must name him John. [14]His birth will make you very happy, and many people will be glad. [15]Your son will be a great servant of the Lord. He must never drink wine or beer, and the power of the Holy Spirit will be with him from the time he is born.

[16]John will lead many people in Israel to turn back to the Lord their God. [17]He will go ahead of the Lord with the same power and spirit that Elijah had. And because of John, parents will be more thoughtful of their children. And people who now disobey God will begin to think as they ought to. That is how John will get people ready for the Lord.

[18]Zechariah said to the angel, "How will I know this is going to happen? My wife and I are both very old."

[19]The angel answered, "I am Gabriel, God's servant, and I was sent to tell you this good news. [20]You have not believed what I have said. So you will not be able to say a thing until all this happens. But everything will take place when it is supposed to."

---

[a] **1.3** *careful study:* Or "a study from the beginning."

21The crowd was waiting for Zechariah and kept wondering why he was staying so long in the temple. **22**When he did come out, he could not speak, and they knew he had seen a vision. He motioned to them with his hands, but did not say a thing.

23When Zechariah's time of service in the temple was over, he went home. **24**Soon after that, his wife was expecting a baby, and for five months she did not leave the house. She said to herself, **25**"What the Lord has done for me will keep people from looking down on me."

An Angel Tells about the Birth of Jesus

26One month later God sent the angel Gabriel to the town of Nazareth in Galilee **27**with a message for a virgin named Mary. She was engaged to Joseph from the family of King David. **28**The angel greeted Mary and said, "You are truly blessed! The Lord is with you."

29Mary was confused by the angel's words and wondered what they meant. **30**Then the angel told Mary, "Don't be afraid! God is pleased with you, **31**and you will have a son. His name will be Jesus. **32**He will be great and will be called the Son of God Most High. The Lord God will make him king, as his ancestor David was. **33**He will rule the people of Israel forever, and his kingdom will never end."

34Mary asked the angel, "How can this happen? I am not married!"

35The angel answered, "The Holy Spirit will come down to you, and God's power will come over you. So your child will be called the holy Son of God. **36**Your relative Elizabeth is also going to have a son, even though she is old. No one thought she could ever have a baby, but in three months she will have a son. **37**Nothing is impossible for God!"

38Mary said, "I am the Lord's servant! Let it happen as you have said." And the angel left her.

Mary Visits Elizabeth

39A short time later Mary hurried to a town in the hill country of Judea. **40**She went into Zechariah's home, where she greeted Elizabeth. **41**When Elizabeth heard Mary's greeting, her baby moved within her.

The Holy Spirit came upon Elizabeth. **42**Then in a loud voice she said to Mary:

> God has blessed you more than any other woman! He has also blessed the child you will have. **43**Why should the mother of my Lord come to me? **44**As soon as I heard your greeting, my baby became happy and moved within me. **45**The Lord has blessed you because you believed that he will keep his promise.

1.23 *time of service:* Each priest spent some time each year working in the temple. See the note at 1.5 (Zechariah) and the mini-article called "Israel's Priests," p. 171.

1.26 *Nazareth in Galilee:* This small town is never mentioned in the Old Testament. In 63 B.C., the Romans made Galilee part of their empire and ruled it during the time Jesus lived. See the map on p. 197.

1.27 *Mary . . . Joseph:* Joseph was from the family of David, who was considered Israel's greatest king. Israelite prophets said the Messiah would come from David's family (Isa 11.1-3; Matt 1.18).

1.31 *Jesus:* In Hebrew *Jesus* means "the Lord saves."

1.32 *God Most High:* This name for God goes back to the time of Abraham (Gen 14.17-22). See also the mini-article called "Names of God," p. 179.

1.35 *Holy Spirit:* See the note on p. 24.

1.35 *Son of God:* See the mini-article called "Son of God," p. 189.

1.39 *hill country of Judea:* Judea was an area in the southern part of Palestine. Since many parts of Judea are hilly, it's not clear exactly where in Judea Zechariah and Elizabeth lived.

1.41 *Holy Spirit:* See the note on p. 24.

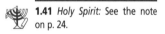
1.32,33 2 Sam 7.12,13,16; Isa 9.7. **1.37** Gen 18.14.

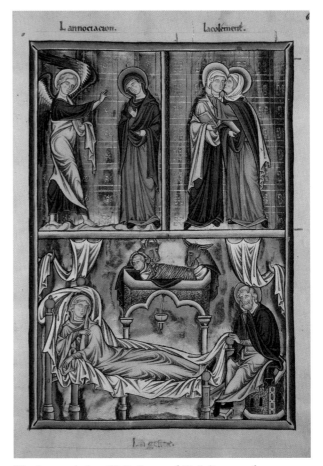

The Annunciation, Visitation, and Nativity, page from an illuminated Psalter, thirteenth century. Psalters are devotional books containing some or all of the Psalms from the Old Testament. This one from France includes images from the life of Jesus' mother Mary. Immediately after an angel tells Mary that she is pregnant (Annunciation, top left), Mary visits her cousin Elizabeth (Visitation, top right), who is pregnant with John the Baptist. The bottom panel (Nativity) shows the baby Jesus lying in a "manger," a box for holding feed for livestock, as two animals look on. (See Luke 1.26-45; 2.1-7.)

 1.46-55 *Mary's song:* Mary's song is a prayer that praises God and is like the song that Hannah sang when God gave her a son (1 Sam 2.1-10). Mary's song is also known by some Christians as the *Magnificat,* which in Latin means "magnify." This song introduces an important theme in LUKE: God is a friend of poor people.

1.48 1 Sam 1.11.

Mary's Song of Praise

⁴⁶Mary said:

> With all my heart I praise the Lord,
> ⁴⁷ and I am glad because of God my Savior.
> ⁴⁸He cares for me, his humble servant.
> From now on, all people will say
> God has blessed me.
> ⁴⁹God All-Powerful has done great things for me,
> and his name is holy.

^{50}He always shows mercy
 to everyone who worships him.
^{51}The Lord has used his powerful arm
 to scatter those who are proud.
^{52}He drags strong rulers from their thrones
 and puts humble people in places of power.
^{53}God gives the hungry good things to eat,
 and sends the rich away
  with nothing.
^{54}He helps his servant Israel
 and is always merciful to his people.
^{55}The Lord made this promise to our ancestors,
 to Abraham and his family forever!

^{56}Mary stayed with Elizabeth about three months. Then she went back home.

The Birth of John the Baptist

^{57}When Elizabeth's son was born, ^{58}her neighbors and relatives heard how kind the Lord had been to her, and they too were glad.

^{59}Eight days later they did for the child what the Law of Moses commands. They were going to name him Zechariah, after his father. ^{60}But Elizabeth said, "No! His name is John."

^{61}The people argued, "No one in your family has ever been named John." ^{62}So they motioned to Zechariah to find out what he wanted to name his son.

^{63}Zechariah asked for a writing tablet. Then he wrote, "His name is John." Everyone was amazed. ^{64}Right away, Zechariah started speaking and praising God.

^{65}All the neighbors were frightened because of what had happened, and everywhere in the hill country people kept talking about these things. ^{66}Everyone who heard about this wondered what this child would grow up to be. They knew that the Lord was with him.

Zechariah Praises the Lord

^{67}The Holy Spirit came upon Zechariah, and he began to speak:

^{68}Praise the Lord, the God of Israel!
 He has come to save his people.
^{69}Our God has given us a mighty Savior^{b}
 from the family of David his servant.
^{70}Long ago the Lord promised
 by the words of his holy prophets
^{71}to save us from our enemies
 and from everyone who hates us.
^{72}God said he would be kind to our people

1.55 *our ancestors, to Abraham:* This refers to the people of Israel, all of whom can trace their families back to Abraham and Sarah. God made an agreement (covenant) with Abraham many centuries before Jesus was born (Gen 12.1-3; 17.4-8). Abraham agreed to follow God, and God promised Abraham that he and Sarah would be the parents of a great nation (Gen 15.1-6). See also the mini-articles called "Abraham," p. 155, and "Israel," p. 170.

1.59 *what the Law of Moses commands:* The Law of Moses commanded that all Jewish boys had to have the foreskin on their penis cut off eight days after they were born to show that they belonged to the Lord (Gen 17.9-14; Lev 12.3). This ritual is called circumcision. See also the mini-article called "Circumcision," p. 158.

1.67 *Holy Spirit:* See the note on p. 24.

1.70 *holy prophets:* The prophets of Israel were special messengers who spoke for God. They told about God's promise to send a Messiah who would save the people (see Isa 7.14; 9.6,7; Mic 5.2). See the article called "Prophets and Prophecy," p. 129.

1.69 *David his servant:* This refers to Israel's King David. See also the mini-article called "David," p. 160.

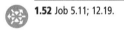

1.52 Job 5.11; 12.19.

---

^{b}**1.69** *mighty Savior:* The Greek text has "a horn of salvation." In the Scriptures animal horns are often a symbol of great strength.

1.73 *ancestor Abraham:* See the note at 1.55.

1.68-79 *Zechariah's song:* Zechariah praised God and offered a prophecy or vision of what his son, John, would do. Zechariah's song is in the form of a blessing much like those found in PSALMS. See Ps 41.13; 106.48.

1.80 *God's Spirit:* See the note on p. 24 (Holy Spirit). The time between John's birth and his preaching in the desert was about thirty years.

1.80 *desert:* John probably lived in the desert of Judea, which is between Jerusalem and the Dead Sea. See the map on p. 197.

2.1 *Emperor Augustus:* The Roman emperor at the time Jesus was born. His actual name was Octavian, but he was better known by his title, Caesar Augustus. Under the rule of Augustus, Rome controlled almost all the land surrounding the Mediterranean Sea. See the article called "The World of Jesus: Peoples, Powers, and Politics," p. 133.

2.1 *names . . . listed in record books:* This was done so that everyone living in Roman-held territories could be made to pay taxes to the Roman emperor. All the people were supposed to register in their hometowns (2.3).

1.76 Mal 3.1. **1.79** Isa 9.2.

and keep his sacred promise.
[73] He told our ancestor Abraham
[74] that he would rescue us from our enemies.
 Then we could serve him without fear,
[75] by being holy and good as long as we live.

[76] You, my son, will be called
  a prophet of God in heaven above.
 You will go ahead of the Lord
  to get everything ready for him.
[77] You will tell his people
  that they can be saved when their sins are forgiven.
[78] God's love and kindness will shine upon us
  like the sun that rises in the sky.[c]
[79] On us who live in the dark shadow of death
 this light will shine
  to guide us into a life of peace.

[80] As John grew up, God's Spirit gave him great power. John lived in the desert until the time he was sent to the people of Israel.

The Birth of Jesus
(Matthew 1.18-25)

2 About that time Emperor Augustus gave orders for the names of all the people to be listed in record books. [2] These first records were made when Quirinius was governor of Syria.

[3] Everyone had to go to their own hometown to be listed. [4] So Joseph had to leave Nazareth in Galilee and go to Bethlehem in Judea. Long ago Bethlehem had been King David's hometown, and Joseph went there because he was from David's family.

[5] Mary was engaged to Joseph and traveled with him to Bethlehem. She was soon going to have a baby, [6] and while they were there, [7] she gave birth to her first-born son. She dressed him in baby clothes[d] and laid him on a bed of hay, because there was no room for them in the inn.

The Shepherds

[8] That night in the fields near Bethlehem some shepherds were guarding their sheep. [9] All at once an angel came down to them from the Lord, and the brightness of the Lord's glory flashed around them. The shepherds were frightened. [10] But the angel said, "Don't be afraid! I have good news for you, which will make everyone happy. [11] This very day in King David's hometown a Savior was born for you. He is Christ the Lord. [12] You will know who he is, because you will find him dressed in baby clothes and lying on a bed of hay."

---

[c] **1.78** *like the sun that rises in the sky:* Or "like the Messiah coming from heaven."
[d] **2.7** *dressed him in baby clothes:* The Greek text has "wrapped him in wide strips of cloth," which was how infants were first dressed.

Judean Desert. The deserts in Palestine are dry areas of land that support little plant or animal life, but where flash flooding sometimes occurs during the winter months. LUKE says that John lived in the desert until the time he was sent to tell the people to turn back to God and to be baptized (Luke 1.80; 3.3). He wore clothes made out of camel's hair and ate grasshoppers and wild honey (see Mark 1.6).

2.2 *Quirinius:* Quirinius was made governor of Syria in A.D. 6. According to the Jewish historian Josephus, Quirinius ordered a counting of people (called a census) to be made in A.D. 6 or 7. Jesus was born during the rule of Herod the Great, who is reported to have died in 4 B.C. So, the exact date of the record-taking mentioned in LUKE is not known.

2.4 *Nazareth . . . Bethlehem in Judea:* See the note at 1.26 (Nazareth). In Hebrew, Bethlehem means "house of bread." It is located south of Jerusalem and stands about 2,500 feet above sea level. See the map on p. 197.

2.7 *first-born son:* According to the Law of Moses, the first-born son in each of their families belonged to the LORD (Exod 34.19).

2.7 *bed of hay:* This refers to an animal's feedbox, traditionally called a manger.

2.11 *King David's hometown:* Bethlehem (see the note at 2.4).

2.11 *Savior . . . Christ:* A savior is one who rescues or sets people free. See Isa 43.11; Matt 1.21. "Christ" is from the Greek word, *christos,* which means Messiah or "chosen one." See the mini-article called "Messiah (Chosen One)," p. 176.

2.13-15 *angels:* The word "angel" means "messenger." In the Bible, angels act both as messengers and as servants of God. See also the mini-article called "Angels," p. 157.

2.21 *what the Law of Moses commands:* See the note at 1.59. See also Luke 1.31 and the mini-article called "Law," p. 175.

¹³Suddenly many other angels came down from heaven and joined in praising God. They said:

¹⁴"Praise God in heaven!
Peace on earth to everyone who pleases God."

¹⁵After the angels had left and gone back to heaven, the shepherds said to each other, "Let's go to Bethlehem and see what the Lord has told us about." ¹⁶They hurried off and found Mary and Joseph, and they saw the baby lying on a bed of hay. ¹⁷When the shepherds saw Jesus, they told his parents what the angel had said about him. ¹⁸Everyone listened and was surprised. ¹⁹But Mary kept thinking about all this and wondering what it meant.

²⁰As the shepherds returned to their sheep, they were praising God and saying wonderful things about him. Everything they had seen and heard was just as the angel had said.

²¹Eight days later Jesus' parents did for him what the Law of Moses commands. And they named him Jesus, just as the angel had told Mary when he promised she would have a baby.

SHEPHERDS

In Jesus' day, shepherds either wandered from place to place living in tents, or lived in villages. Peasant shepherds who lived in a village had the right to let their flocks feed in the pastures near the village. When food supplies got scarce, they would move their herds to higher pastures in the hot summer or to warmer valleys in the winter.

Life was often difficult for shepherds. They spent most of their time outside watching over the herd and often slept near their flock to protect it from robbers and wild animals. At night, they gathered their flocks into places called sheepfolds. These could be stone walls made by the shepherds or natural enclosures like a cave. Shepherds counted their flocks when they came into the fold at night by separating the sheep from the goats with a walking stick. They counted them again in the morning when they left for the pastures.

A flock often included both sheep and goats. Sheep are timid animals that need constant protection. Goats are harder to handle than sheep, because they like to climb up the rocky hillsides. Sheep produce wool for clothing and meat for special meals. Many sheep were also used for sacrifices at the temple in Jerusalem. It is likely that some of the sheep in the fields near Bethlehem at the time of Jesus' birth were intended to be offered as temple sacrifices on one of the important Jewish festivals.

Jesus identified with shepherds, even though many in society looked down on them. Jesus called himself the Good Shepherd who would lay down his life for his sheep (John 10.11-16). The writers of the Psalms (Ps 23.1 and 100.3) and the prophet Ezekiel pictured God as a shepherd who would save his flock, the Israelite people (Ezek 34.11-16).

JESUS AS A CHILD

LUKE is the only one of the four Gospels that tells about Jesus' childhood or youth.

Simeon Praises the Lord

²²The time came for Mary and Joseph to do what the Law of Moses says a mother is supposed to do after her baby is born.

They took Jesus to the temple in Jerusalem and presented him to the Lord, ²³just as the Law of the Lord says, "Each first-born baby boy belongs to the Lord." ²⁴The Law of the Lord also says that parents have to offer a sacrifice, giving at least a pair of doves or two young pigeons. So that is what Mary and Joseph did.

²⁵At this time a man named Simeon was living in Jerusalem. Simeon was a good man. He loved God and was waiting for God to save the people of Israel. God's Spirit came to him ²⁶and told him that he would not die until he had seen Christ the Lord.

²⁷When Mary and Joseph brought Jesus to the temple to do what the Law of Moses says should be done for a new baby, the Spirit told Simeon to go into the temple. ²⁸Simeon took the baby Jesus in his arms and praised God,

²⁹"Lord, I am your servant,
> and now I can die in peace,
>> because you have kept your promise to me.
³⁰With my own eyes I have seen
> what you have done to save your people,
³¹   and foreign nations will also see this.
³²Your mighty power is a light for all nations,
> and it will bring honor to your people Israel."

³³Jesus' parents were surprised at what Simeon had said. ³⁴Then he blessed them and told Mary, "This child of yours will cause many people in Israel to fall and others to stand. The child will be like a warning sign. Many people will reject him, ³⁵and you, Mary, will suffer as though you had been stabbed by a dagger. But all this will show what people are really thinking."

Anna Speaks about the Child Jesus

³⁶The prophet Anna was also there in the temple. She was the daughter of Phanuel from the tribe of Asher, and she was very old. In her youth she had been married for seven years, but her husband died. ³⁷And now she was eighty-four years old.ᵉ Night and day she served God in the temple by praying and often going without eating. ³⁸At that time Anna came in and praised God. She spoke about the child Jesus to everyone who hoped for Jerusalem to be set free.

ᵉ**2.37** *And now she was eighty-four years old:* Or "And now she had been a widow for eighty-four years."

2.22 *after her baby is born:* After a Jewish mother gave birth to a child, she was considered ritually "unclean" (Lev 12.1-8). When a woman gave birth to a son, she had to stay home for seven days, and on the eighth day, a baby son was circumcised (see the note at 1.59). Then the mother had to stay home for another thirty-three days. After this period apart from society, she offered a sacrifice to the Lord to make herself "clean" again (2.24).

2.23 *first-born:* See the note at 2.7 (first-born son). See also Exod 13.2,12.

2.28-32 *Simeon . . . praised God:* Simeon's song is also known by some Christians as the "Nunc Dimittis," which in Latin means "Now you let [me] leave."

2.32 *a light for all nations:* Simeon was referring to Isaiah 42.6; 49.6; 52.10. See also Acts 13.46,47, where Paul and Barnabas say that they have been chosen to carry on the work of Jesus by taking his message to the Gentiles (all nations).

2.36 *prophet Anna . . . from the tribe of Asher:* Little is known about the prophet Anna or her father Phanuel. Though most prophets were male, LUKE has a number of examples of women who, like Anna, spoke God's messages or participated as Jesus' followers. One of the twelve tribes of Israel was named for Asher, one of Jacob's twelve sons (Gen 30.9-12).

2.37 *going without eating:* The Jewish people sometimes went without eating (also called "fasting") to show their love for God or to show sorrow for their sins.

2.41 *Passover:* Passover was celebrated as a remembrance of how God helped the people of Israel escape from slavery in Egypt (Exod 12.1-27; Deut 16.1-8). See also the mini-article called "Passover and the Festival of Thin Bread," p.94.

2.42 *twelve years old:* At twelve years old, Jewish boys prepared to take their full place in the religious community when they turned thirteen.

2.46 *teachers:* Probably refers to men who taught the Law of Moses and the Jewish Scriptures.

3.1,2 *Tiberius . . . Annas and Caiaphas:* Tiberius Claudius Caesar ruled the Roman Empire from A.D. 14 to 37. If he had ruled for fifteen years, that would make the year A.D. 28 or 29. Tiberius appointed Pontius Pilate to be the governor of Judea from A.D. 26 to 36.

The Herod who ruled Galilee at this time was Herod Antipas, the son of Herod the Great (see the note at 1.5). Herod Antipas was the governor of Galilee from 4 B.C. to A.D. 39. The Romans appointed Philip, Herod Antipas' brother, as ruler of Iturea and Trachonitis. Little is known about Lysanias, ruler of Abilene. See the map on p. 196 for the locations mentioned here.

Annas was the Jewish high priest from A.D. 6 to 15. His son-in-law Caiaphas was high priest from A.D. 18 to 37. See also the note at 22.54 and the mini-article called "Israel's Priests," p. 171.

3.3 *Jordan Valley:* See the map on p. 197 for the location of this valley.

3.8 *children for Abraham:* John warned the Jewish people not to think that they could live any way they wanted, just because they were descendants of Abraham and Sarah. See also John 8.33.

3.8 *sins:* See the mini-article called "Sin," p. 187.

2.52 1 Sam 2.26; Prov 3.4.

The Return to Nazareth

³⁹After Joseph and Mary had done everything that the Law of the Lord commands, they returned home to Nazareth in Galilee. ⁴⁰The child Jesus grew. He became strong and wise, and God blessed him.

The Boy Jesus in the Temple

⁴¹Every year Jesus' parents went to Jerusalem for Passover. ⁴²And when Jesus was twelve years old, they all went there as usual for the celebration. ⁴³After Passover his parents left, but they did not know that Jesus had stayed on in the city. ⁴⁴They thought he was traveling with some other people, and they went a whole day before they started looking for him. ⁴⁵When they could not find him with their relatives and friends, they went back to Jerusalem and started looking for him there.

⁴⁶Three days later they found Jesus sitting in the temple, listening to the teachers and asking them questions. ⁴⁷Everyone who heard him was surprised at how much he knew and at the answers he gave.

⁴⁸When his parents found him, they were amazed. His mother said, "Son, why have you done this to us? Your father and I have been very worried, and we have been searching for you!"

⁴⁹Jesus answered, "Why did you have to look for me? Didn't you know that I would be in my Father's house?"[f] ⁵⁰But they did not understand what he meant.

⁵¹Jesus went back to Nazareth with his parents and obeyed them. His mother kept on thinking about all that had happened.

⁵²Jesus became wise, and he grew strong. God was pleased with him and so were the people.

JESUS IS GOD'S OWN SON

John preaches in the desert, preparing people for the coming of God's chosen one, Jesus. Jesus is baptized by John and identified as God's Son, and a list of Jesus' ancestors is given. Jesus then goes into the desert where he is tested by the devil.

The Preaching of John the Baptist
(Matthew 3.1-12; Mark 1.1-8; John 1.19-28)

3 For fifteen years Emperor Tiberius had ruled that part of the world. Pontius Pilate was governor of Judea, and Herod was the ruler of Galilee. Herod's brother, Philip, was the ruler in the countries of Iturea and Trachonitis, and Lysanias was the ruler of Abilene. ²Annas and Caiaphas were the Jewish high priests.

---

[f] **2.49** *in my Father's house:* Or "doing my Father's work."

At that time God spoke to Zechariah's son John, who was living in the desert. ³So John went along the Jordan Valley, telling the people, "Turn back to God and be baptized! Then your sins will be forgiven." ⁴Isaiah the prophet wrote about John when he said,

"In the desert someone is shouting,
'Get the road ready for the Lord!
    Make a straight path for him.
⁵ Fill up every valley and level every mountain and hill.
    Straighten the crooked paths
        and smooth out the rough roads.
⁶ Then everyone will see the saving power of God.'"

⁷Crowds of people came out to be baptized, but John said to them, "You bunch of snakes! Who warned you to run from the coming judgment? ⁸Do something to show that you really have given up your sins. Don't start saying that you belong to Abraham's family. God can turn these stones into children for Abraham. ⁹An ax is ready to cut the trees down at their roots. Any tree that doesn't produce good fruit will be cut down and thrown into a fire."

¹⁰The crowds asked John, "What should we do?"

¹¹John told them, "If you have two coats, give one to someone who doesn't have any. If you have food, share it with someone else."

¹²When tax collectors came to be baptized, they asked John, "Teacher, what should we do?"

¹³John told them, "Don't make people pay more than they owe."

¹⁴Some soldiers asked him, "And what about us? What do we have to do?"

John told them, "Don't force people to pay money to make you leave them alone. Be satisfied with your pay."

¹⁵Everyone became excited and wondered, "Could John be the Messiah?"

¹⁶John said, "I am just baptizing with water. But someone more powerful is going to come, and I am not good enough even to untie his sandals. He will baptize you with the Holy Spirit and with fire. ¹⁷His threshing fork is in his hand, and he is ready to separate the wheat from the husks. He will store the wheat in his barn and burn the husks with a fire that never goes out."

¹⁸In many different ways John preached the good news to the people. ¹⁹But to Herod the ruler, he said, "It was wrong for you to take Herodias, your brother's wife." John also said that Herod had done many other bad things. ²⁰Finally, Herod put John in jail, and this was the worst thing he had done.

The Baptism of Jesus
(Matthew 3.13-17; Mark 1.9-11)

²¹While everyone else is being baptized, Jesus himself was

3.12 *tax collectors:* The Romans issued contracts for the right to collect taxes. These contracts were usually given to wealthy foreigners, who hired local people to collect taxes. These collectors usually took more from people than was actually demanded by Rome. Most Jews in Jesus' day hated tax collectors, considered them ritually unclean, and treated them as traitors.

3.15 *Messiah:* See the note at 2.11 (Savior . . . Christ).

3.16 *baptizing . . . Holy Spirit and with fire:* Baptizing people with water symbolized the old way of life being washed away. Fire may be connected with God's judgment (3.17) or with the Holy Spirit (Acts 2.3). See also the mini-articles called "Baptism," p. 36, "The Holy Spirit," p. 169, and "Fire," p. 164.

3.16 *untie his sandals:* This was the duty of a slave.

3.17 *threshing fork:* Farmers used a threshing fork to pick up the grain and husks and pitch them into the air. Light husks would blow away, but the heavier grain would fall back to the ground to be gathered up.

3.19 *Herodias:* Herodias was Herod's niece and the wife of his brother Philip (Matt 14.3,4; Mark 6.17,18).

3.4-6 Isa 40.3-5 (Septuagint). **3.7** Matt 12.34; 23.33. **3.9** Matt 7.19.

3.23-38 *son of Joseph . . . God:* Family roots were very important to the Jewish people. They believed that the Messiah would come from the family of David (Isa 11.1-11). LUKE traces Jesus' personal history all the way back to Adam and to God. Compare this list of ancestors (called a genealogy) with the one MATTHEW gives at Matthew 1.1-17.

3.22 Gen 22.2; Ps 2.7; Isa 42.1; Matt 3.17; Mark 1.11; Luke 9.35.

baptized. Then as he prayed, the sky opened up, [22]and the Holy Spirit came down upon him in the form of a dove. A voice from heaven said, "You are my own dear Son, and I am pleased with you."

The Ancestors of Jesus
(Matthew 1.1-17)

[23]When Jesus began to preach, he was about thirty years old. Everyone thought he was the son of Joseph. But his family went back through Heli, [24]Matthat, Levi, Melchi, Jannai, Joseph, [25]Mattathias, Amos, Nahum, Esli, Naggai, [26]Maath, Mattathias, Semein, Josech, Joda;

BAPTISM

The English word "baptism" comes from the Greek verb that means "to dip in water." In the Jewish Scriptures there were laws that required priests to wash themselves before they could offer sacrifices to God (Exod 40.12-15). The high priest had to bathe himself before and after he went into the most holy place inside the sacred tent or the temple to make the sacrifice on the Day of Atonement (Lev 16.4,23,24).

The prophets of Israel instructed the people to bathe themselves as a way of showing that they wanted to be pure and to do what God wanted them to do (Isa 1.16,17). At the site of the religious community in Qumran, archaeologists discovered a pool with a set of steps that the members used to walk down to the water and back up. These steps made it possible for members to wash themselves as a way of showing that they wanted their lives to be pure. During the same period in Israel's history John the Baptist began preaching in the Jordan Valley. John told people to be baptized as a way of preparing themselves for the coming of someone who would be more powerful than he was, and who would bring the Holy Spirit to God's people (Luke 3.15-17).

Jesus may not have actually baptized anyone during his earthly ministry (see John 4.1-2), but he did tell people he had healed to undergo the ritual cleansing required by the Law of Moses (John 9.6,7).

And later, before Jesus was taken up to heaven, he told his disciples to teach and to baptize people of all nations (Matt 28.18-20). His disciples obeyed his command, and ACTS is full of accounts of how Jesus' disciples baptized new members, making them part of the Christian church. These new members were baptized to show that they wanted to stop sinning, turn away from their old way of life, and show that they were ready to enter a new life of obedience to God (Rom 6.1-4).

ACTS begins with the story of how the Holy Spirit was sent to the church on the Day of Pentecost and how 3,000 new members were baptized (Acts 2.41). As the Good News of Jesus spread throughout Judea and across Asia Minor, new members were baptized, including many who were not Jews: Samaritans (Acts 8.12), an Ethiopian official (Acts 8.38), a Roman army officer (Acts 10.47,48), and a wealthy Greek woman (Acts 16.15). The apostle Paul wrote letters to local churches explaining that those who are baptized should make a break with their past life and become part of the people of faith (Rom 6.1-4; Col 2.11,12). Just as God saved Noah from the flood, and just as God raised Jesus from the dead, so God's new people are saved from the power of death, made acceptable to God, and welcomed into God's family when they are baptized (1 Pet 3.18-22).

²⁷Joanan, Rhesa, Zerubbabel, Shealtiel, Neri, ²⁸Melchi, Addi, Cosam, Elmadam, Er, ²⁹Joshua, Eliezer, Jorim, Matthat, Levi;

³⁰Simeon, Judah, Joseph, Jonam, Eliakim, ³¹Melea, Menna, Mattatha, Nathan, David, ³²Jesse, Obed, Boaz, Salmon, Nahshon;

³³Amminadab, Admin, Arni, Hezron, Perez, Judah, ³⁴Jacob, Isaac, Abraham, Terah, Nahor, ³⁵Serug, Reu, Peleg, Eber, Shelah;

³⁶Cainan, Arphaxad, Shem, Noah, Lamech, ³⁷Methuselah, Enoch, Jared, Mahalaleel, Kenan, ³⁸Enosh, and Seth.

The family of Jesus went all the way back to Adam and then to God.

A voice from heaven said, "You are my own dear son, and I am pleased with you."
Luke 3.22

Temptation of Christ, from a fifteenth century illuminated *Book of Hours* by the Limbourg brothers. After Jesus was baptized by John, he went into the desert to pray. The devil appeared to him and tested (tempted) him three times. The devil took Jesus to a high place and offered him "power and glory," but Jesus answered him by quoting the Scriptures: "Worship the Lord your God and serve only him!" (See 4.1-8.)

4.1 *Jordan River . . . desert:* The desert of Judea stretched about twenty miles eastward from the highlands around Jerusalem down to the Jordan River and the Dead Sea. See the map on p. 197.

4.2 *forty days:* The forty days and nights Jesus spent in the desert are the same number of days that Moses (Exod 24.18; 34.28) and Elijah (1 Kgs 19.8) spent preparing for the important work they had to do among God's people. See also the chart called "Numbers in the Bible," p. 180.

4.2 *went without eating:* See the note at 2.37.

4.3 *devil:* By the time of Jesus, the devil (Satan), was identified as the leader of the forces that are against God and God's people. For more, see the mini-article called "Satan," p. 185.

4.14 *Galilee:* Jesus' home region. See the note at 1.26.

4.14 *power of the Spirit:* See the note on p. 24 (Holy Spirit). LUKE often notes that God's Spirit is at work directing Jesus and others.

Jesus and the Devil
(Matthew 4.1-11; Mark 1.12,13)

4 When Jesus returned from the Jordan River, the power of the Holy Spirit was with him, and the Spirit led him into the desert. ²For forty days Jesus was tested by the devil, and during that time he went without eating. When it was all over, he was hungry.

³The devil said to Jesus, "If you are God's Son, tell this stone to turn into bread."

⁴Jesus answered, "The Scriptures say, 'No one can live only on food.' "

⁵Then the devil led Jesus up to a high place and quickly showed him all the nations on earth. ⁶The devil said, "I will give all this power and glory to you. It has been given to me, and I can give it to anyone I want to. ⁷Just worship me, and you can have it all."

⁸Jesus answered, "The Scriptures say:

'Worship the Lord your God
    and serve only him!' "

⁹Finally, the devil took Jesus to Jerusalem and had him stand on top of the temple. The devil said, "If you are God's Son, jump off. ¹⁰⁻¹¹The Scriptures say:

'God will tell his angels to take care of you.
They will catch you in their arms,
    and you will not hurt your feet on the stones.' "

¹²Jesus answered, "The Scriptures also say, 'Don't try to test the Lord your God!' "

¹³After the devil had finished testing Jesus in every way possible, he left him for a while.

QUESTIONS ABOUT LUKE 1.1—4.13

1. What message did the angel Gabriel bring to Zechariah? to Mary? (1.5-38) How did each of them respond to the angel's message?

2. Why did Mary visit Elizabeth? (1.39-45) Mary sings about the promise God has made (1.46-55). What is the promise? Where do you see signs of this promise in the world today? What are some of these signs?

3. Describe how each of the following reacted to the birth of Jesus: (a) the shepherds, (b) Simeon, (c) Anna (2.1-38). What is the promise that Simeon sings about? What would you say is special about Jesus' birth?

4. What was John's main message? (3.1-20) What does John's message have for people today? John was later killed for speaking the truth about God and how God wants people to live. What situations can you think of in the world today that might be like what happened to John?

5. In what ways does the devil test Jesus? (4.1-13) How does Jesus challenge this testing? Has anyone ever tried to persuade you to do something that you knew was wrong? How did you handle it? Where do you turn for help in facing temptations or times of testing?

Jesus Preaches and Heals in Galilee

Led by the Spirit, Jesus returns to Galilee to teach, work miracles, and choose his disciples. He also runs into trouble from teachers and experts in the Law of Moses. Twice in this section Jesus talks about his coming death, but it is clear that the disciples don't yet know why this needs to happen.

MIXED REACTIONS TOWARD JESUS

*Jesus is rejected in his hometown
but gains a big following in other places.*

Jesus Begins His Work
(Matthew 4.12-17; Mark 1.14,15)

[14]Jesus returned to Galilee with the power of the Spirit. News about him spread everywhere. [15]He taught in the Jewish meeting places, and everyone praised him.

The People of Nazareth
Turn against Jesus
(Matthew 13.53-58; Mark 6.1-6)

[16]Jesus went back to Nazareth, where he had been brought up, and as usual he went to the meeting place on the Sabbath. When he stood up to read from the Scriptures, [17]he was given the book of Isaiah the prophet. He opened it and read,

> [18]"The Lord's Spirit has come to me,
>   because he has chosen me
>   to tell the good news to the poor.
> The Lord has sent me to announce
>   freedom for prisoners,
>   to give sight to the blind, to free everyone who suffers,
> [19]   and to say, 'This is the year the Lord has chosen.'"

[20]Jesus closed the book, then handed it back to the man in charge and sat down. Everyone in the meeting place looked straight at Jesus.
[21]Then Jesus said to them, "What you have just heard me read has come true today."
[22]All the people started talking about Jesus and were amazed at the wonderful things he said. They kept on asking, "Isn't he Joseph's son?"
[23]Jesus answered:

> You will certainly want to tell me this saying, "Doctor, first make yourself well." You will tell me to do the same things here in my own hometown that you heard I did in Capernaum. [24]But you can be sure that no prophets are liked by the people of their own hometown.

4.15 *Jewish meeting places:* This phrase translates the Greek word *synagogue,* which means "gathering." See also the mini-article called "Synagogues," p. 191.

4.16 *Nazareth:* See the note at 1.26.

4.16 *Sabbath:* The Jewish day of rest. The Sabbath was the seventh day of the week, the day that God rested after creating the world (Gen 2.2,3). For more, see the chart called "Jewish Calendar and Festivals," p. 114.

4.16 *Scriptures:* These are the Jewish Scriptures, which Christians call the Old Testament.

4.17 *Isaiah the prophet:* Isaiah was a prophet in Judah from about 740 to 701 B.C.

4.20 *book:* The books of the Jewish Scriptures were written on long parchment or leather scrolls. See also the article called "How the Bible Came to Us," p. 3, and the mini-article called "Scrolls," p. 186.

4.4 Deut 8.3. **4.8** Deut 6.13 **4.10-11** Ps 91.11,12. **4.12** Deut 6.16. **4.18,19** Isa 61.1,2 (Septuagint). **4.24** John 4.44.

4.25-27 *many widows . . . Naaman:* See 1 Kgs 17.1-15 and 2 Kgs 5.1-14. Both the widow of Zarephath and Naaman of Syria were Gentiles. Jesus told these stories to show how God cares about all people.

4.27 *leprosy:* The word translated as "leprosy" was used for many different kinds of skin diseases. According to Leviticus 13 and 14, certain skin diseases made a person unacceptable to join the community in worshiping God. Such people were considered "unclean." Members of the Jewish community who touched an "unclean" person or thing had to go through a washing ceremony so they could again take part in the life of the community. See also the mini-article called "Purity (Clean and Unclean)," p. 183.

4.33 *Jewish meeting place:* See the note at 4.15.

4.33-35 *evil spirit . . . demon:* Demons are evil spirits that work for the devil. In Jesus' day, demons were understood to be the cause of many kinds of sickness and mental illness. This demon recognized who Jesus was and called him "God's Holy One." See also the article called "Miracles, Magic, and Medicine," p. 144.

4.38 *Simon's home:* Simon, also known as Peter, was one of the first of the disciples Jesus chose (5.3-10).

4.41 *Son of God:* See the mini-article called "Son of God," p. 189.

4.41 *Messiah:* See the notes at 2.11.

4.32 Matt 7.28,29.

---

[25]Once during the time of Elijah there was no rain for three and a half years, and people everywhere were starving. There were many widows in Israel, [26]but Elijah was sent only to a widow in the town of Zarephath near the city of Sidon. [27]During the time of the prophet Elisha, many men in Israel had leprosy. But no one was healed, except Naaman who lived in Syria.

[28]When the people in the meeting place heard Jesus say this, they became so angry [29]that they got up and threw him out of town. They dragged him to the edge of the cliff on which the town was built, because they wanted to throw him down from there. [30]But Jesus slipped through the crowd and got away.

A Man with an Evil Spirit
(Mark 1.21-28)

[31]Jesus went to the town of Capernaum in Galilee and taught the people on the Sabbath. [32]His teaching amazed them because he spoke with power. [33]There in the Jewish meeting place was a man with an evil spirit. He yelled out, [34]"Hey, Jesus of Nazareth, what do you want with us? Are you here to get rid of us? I know who you are! You are God's Holy One."

[35]Jesus ordered the evil spirit to be quiet and come out. The demon threw the man to the ground in front of everyone and left without harming him.

[36]They all were amazed and kept saying to each other, "What kind of teaching is this? He has power to order evil spirits out of people!" [37]News about Jesus spread all over that part of the country.

JESUS HEALS MANY PEOPLE AND CHOOSES HIS DISCIPLES

Jesus Heals Many People
(Matthew 8.14-17; Mark 1.29-34)

[38]Jesus left the meeting place and went to Simon's home. When Jesus got there, he was told that Simon's mother-in-law was sick with a high fever. [39]So Jesus went over to her and ordered the fever to go away. Right then she was able to get up and serve them a meal.

[40]After the sun had set, people with all kinds of diseases were brought to Jesus. He put his hands on each one of them and healed them. [41]Demons went out of many people and shouted, "You are the Son of God!" But Jesus ordered the demons not to speak because they knew he was the Messiah.

[42]The next morning Jesus went out to a place where he could be alone, and crowds came looking for him. When they found him, they tried to stop him from leaving. [43]But Jesus said, "People

Jesus Chooses His First Disciples:
"From now on you will bring in people instead of fish."
See Luke 5.1-11

Jesus Teaches His Disciples (The Sermon on the Mount):
"God blesses those people who depend only on Him."
See Matt 5.1-12

Gennessaret
Chorazin
Magdala
Capernaum
Bethsaida
Jordan River
Tiberias
LAKE GALILEE
Gergasa
Sennabris
Jordan River
Yarmuk River
Gadara

Jesus Calms a Storm:
"Why were you afraid? Don't you have any faith?"
See Mark 4.35-41

Jesus Heals the Man with Many Demons:
"Go back home and tell everyone how much God has done for you."
See Luke 8.26-39

Jesus Feeds Five Thousand:
"Jesus took the five loaves and the two fish. He looked up toward heaven and blessed the food. Then he broke the bread and handed it to his disciples to give to the people. He also divided the two fish so that everyone could have some."
See Mark 6.30-44

Jesus at Lake Galilee. Jesus was born and died in Judea, the Roman province to the west of the Dead Sea, and he grew up in the Nazareth in the province of Galilee in the north. Most of his healing and preaching ministry took place in the small towns around the large, fresh-water Lake Galilee. On the shores of this lake Jesus chose his first disciples and gave his famous "Sermon on the Mount." (The Church of the Beatitudes, shown here, marks the traditional site of the sermon.) The Gospels describe many miracles Jesus performed in this area. Once, when Jesus was asleep in a boat, a storm broke out and caused Jesus' disciples to panic. Jesus commanded the storm to stop and the wind and sea obeyed him. (Shown above is a 2000-year-old fishing boat discovered in 1986 in the mud of Lake Galilee. This discovery has given archaeologists a better understanding of what boats from Jesus' day looked like; see the reconstructed model to the left.) In one of the towns near Lake Galilee (perhaps Gadara or Gerasa), Jesus ordered demons to come out of a man and then commanded them to go into a herd of swine who rushed off the cliffs into the sea. In one of Jesus' most famous miracles, a crowd who had gathered to hear him preach became hungry, and Jesus fed all five thousand of them with just five loaves of bread and two fish.

4.43 *good news about God's kingdom:* Jesus first told why he was sent in 4.18,19. This is the "good news." God's kingdom is anywhere God's people do what God wants them to do, like serving others and telling the good news.

4.44 *Judea:* This is the Greek name for the territory of Palestine that had once been known as Judah. In Jesus' day the three main divisions in Palestine were Judea, Samaria, and Galilee. The capital and religious center for the Jewish people was Jerusalem, in Judea. See the map on p. 197.

5.1 *Lake Gennesaret:* This is another name for Lake Galilee, a lake in the northern part of the Jordan River Valley. It is about 14 miles long and 6 miles wide. The Romans called it Lake Tiberias (John 6.1; 21.1) after one of their emperors. See the illustration on p. 41.

5.2 *fishermen . . . wash their nets:* See the mini-article called "Fish and Fishing," p. 165. Fishermen washed their nets to keep the oil from the fish from drying and making the nets brittle.

5.3 *Jesus sat down:* Teachers in the ancient world usually sat down when they taught (see also Matt 5.1).

5.8 *Simon Peter:* Simon's Greek name (Peter) and his Hebrew nickname Cephas mean "rock." See also 9.20 and the note at 4.38.

5.8 *I am a sinner:* Genesis 3 tells how sin entered the world. See also Rom 3.23. Peter recognized God's glory in Jesus. This made Peter realize that he himself was sinful. See also the mini-article called "Sin," p. 187.

5.1-3 Matt 13.1,2; Mark 3.9,10; 4.1. **5.5,6** John 21.3,6.

Jesus Calls His First Disciples, mosaic from Sant'Apollinare Nuovo, Ravenna, Italy, around A.D. 530. Jesus did not choose priests or other established religious leaders to be his disciples. Instead, he chose people like Simon (Peter) and his business partners, James and John, who were simple fishermen. Jesus told Peter where to cast his net so that he would catch so many fish he wouldn't be able to pull in the net alone. Then he told the amazed fisherman, "From now on you will bring in people instead of fish!" (See 5.1-11.)

in other towns must hear the good news about God's kingdom. That's why I was sent." [44]So he kept on preaching in the Jewish meeting places in Judea.[g]

Jesus Chooses His First Disciples
(Matthew 4.18-22; Mark 1.16-20)

5 Jesus was standing on the shore of Lake Gennesaret, teaching the people as they crowded around him to hear God's message. [2]Near the shore he saw two boats left there by some fishermen who had gone to wash their nets. [3]Jesus got into the boat that belonged to Simon and asked him to row it out a little way from the shore. Then Jesus sat down in the boat to teach the crowd.

[4]When Jesus had finished speaking, he told Simon, "Row the boat out into the deep water and let your nets down to catch some fish."

[5]"Master," Simon answered, "we have worked hard all night long and have not caught a thing. But if you tell me to, I will let the nets down." [6]They did it and caught so many fish that their nets began ripping apart. [7]Then they signaled for their partners in the

---

[g] **4.44** *Judea:* Some manuscripts have "Galilee."

other boat to come and help them. The men came, and together they filled the two boats so full that they both began to sink.

[8]When Simon Peter saw this happen, he knelt down in front of Jesus and said, "Lord, don't come near me! I am a sinner." [9]Peter and everyone with him were completely surprised at all the fish they had caught. [10]His partners James and John, the sons of Zebedee, were surprised too.

Jesus told Simon, "Don't be afraid! From now on you will bring in people instead of fish." [11]The men pulled their boats up on the shore. Then they left everything and went with Jesus.

Jesus Heals a Man
(Matthew 8.1-4; Mark 1.40-45)

[12]Jesus came to a town where there was a man who had leprosy. When the man saw Jesus, he knelt down to the ground in front of Jesus and begged, "Lord, you have the power to make me well, if only you wanted to."

[13]Jesus put his hand on him and said, "I want to! Now you are well." At once the man's leprosy disappeared. [14]Jesus told him, "Don't tell anyone about this, but go and show yourself to the priest. Offer a gift to the priest, just as Moses commanded, and everyone will know that you have been healed."

[15]News about Jesus kept spreading. Large crowds came to listen to him teach and to be healed of their diseases. [16]But Jesus would often go to some place where he could be alone and pray.

Jesus Heals a Crippled Man
(Matthew 9.1-8; Mark 2.1-12)

[17]One day some Pharisees and experts in the Law of Moses sat listening to Jesus teach. They had come from every village in Galilee and Judea and from Jerusalem.

God had given Jesus the power to heal the sick, [18]and some people came carrying a crippled man on a mat. They tried to take him inside the house and put him in front of Jesus. [19]But because of the crowd, they could not get him to Jesus. So they went up on the roof, where they removed some tiles and let the mat down in the middle of the room.

[20]When Jesus saw how much faith they had, he said to the crippled man, "My friend, your sins are forgiven."

[21]The Pharisees and the experts began arguing, "Jesus must think he is God! Only God can forgive sins."

[22]Jesus knew what they were thinking, and he said, "Why are you thinking that? [23]Is it easier for me to tell this crippled man that his sins are forgiven or to tell him to get up and walk? [24]But now you will see that the Son of Man has the right to forgive sins here on earth." Jesus then said to the man, "Get up! Pick up your mat and walk home."

5.10 *James and John, the sons of Zebedee:* James and John became disciples of Jesus (5.11; 6.14). He nicknamed them "Boanerges," which means "Thunderbolts" (Mark 3.17).

5.12 *leprosy:* See the note at 4.27.

5.14 *Don't tell anyone about this:* Jesus often told people he helped not to tell what he had done for them (Mark 3.10-12; 7.34-36). He may have wanted the miracle to speak for itself. Or he may have wanted to avoid drawing crowds of people who were more interested in miracles than in hearing about God's new kingdom.

5.14 *show yourself to the priest:* People with leprosy had to be examined by a priest to have their healing confirmed before they could once again live in the Jewish community (Lev 13). The gift that was required for this was the sacrifice of some lambs and flour mixed with olive oil (Lev 14.1-32).

5.17 *Pharisees and experts in the Law of Moses:* The Pharisees met in homes to pray and to study the Jewish Scriptures. The experts in the Law of Moses were teachers who studied the first five books of the Jewish Scriptures. Like the Pharisees, they believed that only God could forgive sins. See also the article, called "The World of Jesus: Peoples, Powers, and Politics," p. 133.

5.19 *roof:* In Palestine, houses usually had flat roofs. Stairs on the outside led up to the roof, which was made of beams and boards covered with packed earth. Roofs of fancier houses were sometimes made of clay tiles. See the illustration on p. 192.

5.24 *Son of Man:* See the mini-article called "Son of Man," p. 190.

5.21 Isa 43.25.

5.27 *tax collector named Levi:* Levi is also called Matthew (Matt 9.9-13). He was probably collecting taxes from people and merchants as they traveled past him on a major highway.

5.30 *Pharisees and . . . teachers of the Law of Moses:* See the note at 5.17.

5.33 *John's followers:* This refers to followers of John the Baptist.

5.33 *go without eating:* See the note at 2.37.

5.34 *bridegroom:* Jesus was referring to himself. See also 9.22 and 17.22.

5.36-38 *patch . . . wineskins:* A patch made of new, unwashed cloth could shrink after being washed. If it had been used to patch a hole in an old piece of clothing, it could tear away from the garment and make a bigger tear.

Similarly, when the juice from grapes becomes wine, gas is produced which can swell and stretch the fresh wineskins where it is being stored. If new wine was put into old skins that had become stiff, the skins could burst. See also the mini-article called "Wine," p. 193.

6.1 *walking through some wheat fields:* It was the custom among the Jewish people to let hungry travelers pick grains of wheat (Deut 23.25).

6.2 *picking grain on the Sabbath:* The Pharisees believed that all Jews should be strict about following the Laws of Moses. One important law said that it was wrong to do any work on the Sabbath (see Exod 20.10; Deut 5.14). The Pharisees said that picking grain on the Sabbath broke this law.

---

^{25}At once the man stood up in front of everyone. He picked up his mat and went home, giving thanks to God. ^{26}Everyone was amazed and praised God. What they saw surprised them, and they said, "We have seen a great miracle today!"

Jesus Chooses Levi
(Matthew 9.9-13; Mark 2.13-17)

^{27}Later, Jesus went out and saw a tax collector named Levi sitting at the place for paying taxes. Jesus said to him, "Come with me." ^{28}Levi left everything and went with Jesus.

^{29}In his home Levi gave a big dinner for Jesus. Many tax collectors and other guests were also there.

^{30}The Pharisees and some of their teachers of the Law of Moses grumbled to Jesus' disciples, "Why do you eat and drink with those tax collectors and other sinners?"

^{31}Jesus answered, "Healthy people don't need a doctor, but sick people do. ^{32}I didn't come to invite good people to turn to God. I came to invite sinners."

JESUS CONTINUES HIS WORK IN GALILEE

Jesus continues to do his work of teaching, healing, and working miracles. He also chooses his twelve disciples and has to face many questions about his actions and his message.

People Ask about Going without Eating
(Matthew 9.14-17; Mark 2.18-22)

^{33}Some people said to Jesus, "John's followers often pray and go without eating, and so do the followers of the Pharisees. But your disciples never go without eating or drinking."

^{34}Jesus told them, "The friends of a bridegroom don't go without eating while he is still with them. ^{35}But the time will come when he will be taken from them. Then they will go without eating."

^{36}Jesus then told them these sayings:

No one uses a new piece of cloth to patch old clothes. The patch would shrink and make the hole even bigger.

^{37}No one pours new wine into old wineskins. The new wine would swell and burst the old skins. Then the wine would be lost, and the skins would be ruined. ^{38}New wine must be put only into new wineskins.

^{39}No one wants new wine after drinking old wine. They say, "The old wine is better."

A Question about the Sabbath
(Matthew 12.1-8; Mark 2.23-28)

6 One Sabbath when Jesus and his disciples were walking through

some wheat fields, the disciples picked some wheat. They rubbed the husks off with their hands and started eating the grain.

²Some Pharisees said, "Why are you picking grain on the Sabbath? You're not supposed to do that!"

³Jesus answered, "You surely have read what David did when he and his followers were hungry. ⁴He went into the house of God and took the sacred loaves of bread that only priests were supposed to eat. He not only ate some himself, but even gave some to his followers."

⁵Jesus finished by saying, "The Son of Man is Lord over the Sabbath."

A Man with a Crippled Hand
(Matthew 12.9-14; Mark 3.1-6)

⁶On another Sabbath[h] Jesus was teaching in a Jewish meeting place, and a man with a crippled right hand was there. ⁷Some Pharisees and teachers of the Law of Moses kept watching Jesus to see if he would heal the man. They did this because they wanted to accuse Jesus of doing something wrong.

⁸Jesus knew what they were thinking. So he told the man to stand up where everyone could see him. And the man stood up. ⁹Then Jesus asked, "On the Sabbath should we do good deeds or evil deeds? Should we save someone's life or destroy it?"

¹⁰After he had looked around at everyone, he told the man, "Stretch out your hand." He did, and his bad hand became completely well.

¹¹The teachers and the Pharisees were furious and started saying to each other, "What can we do about Jesus?"

Jesus Chooses His Twelve Apostles
(Matthew 10.1-4; Mark 3.13-19)

¹²About that time Jesus went off to a mountain to pray, and he spent the whole night there. ¹³The next morning he called his disciples together and chose twelve of them to be his apostles. ¹⁴One was Simon, and Jesus named him Peter. Another was Andrew, Peter's brother. There were also James, John, Philip, Bartholomew, ¹⁵Matthew, Thomas, and James the son of Alphaeus. The rest of the apostles were Simon, known as the Eager One,[i] ¹⁶Jude, who was the son of James, and Judas Iscariot,[j] who later betrayed Jesus.

---

[h] **6.6** *On another Sabbath:* Some manuscripts have a reading which may mean "the Sabbath after the next." [i] **6.15** *known as the Eager One:* The word "eager" translates the Greek word "zealot," which was a name later given to the members of a Jewish group that resisted and fought against the Romans. See also the article called "The World of Jesus: People, Powers, and Politics," p. 1709. [j] **6.16** *Iscariot:* This may mean "a man from Kerioth" (a place in Judea). But more probably it means "a man who was a liar" or "a man who was a betrayer."

Jesus answered, "Healthy people don't need a doctor, but sick people do."
Luke 5.31

6.3,4 *David . . . only priests:* David was from the tribe of Judah. See 1 Sam 21.1-6. Only the priests (descendants of Aaron, from the tribe of Levi) were allowed to eat the holy bread. See also Lev 24.8,9.

6.5 *Son of Man:* What Jesus teaches and does has more authority than the Law of Moses, which includes the laws about the Sabbath. See also Heb 2.1—3.6.

6.6 *Jewish meeting place:* See the note at 4.15.

6.7 *Pharisees and teachers of the Law of Moses:* See the note at 5.17.

6.9 *On the Sabbath . . . good deeds:* See the note at 4.16 (Sabbath). Since any work done on the Sabbath was considered breaking the Law, the Pharisees and teachers of the Law thought that Jesus was breaking the Sabbath law when he healed the man with a crippled hand. Jesus showed by his actions that doing a good deed on the Sabbath is not against God's Law.

6.12 *mountain:* Jesus went to a mountain to pray before selecting his apostles. In LUKE mountains are often associated with important moments in Jesus' ministry (see also 4.5; 9.28; and 19.29).

6.13 *disciples . . . twelve . . . apostles:* A *disciple* is a follower who learns from a master teacher, and an *apostle* is someone who is sent to others to carry the teacher's actions and message. The number of disciples (twelve) is the same number as the tribes of Israel. These twelve were later called apostles, as were a few others such as the apostle Paul (1 Cor 9.1). See also the chart, called "Jesus' Twelve Disciples," p. 173.

6.17 *down from the mountain
. . . to some flat, level ground:* It
is not clear exactly where this was. What
Jesus teaches in 6.20-49 is sometimes
called the "Sermon on the Plain." Notice
that many of the things that Jesus says
here are similar to what he says while
teaching from the mountainside in
Matthew 5.1—7.29.

 6.20 *His kingdom:* See the note
at 4.43.

6.22 *Son of Man:* See the mini-
article called "Son of Man," p. 190.

6.23 *heaven:* Living under God's
rule in heaven will be the reward for
those who are faithful. See also the
mini-article called "Heaven," p. 167.

 6.29 *someone slaps you on one
cheek:* A slap on the cheek was
a very bad insult.

6.22 1 Pet 4.14. **6.23** 2 Chr
36.16; Acts 7.52.

Jesus Teaches, Preaches, and Heals
(Matthew 4.23-25)

[17]Jesus and his apostles went down from the mountain and
came to some flat, level ground. Many other disciples were there to
meet him. Large crowds of people from all over Judea, Jerusalem,
and the coastal cities of Tyre and Sidon were there too. [18]These
people had come to listen to Jesus and to be healed of their diseases. All who were troubled by evil spirits were also healed.
[19]Everyone was trying to touch Jesus, because power was going out
from him and healing them all.

Blessings and Troubles
(Matthew 5.1-12)

[20]Jesus looked at his disciples and said:

God will bless you people who are poor.
His kingdom belongs to you!
[21]God will bless you hungry people.
You will have plenty to eat!
God will bless you people who are crying.
You will laugh!

[22]God will bless you when others hate you and
won't have anything to do with you. God will bless you
when people insult you and say cruel things about you,
all because you are a follower of the Son of Man. [23]Long
ago your own people did these same things to the prophets. So when this happens to you, be happy and jump for
joy! You will have a great reward in heaven.

[24]But you rich people are in for trouble.
You have already had an easy life!
[25]You well-fed people are in for trouble.
You will go hungry!
You people who are laughing now are in for trouble.
You are going to cry and weep!

[26]You are in for trouble when everyone says good
things about you. That is what your own people said
about those prophets who told lies.

Love for Enemies
(Matthew 5.38-48; 7.12a)

[27]This is what I say to all who will listen to me:
Love your enemies, and be good to everyone who
hates you. [28]Ask God to bless anyone who curses you, and
pray for everyone who is cruel to you. [29]If someone slaps
you on one cheek, don't stop that person from slapping you
on the other cheek. If someone wants to take your coat,
don't try to keep back your shirt. [30]Give to everyone who

asks and don't ask people to return what they have taken from you. ³¹Treat others just as you want to be treated.

³²If you love only someone who loves you, will God praise you for that? Even sinners love people who love them. ³³If you are kind only to someone who is kind to you, will God be pleased with you for that? Even sinners are kind to people who are kind to them. ³⁴If you lend money only to someone you think will pay you back, will God be pleased with you for that? Even sinners lend to sinners because they think they will get it all back.

³⁵But love your enemies and be good to them. Lend without expecting to be paid back.ᵏ Then you will get a great reward, and you will be the true children of God in heaven. He is good even to people who are unthankful and cruel. ³⁶Have pity on others, just as your Father has pity on you.

Judging Others
(Matthew 7.1-5)

³⁷Jesus said:

Don't judge others, and God won't judge you. Don't be hard on others, and God won't be hard on you. Forgive others, and God will forgive you. ³⁸If you give to others, you will be given a full amount in return. It will be packed down, shaken together, and spilling over into your lap. The way you treat others is the way you will be treated.

³⁹Jesus also used some sayings as he spoke to the people. He said:

Can one blind person lead another blind person? Won't they both fall into a ditch? ⁴⁰Are students better than their teacher? But when they are fully trained, they will be like their teacher.

⁴¹You can see the speck in your friend's eye. But you don't notice the log in your own eye. ⁴²How can you say, "My friend, let me take the speck out of your eye," when you don't see the log in your own eye? You show-offs! First, get the log out of your own eye. Then you can see how to take the speck out of your friend's eye.

A Tree and Its Fruit
(Matthew 7.17-20; 12.34b, 35)

⁴³A good tree cannot produce bad fruit, and a bad tree cannot produce good fruit. ⁴⁴You can tell what a tree is like by the fruit it produces. You cannot pick figs or grapes from thornbushes. ⁴⁵Good people do good things

---

Jesus said:
Don't be hard on others,
and God won't be hard
on you. Forgive others,
and God will forgive you.
Luke 6.37

6.35 *true children of God:* "Children" is used to describe members of God's family, no matter how young or old they are. Jesus says that the true children of God will act like God by loving their enemies, being generous, and by having pity on others.

6.41 *log in your own eye:* Jesus uses this exaggeration to emphasize how important it is not to judge others before looking closely at one's own life.

6.42 *You show-offs:* The Greek word translated as "show-offs" is often translated into English as "hypocrites."

6.44 *figs or grapes:* Figs are sweet fruits from bushy trees that can grow quite tall. In Jesus' day they were an important source of food. A large fig tree produced two crops each year. Grapes were also an important food. They were eaten fresh or dried, but most were used for making wine. Grapes grow on vines that have to be watered, weeded, and trimmed so that they will produce good grapes. See also Matt 12.33.

6.31 Matt 7.12. **6.39** Matt 15.14. **6.40** Matt 10.24,25; John 13.16; 15.20. **6.45** Matt 12.34.

ᵏ **6.35** *without expecting to be paid back:* Some manuscripts have "without giving up on anyone."

7.1 *Capernaum:* See the note at 4.23.

7.2 *army officer:* The Greek text says that this officer was a centurion, a leader of one hundred men. A centurion commanded and trained his men to fight and die at his command. Since this is Galilee, it is possible that the centurion served in the army of Herod Antipas.

7.3 *Jewish leaders:* These were probably respected local leaders who worked with the government authorities in Capernaum.

7.5 *built us a meeting place:* The Greek word used in this verse is *synagogue* (see the note at 4.15). In recent years, archaeologists have examined the remains of the ancient synagogue at Capernaum. They have found that it was originally a private house that was rebuilt to serve as a meeting place. Later, it was completely rebuilt as a formal place of worship. This type of religious building began to be erected by Jews in the second century A.D.

7.11 *Nain:* This small town was in southern Galilee. See the map on p. 197.

7.12 *people carrying out the body:* The Jewish people usually took the dead body to a tomb on the same day the person died. The family of a dead person often hired professional mourners for funerals. The family and other mourners would wail (cry out loud) and beat on their chests or tear their clothes to show their sadness (see Gen 37.34; Deut 34.8; 1 Sam 31.13).

7.14,15 *Jesus . . . touched the stretcher . . . back to his mother:* Jewish people in the crowd would have been reminded of the prophet Elijah who used God's power to raise a widow's dead son (1 Kgs 17.8-24). The Gospels tell of two other times Jesus raised people from the dead: the daughter of Jairus (Luke 8.40-56) and Lazarus (John 11.38-44).

because of the good in their hearts. Bad people do bad things because of the evil in their hearts. Your words show what is in your heart.

Two Builders
(Matthew 7.24-27)

⁴⁶Why do you keep on saying that I am your Lord, when you refuse to do what I say? ⁴⁷Anyone who comes and listens to me and obeys me ⁴⁸is like someone who dug down deep and built a house on solid rock. When the flood came and the river rushed against the house, it was built so well that it didn't even shake. ⁴⁹But anyone who hears what I say and doesn't obey me is like someone whose house wasn't built on solid rock. As soon as the river rushed against that house, it was smashed to pieces!

Jesus Heals an Army Officer's Servant
(Matthew 8.5-13; John 4.43-54)

7 After Jesus had finished teaching the people, he went to Capernaum. ²In that town an army officer's servant was sick and about to die. The officer liked this servant very much. ³And when he heard about Jesus, he sent some Jewish leaders to ask him to come and heal the servant.

⁴The leaders went to Jesus and begged him to do something. They said, "This man deserves your help! ⁵He loves our nation and even built us a meeting place." ⁶So Jesus went with them.

When Jesus wasn't far from the house, the officer sent some friends to tell him, "Lord, don't go to any trouble for me! I am not good enough for you to come into my house. ⁷And I am certainly not worthy to come to you. Just say the word, and my servant will get well. ⁸I have officers who give orders to me, and I have soldiers who take orders from me. I can say to one of them, 'Go!' and he goes. I can say to another, 'Come!' and he comes. I can say to my servant, 'Do this!' and he will do it."

⁹When Jesus heard this, he was so surprised that he turned and said to the crowd following him, "In all of Israel I've never found anyone with this much faith!"

¹⁰The officer's friends returned and found the servant well.

A Widow's Son

¹¹Soon Jesus and his disciples were on their way to the town of Nain, and a big crowd was going along with them. ¹²As they came near the gate of the town, they saw people carrying out the body of a widow's only son. Many people from the town were walking along with her.

¹³When the Lord saw the woman, he felt sorry for her and said, "Don't cry!"

¹⁴Jesus went over and touched the stretcher on which the people were carrying the dead boy. They stopped, and Jesus said, "Young man, get up!" ¹⁵The boy sat up and began to speak. Jesus then gave him back to his mother.

¹⁶Everyone was frightened and praised God. They said, "A great prophet is here with us! God has come to his people."

¹⁷News about Jesus spread all over Judea and everywhere else in that part of the country.

John the Baptist
(Matthew 11.1-19)

¹⁸⁻¹⁹John's followers told John everything that was being said about Jesus. So he sent two of them to ask the Lord, "Are you the one we should be looking for? Or must we wait for someone else?"

²⁰When these messengers came to Jesus, they said, "John the Baptist sent us to ask, 'Are you the one we should be looking for? Or are we supposed to wait for someone else?'"

²¹At that time Jesus was healing many people who were sick or in pain or were troubled by evil spirits, and he was giving sight to a lot of blind people. ²²Jesus said to the messengers sent by John, "Go and tell John what you have seen and heard. Blind people are now able to see, and the lame can walk. People who have leprosy are being healed, and the deaf can now hear. The dead are raised to life, and the poor are hearing the good news. ²³God will bless everyone who doesn't reject me because of what I do."

²⁴After John's messengers had gone, Jesus began speaking to the crowds about John:

What kind of person did you go out to the desert to see? Was he like tall grass blown about by the wind? ²⁵What kind of man did you really go out to see? Was he someone dressed in fine clothes? People who wear expensive clothes and live in luxury are in the king's palace. ²⁶What then did you go out to see? Was he a prophet? He certainly was! I tell you that he was more than a prophet. ²⁷In the Scriptures, God calls John his messenger and says, "I am sending my messenger ahead of you to get things ready for you." ²⁸No one ever born on this earth is greater than John. But whoever is least important in God's kingdom is greater than John.

²⁹Everyone had been listening to John. Even the tax collectors had obeyed God and had done what was right by letting John baptize them. ³⁰But the Pharisees and the experts in the Law of Moses refused to obey God and be baptized by John.

³¹Jesus went on to say:

What are you people like? What kind of people are you? ³²You are like children sitting in the market and shouting to each other,

7.20 *John the Baptist:* See the note at 1.13.

7.22 *leprosy:* See the note at 4.27.

7.27 *God calls John his messenger:* Jesus says that John is a messenger sent from God (Exod 23.20; Mal 3.1) to prepare the way for Jesus.

7.29,30 *tax collectors . . . Pharisees and the experts in the Law of Moses:* See the notes at 3.12 (tax collectors) and 5.17 (Pharisees and experts). See also Matt 21.32; Luke 3.12.

7.32-34 *children sitting in the market:* Jesus said that some of the Jewish people and their religious leaders were like quarreling children. Some children wanted to play a joyful game, but others wanted to play a sad game. Jesus is saying that some leaders didn't agree with John's ways, because they were so strict. And they didn't like Jesus' ways, because they weren't strict enough.

7.22,23: Isa 35.5,6; 61.1; Luke 4.18. **7.28** Matt 11.11.

7.35 *Wisdom:* Wise people were honored in Jewish society. True wisdom was said to come from God's Law (Ps 19.7). Here Jesus is saying that Wisdom is made visible by the good we do for others. See the mini-article called "Wisdom," p. 194.

7.36 *Pharisee:* See the note at 5.17.

7.36 *got ready to eat:* On special occasions the Jewish people often followed the Greek and Roman custom of lying on their left side while eating with the right hand. This is probably what Jesus was doing when the woman washed his feet (7.38).

7.37 *expensive bottle of perfume:* The bottle was made out of a very soft beautiful stone called alabaster.

7.39 *what kind of woman is touching him:* It is not clear what the woman's sin was. According to Jewish law, someone who touched a sinner would become unclean and would have to live apart from the Jewish community. Simon was a Pharisee who always tried to avoid contact with anyone who could make him unclean. That is why he was surprised that Jesus let the woman touch him.

7.41 *moneylender:* See the mini-article called "Money Changing in the Temple," p. 177.

7.41 *silver coins:* The coin was a denarius, which was equal to about the daily pay of a common laborer (see Matt 20.9).

7.44-46 *wash my feet . . . greet me with a kiss . . . pour olive oil on my head:* The Jewish people believed that it was very important to be friendly to guests. Since most people wore open sandals, guests in a home were usually offered water so they could wash their feet. Guests were also greeted with a kiss on the cheek and often had olive oil poured on their head.

"We played the flute, but you would not dance!
  We sang a funeral song, but you would not cry!"

[33]John the Baptist did not go around eating and drinking, and you said, "John has a demon in him!" [34]But because the Son of Man goes around eating and drinking, you say, "Jesus eats and drinks too much! He is even a friend of tax collectors and sinners." [35]Yet Wisdom is shown to be right by what its followers do.

Simon the Pharisee

[36]A Pharisee invited Jesus to have dinner with him. So Jesus went to the Pharisee's home and got ready to eat.

[37]When a sinful woman in that town found out that Jesus was there, she bought an expensive bottle of perfume. [38]Then she came and stood behind Jesus. She cried and started washing his feet with her tears and drying them with her hair. The woman kissed his feet and poured the perfume on them.

[39]The Pharisee who had invited Jesus saw this and said to himself, "If this man really were a prophet, he would know what kind of woman is touching him! He would know that she is a sinner."

[40]Jesus said to the Pharisee, "Simon, I have something to say to you."

"Teacher, what is it?" Simon replied.

[41]Jesus told him, "Two people were in debt to a moneylender. One of them owed him five hundred silver coins, and the other owed him fifty. [42]Since neither of them could pay him back, the moneylender said that they didn't have to pay him anything. Which one of them will like him more?"

[43]Simon answered, "I suppose it would be the one who had owed more and didn't have to pay it back."

"You are right," Jesus said.

[44]He turned toward the woman and said to Simon, "Have you noticed this woman? When I came into your home, you didn't give me any water so I could wash my feet. But she has washed my feet with her tears and dried them with her hair. [45]You didn't greet me with a kiss, but from the time I came in, she has not stopped kissing my feet. [46]You didn't even pour olive oil on my head, but she has poured expensive perfume on my feet. [47]So I tell you that all her sins are forgiven, and that is why she has shown great love. But anyone who has been forgiven for only a little will show only a little love."

[48]Then Jesus said to the woman, "Your sins are forgiven."

[49]Some other guests started saying to one another, "Who is this who dares to forgive sins?"

[50]But Jesus told the woman, "Because of your faith, you are now saved.[1] May God give you peace!"

---

[1]**7.50** *saved:* Or "healed." The Greek word may have either meaning.

Women Who Helped Jesus

8 Soon after this, Jesus was going through towns and villages, telling the good news about God's kingdom. His twelve apostles were with him, ²and so were some women who had been healed of evil spirits and all sorts of diseases. One of the women was Mary Magdalene, who once had seven demons in her. ³Joanna, Susanna, and many others had also used what they owned to help Jesus and his disciples. Joanna's husband Chuza was one of Herod's officials.

A Story about a Farmer
(Matthew 13.1-9; Mark 4.1-9)

⁴When a large crowd from several towns had gathered around Jesus, he told them this story:

⁵A farmer went out to scatter seed in a field. While the farmer was doing it, some of the seeds fell along the road and were stepped on or eaten by birds. ⁶Other seeds fell on rocky ground and started growing. But the plants did not have enough water and soon dried up. ⁷Some other seeds fell where thornbushes grew up and choked the plants. ⁸The rest of the seeds fell on good ground where they grew and produced a hundred times as many seeds.

When Jesus had finished speaking, he said, "If you have ears, pay attention!"

Why Jesus Used Stories
(Matthew 13.10-17; Mark 4.10-12)

⁹Jesus' disciples asked him what the story meant. ¹⁰So he answered:

I have explained the secrets about God's kingdom to you, but for others I can only use stories. These people look, but they don't see, and they hear, but they don't understand.

Jesus Explains the Story about a Farmer
(Matthew 13.18-23; Mark 4.13-20)

¹¹This is what the story means: The seed is God's message, ¹²and the seeds that fell along the road are the people who hear the message. But the devil comes and snatches the message out of their hearts, so that they will not believe and be saved. ¹³The seeds that fell on rocky ground are the people who gladly hear the message and accept it. But they don't have deep roots, and they believe only for a little while. As soon as life gets hard, they give up.

¹⁴The seeds that fell among the thornbushes are also people who hear the message. But they are so eager for riches and pleasures that they never produce anything. ¹⁵Those seeds that fell on good ground are the people who listen to the message and keep it in good and honest hearts. They last and produce a harvest.

8.1 *good news about God's kingdom:* See the note at 4.43.

8.2 *Mary Magdalene:* Her name means that she was from Magdala, a small town on the shore of Lake Galilee. Some say that she was the sinful woman in 7.36-50, but the Bible gives no hint that this is true. She was present when Jesus died on a cross (Luke 23.49; Mark 15.40,41) and saw where he was buried (Luke 23.55; Mark 15.47). She brought spices to the tomb to use in preparing Jesus' body for burial (Luke 24.1; Mark 16.1) and so became the first person to see Jesus after he was raised from death (Luke 24.9,10; Mark 16.9).

8.3 *Joanna, Susanna and ... Joanna's husband Chuza:* Joanna and Susanna probably traveled with Jesus (Luke 23.49) and helped in his ministry. Women often helped Jewish teachers by giving them money. This is the only place in the Bible where Susanna is mentioned. Joanna is mentioned again in 24.10. Chuza was a manager who worked for Herod Antipas (see the note at 3.1).

8.5 *A farmer went out to scatter seed in a field:* Before planting seeds, a farmer usually prepared an area of ground by breaking up the surface. Then the farmer scattered seeds on the ground a handful at a time. After scattering the seeds, the farmer would plow the seed into the ground along with the stubble from the previous crop, which would act as fertilizer as it decayed. Of course, some seeds stayed on the surface. See also the article called "How People Made a Living in the Time of Jesus," p. 138.

8.10 *God's kingdom:* See the note at 4.43.

8.12 *devil:* See the note at 4.3.

7.37,38 Matt 26.7; Mark 14.3; John 12.3. **7.49** Luke 5.21. **8.1** Luke 6.12-16. **8.10** Isa 6.9 (Septuagint).

8.16 *lamp:* In Jesus' day, people used small clay lamps that burned olive oil. They were small enough to hold in one's hand, and the oil was drawn up from inside the clay lamp by a wick, which gave off light when it burned. See also Matt 5.15; Luke 11.33.

8.19 *Jesus' mother and brothers:* Mark 6.3 gives the names of four brothers and says that Jesus also had sisters.

8.22 *cross the lake:* They were going to go to the eastern shore of Lake Galilee, where most people were not Jewish. See the map on p. 197.

8.26 *Lake Galilee:* See the note at 5.1.

8.26 *town of Gerasa:* Gerasa was probably located about twenty miles east of the Jordan River. It was one of the ten cities that formed what was known as the Decapolis, or "ten towns." Its population, architecture, and style of life were mostly Greek.

8.27 *demons:* See the note at 4.33-35.

8.27 *graveyard:* It was thought that demons and evil spirits lived in graveyards.

8.28 *Son of God in heaven:* The demons knew that Jesus was God's Son, even if people didn't fully believe or understand who Jesus was. Compare this verse to 4.35. See also the mini-article called "Son of God," p. 189.

8.17 Matt 10.26; Luke 12.2.
8.18 Matt 25.29; Luke 19.26.

Light
(Mark 4.21-25)

¹⁶No one lights a lamp and puts it under a bowl or under a bed. A lamp is always put on a lampstand, so that people who come into a house will see the light. ¹⁷There is nothing hidden that will not be found. There is no secret that will not be well known. ¹⁸Pay attention to how you listen! Everyone who has something will be given more, but people who have nothing will lose what little they think they have.

Jesus' Mother and Brothers
(Matthew 12.46-50; Mark 3.31-35)

¹⁹Jesus' mother and brothers went to see him, but because of the crowd they could not get near him. ²⁰Someone told Jesus, "Your mother and brothers are standing outside and want to see you."

²¹Jesus answered, "My mother and my brothers are those people who hear and obey God's message."

A Storm
(Matthew 8.23-27; Mark 4.35-41)

²²One day, Jesus and his disciples got into a boat, and he said, "Let's cross the lake." They started out, ²³and while they were sailing across, he went to sleep.

Suddenly a windstorm struck the lake, and the boat started sinking. They were in danger. ²⁴So they went to Jesus and woke him up, "Master, Master! We are about to drown!"

Jesus got up and ordered the wind and waves to stop. They obeyed, and everything was calm. ²⁵Then Jesus asked the disciples, "Don't you have any faith?"

But they were frightened and amazed. They said to each other, "Who is this? He can give orders to the wind and the waves, and they obey him!"

A Man with Demons in Him
(Matthew 8.28-34; Mark 5.1-20)

²⁶Jesus and his disciples sailed across Lake Galilee and came to shore near the town of Gerasa.^{m 27}As Jesus was getting out of the boat, he was met by a man from that town. The man had demons in him. He had gone naked for a long time and no longer lived in a house, but in the graveyard.

²⁸The man saw Jesus and screamed. He knelt down in front of him and shouted, "Jesus, Son of God in heaven, what do you want with me? I beg you not to torture me!" ²⁹He said this because Jesus had already told the evil spirit to go out of him.

The man had often been attacked by the demon. And even

---

^m **8.26** *Gerasa:* Some manuscripts have "Gergesa."

though he had been bound with chains and leg irons and kept under guard, he smashed whatever bound him. Then the demon would force him out into lonely places.

[30]Jesus asked the man, "What is your name?"

He answered, "My name is Lots." He said this because there were 'lots' of demons in him. [31]They begged Jesus not to send them to the deep pit, where they would be punished.

[32]A large herd of pigs was feeding there on the hillside. So the demons begged Jesus to let them go into the pigs, and Jesus let them go. [33]Then the demons left the man and went into the pigs. The whole herd rushed down the steep bank into the lake and drowned.

[34]When the men taking care of the pigs saw this, they ran to spread the news in the town and on the farms. [35]The people went out to see what had happened, and when they came to Jesus, they also found the man. The demons had gone out of him, and he was sitting there at the feet of Jesus. He had clothes on and was in his right mind. But the people were terrified.

[36]Then all who had seen the man healed told about it. [37]Everyone from around Gerasa begged Jesus to leave, because they were so frightened.

When Jesus got into the boat to start back, [38]the man who had been healed begged to go with him. But Jesus sent him off and said, [39]"Go back home and tell everyone how much God has done for you." The man then went all over town, telling everything that Jesus had done for him.

A Dying Girl and a Sick Woman
(Matthew 9.18-26; Mark 5.21-43)

[40]Everyone had been waiting for Jesus, and when he came back, a crowd was there to welcome him. [41]Just then the man in charge of the Jewish meeting place came and knelt down in front of Jesus. His name was Jairus, and he begged Jesus to come to his home [42]because his twelve-year-old child was dying. She was his only daughter.

While Jesus was on his way, people were crowding all around him. [43]In the crowd was a woman who had been bleeding for twelve years. She had spent everything she had on doctors,[n] but none of them could make her well.

[44]As soon as she came up behind Jesus and barely touched his clothes, her bleeding stopped.

[45]"Who touched me?" Jesus asked.

While everyone was denying it, Peter said, "Master, people are crowding all around and pushing you from every side."[o]

[46]But Jesus answered, "Someone touched me, because I felt power going out from me." [47]The woman knew that she could not

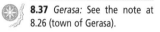

8.31 *deep pit:* The place where evil spirits were kept and punished. This pit may be the place later described as "hell" (see the note at 12.5).

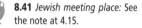

8.32 *herd of pigs:* Jewish people did not have pigs, since the Law of Moses said they could not eat pork. This shows that the area was Gentile, not Jewish.

8.37 *Gerasa:* See the note at 8.26 (town of Gerasa).

8.41 *Jewish meeting place:* See the note at 4.15.

8.43 *doctors:* In New Testament times there were physicians who helped people when they were sick or injured. Though they had many skills, their knowledge of what caused diseases was limited. See the article called "Miracles, Magic, and Medicine," p. 144.

---

[n] **8.43** *She had spent everything she had on doctors:* Some manuscripts do not have these words.   [o] **8.45** *from every side:* Some manuscripts add "and you ask, 'Who touched me?'"

8.51 *Peter, John, James:* Three of the twelve apostles (disciples). All three of them were fishermen when Jesus called them to follow him. James and John were brothers (Luke 5.1-10). All three would see Jesus' true glory (transfiguration) on a mountaintop (Luke 9.28-36), and all of them were with Jesus when he prayed in Gethsemane before his arrest (Mark 14.33).

8.55 *give her something to eat:* Eating was a sign that the girl was alive and not just a spirit. Compare this with Luke 24.30-43. After God raised Jesus from the dead, he met two of his disciples on the road to Emmaus. They recognized him when he shared a meal with them. Later, when he appeared to his disciples, he also ate with them.

9.1 *twelve apostles:* See the note at 6.13.

9.5 *shake the dust from your feet:* This was a customary way of rejecting someone. See Acts 13.51.

9.7 *Herod the ruler:* This is Herod Antipas, one of the sons of Herod the Great (see the note at 3.1). The formal name for Herod's title was "tetrarch," which meant someone who ruled a fourth of a province. Jesus called Herod a fox (13.32), because he thought Herod was clever and dangerous.

9.8 *Elijah had come . . . back:* See the note on p. 24. See also Matt 16.14; Mark 8.28; Luke 9.19.

9.10 *Bethsaida:* Bethsaida was a Jewish town just east of where the Jordan River empties into Lake Galilee. See the map on p. 197.

9.11 *God's kingdom:* See the note at 4.43.

8.55 Luke 7.14,15. **9.3-5** Luke 10.4-11. **9.9** Matt 14.1-12.

hide, so she came trembling and knelt down in front of Jesus. She told everyone why she had touched him and that she had been healed right away.

[48]Jesus said to the woman, "You are now well because of your faith. May God give you peace!"

[49]While Jesus was speaking, someone came from Jairus' home and said, "Your daughter has died! Why bother the teacher anymore?"

[50]When Jesus heard this, he told Jairus, "Don't worry! Have faith, and your daughter will get well."

[51]Jesus went into the house, but he did not let anyone else go with him, except Peter, John, James, and the girl's father and mother. [52]Everyone was crying and weeping for the girl. But Jesus said, "The child isn't dead. She is just asleep." [53]The people laughed at him because they knew she was dead.

[54]Jesus took hold of the girl's hand and said, "Child, get up!" [55]She came back to life and got right up. Jesus told them to give her something to eat. [56]Her parents were surprised, but Jesus ordered them not to tell anyone what had happened.

Instructions for the Twelve Apostles
(Matthew 10.5-15; Mark 6.7-13)

9 Jesus called together his twelve apostles and gave them complete power over all demons and diseases. [2]Then he sent them to tell about God's kingdom and to heal the sick. [3]He told them, "Don't take anything with you! Don't take a walking stick or a traveling bag or food or money or even a change of clothes. [4]When you are welcomed into a home, stay there until you leave that town. [5]If people won't welcome you, leave the town and shake the dust from your feet as a warning to them."

[6]The apostles left and went from village to village, telling the good news and healing people everywhere.

Herod Is Worried
(Matthew 14.1-12; Mark 6.14-29)

[7]Herod the ruler heard about all that was happening, and he was worried. Some people were saying that John the Baptist had come back to life. [8]Others were saying that Elijah had come or that one of the prophets from long ago had come back to life. [9]But Herod said, "I had John's head cut off! Who is this I hear so much about?" Herod was eager to meet Jesus.

Jesus Feeds Five Thousand
(Matthew 14.13-21; Mark 6.30-44; John 6.1-14)

[10]The apostles came back and told Jesus everything they had done. He then took them with him to the village of Bethsaida, where they could be alone. [11]But a lot of people found out about

this and followed him. Jesus welcomed them. He spoke to them about God's kingdom and healed everyone who was sick.

[12]Late in the afternoon the twelve apostles came to Jesus and said, "Send the crowd to the villages and farms around here. They need to find a place to stay and something to eat. There is nothing in this place. It is like a desert!"

[13]Jesus answered, "You give them something to eat."

But they replied, "We have only five small loaves of bread and two fish. If we are going to feed all these people, we will have to go and buy food." [14]There were about five thousand men in the crowd.

Jesus said to his disciples, "Have the people sit in groups of fifty." [15]They did this, and all the people sat down. [16]Jesus took the five loaves and the two fish. He looked up toward heaven and blessed the food. Then he broke the bread and fish and handed them to his disciples to give to the people.

[17]Everyone ate all they wanted. What was left over filled twelve baskets.

WHO JESUS IS AND WHAT HE MUST DO

Jesus wants to make it clear to his disciples who he is and what he must do. Peter, John, and James get to see Jesus' true glory and hear God identify Jesus as "my chosen son." This is the same statement God made when Jesus was baptized (3.22).

Who Is Jesus?
(Matthew 16.13-19; Mark 8.27-29)

[18]When Jesus was alone praying, his disciples came to him, and he asked them, "What do people say about me?"

[19]They answered, "Some say that you are John the Baptist or Elijah or a prophet from long ago who has come back to life."

[20]Jesus then asked them, "But who do you say I am?"

Peter answered, "You are the Messiah sent from God."

[21]Jesus strictly warned his disciples not to tell anyone about this.

Jesus Speaks about His Suffering and Death
(Matthew 16.20-28; Mark 8.30—9.1)

[22]Jesus told his disciples, "The nation's leaders, the chief priests, and the teachers of the Law of Moses will make the Son of Man suffer terribly. They will reject him and kill him, but three days later he will rise to life."

[23]Then Jesus said to all the people:

> If any of you want to be my followers, you must forget about yourself. You must take up your cross each day and follow me. [24]If you want to save your life,[p] you will destroy it.

---

[p] **9.24** *life:* In verses 24, 25 a Greek word which often means "soul" is translated "life" and "yourself."

9.13 *small loaves of bread:* These would have been flat like a pancake, or plump and round like a bun.

9.17 *twelve baskets:* The Jewish people believed that twelve was an especially sacred number. See the chart called "Numbers in the Bible," p. 180.

9.19 *John the Baptist or Elijah:* See the notes at 1.13 and on p. 24. See also Matt 14.1,2; Mark 6.14,15; Luke 9.7,8.

9.20 *Peter:* See the note at 5.8 (Simon Peter).

9.20 *Messiah:* See the notes at 2.11 (Savior . . . Christ). See also John 6.68,69.

9.22 *nation's leaders, the chief priests, and the teachers of the Law of Moses:* The nation's leaders were wealthy older men who had ties to the chief priests. Together, they formed a group that was given some authority by the Romans to make decisions about the local affairs of the Jewish people. See also the note at 5.17.

9.22 *Son of Man:* See the mini-article called "Son of Man," p. 190.

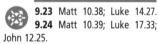

9.23 Matt 10.38; Luke 14.27.
9.24 Matt 10.39; Luke 17.33; John 12.25.

9.26 *Father and the holy angels:* Jesus often referred to God as "Father" (see John 15–17). See also the note at 2.13-15 (angels).

9.27 *God's kingdom:* See the note at 4.43.

 9.28 *Peter, John, and James:* These disciples were the same ones who went with Jesus into the home of Jairus (8.51).

9.28 *mountain:* The exact location of this mountain is not clear.

9.30 *Moses and Elijah:* Moses was very important in the history of Israel. God revealed his name, "I Am," to Moses and chose him to lead the people out of slavery in Egypt. Moses' face glowed with light when he met God on Mount Sinai (Exod 34.29,30). For more, see the mini-article called "Moses," p. 178.
See also the note on p. 24 (Elijah). Both Moses and Elijah were chosen to call God's people to live a new way of life, just as Jesus was.

9.39 *demon:* See the note at 4.33-35. The boy appears to be having some kind of epileptic seizures. See the article called "Miracles, Magic, and Medicine," p. 144.

9.28-35 2 Pet 1.17,18. **9.35** 3.22.

But if you give up your life for me, you will save it. [25]What will you gain, if you own the whole world but destroy yourself or waste your life? [26]If you are ashamed of me and my message, the Son of Man will be ashamed of you when he comes in his glory and in the glory of his Father and the holy angels. [27]You can be sure that some of the people standing here will not die before they see God's kingdom.

The True Glory of Jesus
(Matthew 17.1-8; Mark 9.2-8)

[28]About eight days later Jesus took Peter, John, and James with him and went up on a mountain to pray. [29]While he was praying, his face changed, and his clothes became shining white. [30]Suddenly Moses and Elijah were there speaking with him. [31]They appeared in heavenly glory and talked about all that Jesus' death[q] in Jerusalem would mean.

[32]Peter and the other two disciples had been sound asleep. All at once they woke up and saw how glorious Jesus was. They also saw the two men who were with him.

[33]Moses and Elijah were about to leave, when Peter said to Jesus, "Master, it is good for us to be here! Let us make three shelters, one for you, one for Moses, and one for Elijah." But Peter did not know what he was talking about.

[34]While Peter was still speaking, a shadow from a cloud passed over them, and they were frightened as the cloud covered them. [35]From the cloud a voice spoke, "This is my chosen Son. Listen to what he says!"

[36]After the voice had spoken, Peter, John, and James saw only Jesus. For some time they kept quiet and did not say anything about what they had seen.

Jesus Heals a Boy
(Matthew 17.14-18; Mark 9.14-27)

[37]The next day Jesus and his three disciples came down from the mountain and were met by a large crowd. [38]Just then someone in the crowd shouted, "Teacher, please do something for my son! He is my only child! [39]A demon often attacks him and makes him scream. It shakes him until he foams at the mouth, and it won't leave him until it has completely worn the boy out. [40]I begged your disciples to force out the demon, but they couldn't do it."

[41]Jesus said to them, "You people are stubborn and don't have any faith! How much longer must I be with you? Why do I have to put up with you?"

Then Jesus said to the man, "Bring your son to me." [42]While

---

[q] **9.31** *Jesus' death:* In Greek this is "his departure," which probably includes his rising to life and his return to heaven.

the boy was being brought, the demon attacked him and made him shake all over. Jesus ordered the demon to stop. Then he healed the boy and gave him back to his father. [43]Everyone was amazed at God's great power.

Jesus Again Speaks about His Death
(Matthew 17.22,23; Mark 9.30-32)

While everyone was still amazed at what Jesus was doing, he said to his disciples, [44]"Pay close attention to what I am telling you! The Son of Man will be handed over to his enemies." [45]But the disciples did not know what he meant. The meaning was hidden from them. They could not understand it, and they were afraid to ask.

Who Is the Greatest?
(Matthew 18.1-5; Mark 9.33-37)

[46]Jesus' disciples were arguing about which one of them was the greatest. [47]Jesus knew what they were thinking, and he had a child stand there beside him. [48]Then he said to his disciples, "When you welcome even a child because of me, you welcome me. And when you welcome me, you welcome the one who sent me. Whichever one of you is the most humble is the greatest."

For or against Jesus
(Mark 9.38-40)

[49]John said, "Master, we saw a man using your name to force demons out of people. But we told him to stop, because he isn't one of us."
[50]"Don't stop him!" Jesus said. "Anyone who isn't against you is for you."

> *Jesus said to his disciples, "Whichever one of you is the most humble is the greatest."*
> Luke 9.48

9.22 *Son of Man:* See the mini-article called "Son of Man," p. 190.

9.49 *demons:* See the note at 4.33-35.

9.48 Matt 10.40; Luke 10.16; John 13.20.

QUESTIONS ABOUT LUKE 4.14 — 9.50

1. What did Jesus mean when he said, "This is the year the Lord has chosen"? (4.19) What did Jesus announce? How did the people of his hometown of Nazareth react to his announcement? Why? What is your reaction to Jesus' announcement?

2. In this section Luke gives two accounts of Jesus choosing his disciples (5.1-11; 5.27-32). How are these two stories different? How are they similar? What do they show about the kind of teacher Jesus was? Also in this section, Luke gives the names of the disciples Jesus called to be apostles (6.12-16). What were their names? What did Jesus do before choosing them?

3. What can we learn from Jesus' teachings about loving our enemies and about judging others? (6.27-36; 6.37-42) When are these teachings hard to follow? Explain.

4. This section contains a number of stories about people Jesus healed (4.31-41; 5.12-26; 6.6-11; 7.1-17; 8.26-56; 9.37-43). Who are some of these people? Which story moved you the most? Why? What took place after each healing described?

9.51 *Jerusalem:* Jerusalem was the religious center for the Jewish people. Although the Romans controlled Jerusalem in Jesus' day the Jewish people were still allowed to worship at the temple. Jesus went to the temple to face the Jewish religious leaders, who were against him, and to preach his message to the Jewish people who worshiped there. See also the article called "People of the Law: The Religion of Israel," p. 109, and the mini-article called "Jerusalem," p. 172.

Jesus Goes to Jerusalem

Jesus gives his apostles special powers and prepares them for what is going to happen to him. He has made up his mind to go to Jerusalem. All that he says and does along the way has a purpose. Jesus now prepares his followers for his death and helps them understand how they can continue the work that he has begun.

FOLLOWERS AND UNBELIEVERS

On his way to Jerusalem Jesus encounters many people. Some understand his teachings and decide to follow Jesus. Some do not understand or are unwilling to do what is required to be a follower.

A Samaritan Village Refuses To Receive Jesus

[51]Not long before it was time for Jesus to be taken up to heaven, he made up his mind to go to Jerusalem. [52]He sent some messengers on ahead to a Samaritan village to get things ready for

BURIAL

The people of Israel and the other countries of the ancient Near East considered it very important to honor those who had died by giving them a proper burial. Because of the warm climate in Palestine it was important to bury people within twenty-four hours after they died. In fact, Jewish law required that a dead person should be buried before sunset (Deut 21.23). To let a loved-one's body decay above ground where vultures and dogs could eat it was considered a serious dishonor.

There is no complete description in the Bible of how Jewish people prepared a body for burial. However, it is known that the body was washed (Acts 9.37), anointed with scented ointments (Luke 24.1), and wrapped in cloth (Matt 27.59; John 11.44).

Most ancient Hebrews were buried in caves or in trenches dug in the ground. Sarah and Abraham were buried in Machpelah Cave near Hebron (Gen 23.19; 25.9,10). Later, tombs cut out of rock were used for burying the dead. Some tombs could only hold one body, others could hold several and were used by families. Because touching a corpse, even accidentally, made a person ceremonially unclean according to Jewish

law, tombs were clearly marked. After the flesh had rotted away in the tomb, the bones would be collected in a box (called an *ossuary*). Then the level place where the dead body had been could be used to receive the body of another person who died.

Greeks, Romans, and Canaanites often burned (cremated) the bodies of people who died. Jewish people saw this as a dishonor and did this only if a body was already in an advanced state of decay (1 Sam 31.12) or during a time of plague (Amos 6.10). The dead bodies of people who had disobeyed God's law were also sometimes burned (Lev 20.14; Josh 7.25).

Burial ceremonies centered on the family's mourning for the dead person (see the note at 7.12) and the carrying of the body to the place of burial. The bodies of the dead were put on wooden frames and carried to the place of burial (2 Sam 3.31; Luke 7.11-15). After the burial, those who handled the body were considered unclean and had to undergo a cleansing ceremony in order to be part of the community again (Num 19.11-20). There is no evidence that the Jewish people of Jesus' day performed funeral services to honor the dead.

Left: Perfume bottles from burial caves in Jerusalem, 6th to 5th centuries B.C.
Right: First-century tomb near Jerusalem.

him. [53]But he was on his way to Jerusalem, so the people there refused to welcome him. [54]When the disciples James and John saw what was happening, they asked, "Lord, do you want us to call down fire from heaven to destroy these people?"[r]

[55]But Jesus turned and corrected them for what they had said.[s] [56]Then they all went on to another village.

Three People Who Wanted To Be Followers
(Matthew 8.19-22)

[57]Along the way someone said to Jesus, "I'll go anywhere with you!"

[58]Jesus said, "Foxes have dens, and birds have nests, but the Son of Man doesn't have a place to call his own."

[59]Jesus told someone else to come with him. But the man said, "Lord, let me wait until I bury my father."

[60]Jesus answered, "Let the dead take care of the dead, while you go and tell about God's kingdom."

[61]Then someone said to Jesus, "I want to go with you, Lord, but first let me go back and take care of things at home."

[62]Jesus answered, "Anyone who starts plowing and keeps looking back isn't worth a thing to God's kingdom!"

9.52 *Samaritan village:* The exact location of this village is not known. Samaria was a region north of Jerusalem. In Jesus' day the Jews and the Samaritans distrusted one another. The Samaritans had their own temple (on Mt. Gerizim) and their own priests. Also, they followed their own version of the Law of Moses. See Luke 10.25-37 and 17.11-19 for two other meetings Jesus had with Samaritans.

9.54 *James and John:* See the note at 5.10. See also 1 Kgs 18.16-39; 2 Kings 1.9-16.

9.22 *Son of Man:* See the mini-article called "Son of Man," p. 190.

9.60 *God's kingdom:* See the note at 4.43.

9.61 1 Kgs 19.20.

[r]**9.54** *to destroy these people:* Some manuscripts add "as Elijah did." [s]**9.55** *what they had said:* Some manuscripts add, "and said, 'Don't you know what spirit you belong to? The Son of Man did not come to destroy people's lives, but to save them.'"

Notes (left column)

10.1 *seventy-two:* According to Genesis 10, where the descendants of Noah are listed, there were seventy nations on earth. (But the ancient Greek translation of the Old Testament has "seventy-two" in place of seventy.) Jesus probably chose this number of followers to show that his message was for everyone in the world.

10.4 *waste time greeting people on the road:* In Jesus' day a polite greeting could take a long time.

10.11 *shaking the dust from our feet:* See the note at 9.5.

10.13 *Chorazin . . . Bethsaida . . . Tyre and Sidon:* Chorazin, Bethsaida, and Capernaum were Jewish towns on the northern end of Lake Galilee. Tyre and Sidon were important non-Jewish port cities on the Mediterranean Sea coast. See the map on p. 197. While the people in these Jewish towns did not respond to Jesus' message and miracles, Jesus says that the people in cities like Tyre and Sidon would be more willing to turn to God.

10.13 *sackcloth and . . . ashes:* Sackcloth is dark cloth (see Rev 6.12) made of camel's hair or goat's hair. The Greek word for "ashes" in this verse refers to a kind of smoky soot. People wore sackcloth or put ashes on their head in times of deep sadness or when they wanted to show that they were sorry for their sins (see Esth 4.1, 3; Job 2.8).

10.14 *day of judgment:* This day was expected to be a time when God would judge the people of the world. Those who put their trust in Christ will be saved, but those who did not will experience God's anger and punishment (see Matt 13.47-50; 25.31-46; John 12.44-50). See also the mini-article called "Day of the Lord," p. 161.

10.2 Matt 9.37,38. **10.3** Matt 10.16. **10.7** 1 Cor 9.14; 1 Tim 5.18. **10.4-11** Matt 10.7-14; Mark 6.8-11; Luke 9.3-5. **10.12** Gen 19.24-28; Matt 11.24; Matt 10.15. **10.13** Isa 23.1-18; Ezek 26.1—28.26; Joel 3.4-8; Amos 1.9,10; Zech 9.2-4.

The Work of the Seventy-Two Followers

10 Later the Lord chose seventy-two[t] other followers and sent them out two by two to every town and village where he was about to go. ²He said to them:

A large crop is in the fields, but there are only a few workers. Ask the Lord in charge of the harvest to send out workers to bring it in. ³Now go, but remember, I am sending you like lambs into a pack of wolves. ⁴Don't take along a moneybag or a traveling bag or sandals. And don't waste time greeting people on the road. ⁵As soon as you enter a home, say, "God bless this home with peace." ⁶If the people living there are peace-loving, your prayer for peace will bless them. But if they are not peace-loving, your prayer will return to you. ⁷Stay with the same family, eating and drinking whatever they give you, because workers are worth what they earn. Don't move around from house to house.

⁸If the people of a town welcome you, eat whatever they offer. ⁹Heal their sick and say, "God's kingdom will soon be here!"[u]

¹⁰But if the people of a town refuse to welcome you, go out into the street and say, ¹¹"We are shaking the dust from our feet as a warning to you. And you can be sure that God's kingdom will soon be here!"[u] ¹²I tell you that on the day of judgment the people of Sodom will get off easier than the people of that town!

The Unbelieving Towns
(Matthew 11.20-24)

¹³You people of Chorazin are in for trouble! You people of Bethsaida are also in for trouble! If the miracles that took place in your towns had happened in Tyre and Sidon, the people there would have turned to God long ago. They would have dressed in sackcloth and put ashes on their heads. ¹⁴On the day of judgment the people of Tyre and Sidon will get off easier than you will. ¹⁵People of Capernaum, do you think you will be honored in heaven? Well, you will go down to hell!

¹⁶My followers, whoever listens to you is listening to me. Anyone who says "No" to you is saying "No" to me. And anyone who says "No" to me is really saying "No" to the one who sent me.

The Return of the Seventy-Two

¹⁷When the seventy-two[v] followers returned, they were

---

[t]**10.1** *seventy-two:* Some manuscripts have "seventy." [u]**10.9** *will soon be here:* Or "is already here."" [v]**10.17** *seventy-two:* See the footnote at 10.1.

excited and said, "Lord, even the demons obeyed when we spoke in your name!"

[18]Jesus told them:

> I saw Satan fall from heaven like a flash of lightning. [19]I have given you the power to trample on snakes and scorpions and to defeat the power of your enemy Satan. Nothing can harm you. [20]But don't be happy because evil spirits obey you. Be happy that your names are written in heaven!

Jesus Thanks His Father
(Matthew 11.25-27; 13.16,17)

[21]At that same time, Jesus felt the joy that comes from the Holy Spirit,[w] and he said:

> My Father, Lord of heaven and earth, I am grateful that you hid all this from wise and educated people and showed it to ordinary people. Yes, Father, that is what pleased you.
>
> [22]My Father has given me everything, and he is the only one who knows the Son. The only one who really knows the Father is the Son. But the Son wants to tell others about the Father, so that they can know him too.

[23]Jesus then turned to his disciples and said to them in private, "You are really blessed to see what you see! [24]Many prophets and kings were eager to see what you see and to hear what you hear. But I tell you that they did not see or hear."

The Good Samaritan

[25]An expert in the Law of Moses stood up and asked Jesus a question to see what he would say. "Teacher," he asked, "what must I do to have eternal life?"

[26]Jesus answered, "What is written in the Scriptures? How do you understand them?"

[27]The man replied, "The Scriptures say, 'Love the Lord your God with all your heart, soul, strength, and mind.' They also say, 'Love your neighbors as much as you love yourself.'"

[28]Jesus said, "You have given the right answer. If you do this, you will have eternal life."

[29]But the man wanted to show that he knew what he was talking about. So he asked Jesus, "Who are my neighbors?"

[30]Jesus replied:

> As a man was going down from Jerusalem to Jericho, robbers attacked him and grabbed everything he had. They beat him up and ran off, leaving him half dead. [31]A priest happened to be going down the same

10.15 *Capernaum:* See the notes at 10.13 (Chorazin . . . Bethsaida . . . Tyre and Sidin) and 4.23.

10.15 *hell:* See the notes at 8.31 and 12.5.

10.16 *the one who sent me:* Jesus is referring to God. See also Matt 10.40; Mark 9.37; Luke 9.48; John 13.20.

10.17 *demons:* See the note at 4.33-35.

10.18 *Satan:* See the note at 4.3.

10.20 *names are written in heaven:* Living under God's rule will be the reward for those who are faithful. Hebrews 12.23 also says that the names of the faithful will be written down in heaven. References to a "book" of life can be found in Ps 69.28; Dan 12.1; Phil 4.3; Rev 3.5.

10.25 *expert in the Law of Moses:* See the note at 5.17.

10.25 *eternal life:* By the time of Jesus, many Jewish people had come to believe in and hope for life after death. But some, like the Sadducees, did not accept the concept of eternal life, because it was not specifically mentioned in the Law of Moses (see the article called "The World of Jesus: Peoples, Powers, and Politics," p. 133. Jesus says that all who have faith in him will have eternal life. For more, see the mini-article called "Eternal Life," p. 163.

10.26 *Scriptures:* See the note at 4.16.

10.30 *down from Jerusalem to Jericho:* Jericho is eight hundred feet below sea level and is located about sixteen miles northeast of Jerusalem. Since Jerusalem is 2,500 feet above sea level, the route to Jericho is downhill. See the map on p. 197.

10.18 Isa 14.12. **10.19** Ps 91.13. **10.22** John 3.35; John 10.15. **10.25-28** Matt 22.35-40; Mark 12.28-34. **10.27,28** Deut 6.5; Lev 19.18; Lev 18.5.

---

[w] **10.21** *the Holy Spirit:* Some manuscripts have "his spirit."

The Good Samaritan by Vincent Van Gogh, 1890. When an expert in the Law of Moses asked Jesus who were his "neighbors" that he should love like himself, Jesus answered by telling him a story. In the story a man was beaten and robbed and left along the side of the road. The person who helped this man was not a priest or temple worker, as the expert in the Law would have expected, but a Samaritan, a man from a nearby land that was not friendly with the Jewish people in Jesus' day. (See 10.25-37.)

10.31,32 *priest . . . temple helper:* Jewish priests were descendants of Moses' brother Aaron (see Num 18.20-32). A priest knew that touching a dead body or the blood of an injured man would make him unclean according to the Law of Moses. If he became unclean, he would have to go through a cleansing ceremony before he could serve in the temple again. Temple helpers were Levites who assisted the priests at the temple. This temple helper was also afraid of becoming unclean. See also the note at 4.27 and the mini-article called "Israel's Priests," p. 171.

10.33 *man from Samaria:* People from Samaria were known as Samaritans. See the note at 9.52.

10.34 *olive oil and wine:* In Jesus' day these were used as medicine. Sometimes olive oil was used in healing ceremonies (Jas 5.14).

10.33,34 2 Chr 28.15.

road. But when he saw the man, he walked by on the other side. ³²Later a temple helper came to the same place. But when he saw the man who had been beaten up, he also went by on the other side.

³³A man from Samaria then came traveling along that road. When he saw the man, he felt sorry for him ³⁴and went over to him. He treated his wounds with olive oil and wine and bandaged them. Then he put him on his own donkey and took him to an inn, where he took care of him. ³⁵The next morning he gave the innkeeper two silver coins and said, "Please take care of the man. If you spend more than this on him, I will pay you when I return."

³⁶Then Jesus asked, "Which one of these three people was a real neighbor to the man who was beaten up by robbers?"

³⁷The teacher answered, "The one who showed pity."

Jesus said, "Go and do the same!"

Martha and Mary

[38]The Lord and his disciples were traveling along and came to a village. When they got there, a woman named Martha welcomed him into her home. [39]She had a sister named Mary, who sat down in front of the Lord and was listening to what he said. [40]Martha was worried about all that had to be done. Finally, she went to Jesus and said, "Lord, doesn't it bother you that my sister has left me to do all the work by myself? Tell her to come and help me!"

[41]The Lord answered, "Martha, Martha! You are worried and upset about so many things, [42]but only one thing is necessary. Mary has chosen what is best, and it will not be taken away from her."

JESUS TEACHES MANY THINGS

In this section, Jesus teaches about prayer, evil, being a follower of God, the importance of trust, and the proper use of money. He also criticizes the Pharisees and teachers of the Law of Moses.

Prayer
(Matthew 6.9-13; 7.7-11)

11 When Jesus had finished praying, one of his disciples said to him, "Lord, teach us to pray, just as John taught his followers to pray."

[2]So Jesus told them, "Pray in this way:

'Father, help us to honor your name.
    Come and set up your kingdom.
[3] Give us each day the food we need.[x]
[4] Forgive our sins,
    as we forgive everyone who has done wrong to us.
    And keep us from being tempted.' "

[5]Then Jesus went on to say:

Suppose one of you goes to a friend in the middle of the night and says, "Let me borrow three loaves of bread. [6]A friend of mine has dropped in, and I don't have a thing for him to eat." [7]And suppose your friend answers, "Don't bother me! The door is bolted, and my children and I are in bed. I cannot get up to give you something."

[8]He may not get up and give you the bread, just because you are his friend. But he will get up and give you as much as you need, simply because you are not ashamed to keep on asking.

[9]So I tell you to ask and you will receive, search and you will find, knock and the door will be opened for you.

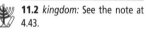

10.38 *village:* This is the village of Bethany, where Mary and Martha lived with their brother Lazarus (John 11.1). Bethany was about two miles east of Jerusalem.

10.38-40 *Martha . . . sister named Mary:* Martha was concerned with practical matters like preparing food and offering hospitality to a traveler (the Greek word is also used to refer to the "service" of a disciple). Mary was more interested in listening to Jesus teach. In JOHN, Martha did not understand what Jesus said about rising from the dead (John 11.17-27).

11.2 *kingdom:* See the note at 4.43.

11.4 *sins:* Sin occurs when people rebel against God and disobey God's Law. Forgiveness removes the sin. According to the Jewish Scriptures, those who disobeyed God's commandments could be forgiven if they turned back to God and stopped committing the sinful acts (repented). The Jewish teachers taught that only God could forgive sin. See also the mini-article called "Sin," p. 187.

---

[x]11.3 *the food we need:* Or "food for today" or "food for the coming day."

11.13,14 *Holy Spirit . . . demon:* See the notes on p. 24 (Holy Spirit) and 4.33-35 (evil spirit . . . demon).

11.15 *Beelzebul, the ruler of the demons:* The name Beelzebul comes from a title of the Canaanite god Baal meaning "prince Baal" or "lord of power." The Hebrew people changed the name slightly to Beelzebub (Matt 12.24), meaning "lord of the flies." See also Matt 9.34.

11.18 *Satan:* See the note at 4.3.

11.23 *gather in the crop:* Jesus is referring to the harvest of believers. Those who don't join with Jesus in this task are against him and his message. See also Mark 9.40.

11.24 *evil spirit:* See the note at 4.33-35.

11.16 Matt 12.38; 16.1; Mark 8.11.

[10]Everyone who asks will receive, everyone who searches will find, and the door will be opened for everyone who knocks. [11]Which one of you fathers would give your hungry child a snake if the child asked for a fish? [12]Which one of you would give your child a scorpion if the child asked for an egg? [13]As bad as you are, you still know how to give good gifts to your children. But your heavenly Father is even more ready to give the Holy Spirit to anyone who asks.

Jesus and the Ruler of Demons
(Matthew 12.22-30; Mark 3.20-27)

[14]Jesus forced a demon out of a man who could not talk. And after the demon had gone out, the man started speaking, and the crowds were amazed. [15]But some people said, "He forces out demons by the power of Beelzebul, the ruler of the demons!"

[16]Others wanted to put Jesus to the test. So they asked him to show them a sign from God. [17]Jesus knew what they were thinking, and he said:

A kingdom where people fight each other will end up in ruin. And a family that fights will break up. [18]If Satan fights against himself, how can his kingdom last? Yet you say that I force out demons by the power of Beelzebul. [19]If I use his power to force out demons, whose power do your own followers use to force them out? They are the ones who will judge you. [20]But if I use God's power to force out demons, it proves that God's kingdom has already come to you.

[21]When a strong man arms himself and guards his home, everything he owns is safe. [22]But if a stronger man comes and defeats him, he will carry off the weapons in which the strong man trusted. Then he will divide with others what he has taken. [23]If you are not on my side, you are against me. If you don't gather in the crop with me, you scatter it.

Return of an Evil Spirit
(Matthew 12.43-45)

[24]When an evil spirit leaves a person, it travels through the desert, looking for a place to rest. But when it doesn't find a place, it says, "I will go back to the home I left." [25]When it gets there and finds the place clean and fixed up, [26]it goes off and finds seven other evil spirits even worse than itself. They all come and make their home there, and that person ends up in worse shape than before.

Being Really Blessed

[27]While Jesus was still talking, a woman in the crowd spoke up, "The woman who gave birth to you and nursed you is blessed!"

[28]Jesus replied, "That's true, but the people who are really blessed are the ones who hear and obey God's message!"[y]

A Sign from God
(Matthew 12.38-42; Mark 8.12)

[29]As crowds were gathering around Jesus, he said:

You people of today are evil! You keep looking for a sign from God. But what happened to Jonah is the only sign you will be given. [30]Just as Jonah was a sign to the people of Nineveh, the Son of Man will be a sign to the people of today. [31]When the judgment comes, the Queen of the South will stand there with you and condemn you. She traveled a long way to hear Solomon's wisdom, and yet here is something far greater than Solomon. [32]The people of Nineveh will also stand there with you and condemn you. They turned to God when Jonah preached, and yet here is something far greater than Jonah.

Light
(Matthew 5.15; 6.22,23)

[33]No one lights a lamp and then hides it or puts it under a clay pot. A lamp is put on a lampstand, so that everyone who comes into the house can see the light. [34]Your eyes are the lamp for your body. When your eyes are good, you have all the light you need. But when your eyes are bad, everything is dark. [35]So be sure that your light isn't darkness. [36]If you have light, and nothing is dark, then light will be everywhere, as when a lamp shines brightly on you.

Jesus Condemns the Pharisees and Teachers of the Law of Moses
(Matthew 23.1-36; Mark 12.38-40; Luke 20.45-47)

[37]When Jesus finished speaking, a Pharisee invited him home for a meal. Jesus went and sat down to eat. [38]The Pharisee was surprised that he did not wash his hands before eating. [39]So the Lord said to him:

You Pharisees clean the outside of cups and dishes, but on the inside you are greedy and evil. [40]You fools! Didn't God make both the outside and the inside?[z] [41]If you would only give what you have to the poor, everything you do would please God.

---

[y] 11.28 *"That's true, but the people who are really blessed...message"*: Or " 'That's not true, the people who are blessed...message.' " [z] 11.40 *Didn't God make both the outside and the inside*: Or "Doesn't the person who washes the outside always wash the inside too?"

Jesus said,
"The people who are really blessed are the ones who hear and obey God's message!"
Luke 11.28

11.29,30 *what happened to Jonah . . . a sign to the people of Nineveh:* After the prophet Jonah refused God's command to bring a message to the Assyrians, Israel's enemies, God sent a big fish to swallow Jonah. He stayed inside the fish for three days before being spit out. Jesus is comparing the time he would spend in the grave (Luke 23.50—24.12) with the time Jonah spent inside the big fish. See also Matt 16.4; Mark 8.12; Jonah 3.4.

11.31,32 *the Queen of the South:* This refers to the queen of Sheba. Sheba was a country in southern Arabia, or possibly northeast Africa. Jesus is saying that if Gentiles like the people of Nineveh (Jonah 3.5) or the Queen of Sheba (1 Kgs 10.1-10; 2 Chr 9.1-12) could learn from Jewish prophets and kings, why can't the leaders of Judah recognize God's message from one of their own people, namely Jesus?

11.33 *lamp:* See the note at 8.16. See also Matt 5.15; Mark 4.21; Luke 8.16.

11.37 *Pharisee:* See the note at 5.17.

11.37 *sat down to eat:* See the note at 7.36 (got ready to eat).

11.38,39 *did not wash his hands:* The Jewish Law taught that what people ate and touched could make them unfit to worship God. This is why they washed their hands and cleansed their dishes before eating. But Jesus was saying that what a person was like inside is more important than following laws that only make a person clean on the outside. See also the mini-article called "Purity (Clean and Unclean)," p. 183.

> Jesus said,
> *"Don't be greedy!*
> *Owning a lot of*
> *things won't make*
> *your life safe."*
> Luke 12.15

11.42 *give God a tenth:* The Pharisees followed the law about giving one tenth of everything back to the Lord (see Deut 14.22 and Lev 27.30), even one tenth of the spices in their gardens. Jesus told them that helping others was just as important.

11.43 *love the front seats . . . like to be greeted with honor:* The Pharisees usually sat at the front of the meetings, because they often taught about the Scriptures. People looked up to the Pharisees and showed them respect in public.

11.44 *unmarked graves:* Tombs were whitewashed so that people would notice them and not touch them. A person who touched a dead body or a tomb was considered unclean and had to go through cleansing ceremony before worshiping again with the rest of the Jewish people.

11.45 *teacher of the Law of Moses:* See the note at 5.17.

11.46 *heavy burdens:* Refers to the laws that the Pharisees and teachers of the Law of Moses taught people to follow. Jesus suggests that these teachers liked to lay down rules, but weren't willing to help those who struggled to keep them. See also the article called "People of the Law: The Religion of Israel," p. 109.

11.49 *Wisdom of God:* Jesus is quoting from an unknown source. God sent messengers before Jesus, but the Jewish people turned their backs on them or even killed them. They failed to listen to what God was saying to them.

12.1 Matt 16.6; Mark 8.15. **12.2** Mark 4.22; Luke 8.17.

[42]You Pharisees are in for trouble! You give God a tenth of the spices from your gardens, such as mint and rue. But you cheat people, and you don't love God. You should be fair and kind to others and still give a tenth to God.

[43]You Pharisees are in for trouble! You love the front seats in the meeting places, and you like to be greeted with honor in the market. [44]But you are in for trouble! You are like unmarked graves that people walk on without even knowing it.

[45]A teacher of the Law of Moses spoke up, "Teacher, you said cruel things about us."

[46]Jesus replied:

You teachers are also in for trouble! You load people down with heavy burdens, but you won't lift a finger to help them carry the loads. [47]Yes, you are really in for trouble. You build monuments to honor the prophets your own people murdered long ago. [48]You must think that was the right thing for your people to do, or else you would not have built monuments for the prophets they murdered.

[49]Because of your evil deeds, the Wisdom of God said, "I will send prophets and apostles to you. But you will murder some and mistreat others." [50]You people living today will be punished for all the prophets who have been murdered since the beginning of the world. [51]This includes every prophet from the time of Abel to the time of Zechariah, who was murdered between the altar and the temple. You people will certainly be punished for all of this.

[52]You teachers of the Law of Moses are really in for trouble! You carry the keys to the door of knowledge about God. But you never go in, and you keep others from going in.

[53]Jesus was about to leave, but the teachers and the Pharisees wanted to get even with him. They tried to make him say what he thought about other things, [54]so that they could catch him saying something wrong.

Warnings

12 As thousands of people crowded around Jesus and were stepping on each other, he told his disciples:

Be sure to guard against the dishonest teaching[a] of the Pharisees! It is their way of fooling people. [2]Everything that is hidden will be found out, and every secret will be known. [3]Whatever you say in the dark will be heard when it is day. Whatever you whisper in a closed room will be shouted from the housetops.

---

[a] **12.1** *dishonest teaching:* The Greek text has "yeast," which is used here to describe a teaching that is not true (see Matt 16.6,12).

The One To Fear
(Matthew 10.28-31)

[4]My friends, don't be afraid of people. They can kill you, but after that, there is nothing else they can do. [5]God is the one you must fear. Not only can he take your life, but he can throw you into hell. God is certainly the one you should fear!

[6]Five sparrows are sold for just two pennies, but God doesn't forget a one of them. [7]Even the hairs on your head are counted. So don't be afraid! You are worth much more than many sparrows.

Telling Others about Christ
(Matthew 10.32,33; 12.32; 10.19,20)

[8]If you tell others that you belong to me, the Son of Man will tell God's angels that you are my followers. [9]But if you reject me, you will be rejected in front of them. [10]If you speak against the Son of Man, you can be forgiven, but if you speak against the Holy Spirit, you cannot be forgiven.

[11]When you are brought to trial in the Jewish meeting places or before rulers or officials, don't worry about how you will defend yourselves or what you will say. [12]At that time the Holy Spirit will tell you what to say.

A Rich Fool

[13]A man in a crowd said to Jesus, "Teacher, tell my brother to give me my share of what our father left us when he died."

[14]Jesus answered, "Who gave me the right to settle arguments between you and your brother?"

[15]Then he said to the crowd, "Don't be greedy! Owning a lot of things won't make your life safe."

[16]So Jesus told them this story:

A rich man's farm produced a big crop, [17]and he said to himself, "What can I do? I don't have a place large enough to store everything."

[18]Later, he said, "Now I know what I'll do. I'll tear down my barns and build bigger ones, where I can store all my grain and other goods. [19]Then I'll say to myself, 'You have stored up enough good things to last for years to come. Live it up! Eat, drink, and enjoy yourself.' "

[20]But God said to him, "You fool! Tonight you will die. Then who will get what you have stored up?"

[21]"This is what happens to people who store up everything for themselves, but are poor in the sight of God."

Worry
(Matthew 6.25-34)

[22]Jesus said to his disciples:

 11.51 *from the time of Abel . . . Zechariah:* Jesus is giving the names of the first and last persons that the Jewish Scriptures say were murdered. Abel is mentioned in Genesis 4.1-16; Zechariah, the brother of King Jeroram is named in 2 Chronicles 24.20-22. (2 CHRONICLES is the last book in the Hebrew Bible; see the chart called "Books of the Hebrew Scriptures," p. 7.

11.52 *teachers of the Law of Moses:* See the note at 5.17.

12.5 *hell:* In Greek the word for hell is "gehenna," which is a form of the Hebrew words that mean "Valley of Hinnom." Even before Jesus was born, some Jewish teachers said that the place where wicked people go when they die is like the burning Valley of Hinnom. See also the mini-article called "Hell," p. 168.

12.6 *Five sparrows . . . two pennies:* The Roman coin referred to here is an assarius, which equals only about one-sixteenth of what a common laborer earned for one day's work. The Law of Moses did not forbid the eating of sparrows. Because they were so cheap, the ordinary person could afford them.

 9.22 *Son of Man:* See the mini-article called "Son of Man," p. 190.

12.8 *God's angels:* See the note at 2.13-15.

12.10 *Holy Spirit:* See the note on p. 24 (Holy Spirit).

12.11 *Jewish meeting places:* See the note at 4.15.

 12.10 Matt 12.32; Mark 3.29. **12.11,12** Matt 10.19,20; Mark 13.11; Luke 21.14,15.

12.27 *Solomon with all his wealth:* The Jewish people thought that King Solomon was the richest person who had ever lived. See also 1 Kgs 10.4-7; 2 Chr 9.3-6; and the mini-article called "Solomon," p. 188.

12.30 *Your Father:* Jesus is referring to God.
12.32 *the kingdom:* See the note at 4.43.
12.33 *heaven:* See the note at 6.23.
9.22 *Son of Man:* See the mini-article called "Son of Man," p. 190.

12.35 Matt 25.1-13. **12.36** Mark 13.34-36. **12.39,40** Matt 24.43,44.

I tell you not to worry about your life! Don't worry about having something to eat or wear. [23]Life is more than food or clothing. [24]Look at the crows! They don't plant or harvest, and they don't have storehouses or barns. But God takes care of them. You are much more important than any birds. [25]Can worry make you live longer?[b] [26]If you don't have power over small things, why worry about everything else?

[27]Look how the wild flowers grow! They don't work hard to make their clothes. But I tell you that Solomon with all his wealth wasn't as well clothed as one of these flowers. [28]God gives such beauty to everything that grows in the fields, even though it is here today and thrown into a fire tomorrow. Won't he do even more for you? You have such little faith!

[29]Don't keep worrying about having something to eat or drink. [30]Only people who don't know God are always worrying about such things. Your Father knows what you need. [31]But put God's work first, and these things will be yours as well.

Treasures in Heaven
(Matthew 6.19-21)

[32]My little group of disciples, don't be afraid! Your Father wants to give you the kingdom. [33]Sell what you have and give the money to the poor. Make yourselves moneybags that never wear out. Make sure your treasure is safe in heaven, where thieves cannot steal it and moths cannot destroy it. [34]Your heart will always be where your treasure is.

Faithful and Unfaithful Servants
(Matthew 24.45-51)

[35]Be ready and keep your lamps burning [36]just like those servants who wait up for their master to return from a wedding feast. As soon as he comes and knocks, they open the door for him. [37]Servants are fortunate if their master finds them awake and ready when he comes! I promise you that he will get ready and have his servants sit down so he can serve them. [38]Those servants are really fortunate if their master finds them ready, even though he comes late at night or early in the morning. [39]You would surely not let a thief break into your home, if you knew when the thief was coming. [40]So always be ready! You don't know when the Son of Man will come.

---

[b] **12.25** *live longer:* Or "grow taller."

[41]Peter asked Jesus, "Did you say this just for us or for everyone?"

[42]The Lord answered:

Who are faithful and wise servants? Who are the ones the master will put in charge of giving the other servants their food supplies at the proper time? [43]Servants are fortunate if their master comes and finds them doing their job. [44]A servant who is always faithful will surely be put in charge of everything the master owns.

[45]But suppose one of the servants thinks that the master won't return until late. Suppose that servant starts beating all the other servants and eats and drinks and gets drunk. [46]If that happens, the master will come on a day and at a time when the servant least expects him. That servant will then be punished and thrown out with the servants who cannot be trusted.

[47]If servants are not ready or willing to do what their master wants them to do, they will be beaten hard. [48]But servants who don't know what their master wants them to do will not be beaten so hard for doing wrong. If God has been generous with you, he will expect you to serve him well. But if he has been more than generous, he will expect you to serve him even better.

Not Peace, but Trouble
(Matthew 10.34-36)

[49]I came to set fire to the earth, and I wish it were already on fire! [50]I am going to be put to a hard test. And

12.41 *Peter:* See the note at 5.8 (Simon Peter).

12.42 *servants:* See the mini-article below called "Slaves and Servants in the Time of Jesus."

12.50 Mark 10.38.

SLAVES AND SERVANTS IN THE TIME OF JESUS

The word in the New Testament usually translated as "servant" actually means "slave," and refers to someone who was owned or controlled by someone else, not just a servant hired to do a certain job. Some slaves performed common household tasks. Others, called "stewards," supervised the work of lesser servants or managed the master's finances. In the time of Jesus, some people were slaves because they were born to slave parents. Others were captured in war and were forced to become slaves. Some people actually sold themselves as slaves because they could have a higher standard of life as a slave than if they had to keep struggling to find housing or food on their own.

Some slaves were better educated than their masters and served as teachers of their master's children. Slaves of rich masters had all kinds of opportunities that they would never have had on their own. But slaves had no freedom, and their owners could do with them whatever they wanted, including selling them to someone else. After slaves became 30 years old, many would become "freedmen," with duties to the former master and his family. Some slaves earned enough money to buy their own freedom, which would mean that their children could be free also.

12.54 *cloud coming up in the west:* Weather systems usually travel from west to east. This is true in Palestine, where there are occasional heavy rain storms in the winter.

13.1 *Pilate:* The Roman governor in charge of Judea from A.D. 26-36. When Pilate was in Jerusalem, he lived at the Antonia, a fortress that overlooked the temple area. Several first-century Jewish historians reported that Pilate was a cruel leader who was disrespectful of the Jewish temple and religious customs. Normally, however, Roman leaders did not interfere with the everyday work and worship at the temple. See also the mini-article called "Pontius Pilate," p. 182. This inscription from a pagan temple in Caesarea includes Pilate's name.

13.2 *sinners:* Those who rebel against God and disobey God's Law. People in Jesus' day generally believed that bad things happened to someone who was sinful. Jesus is saying that all people are sinful and need to turn to God. See also the note at 11.4.

13.4 *tower in Siloam:* This tower was probably by the Pool of Siloam, inside the southeast wall of Jerusalem (see the map on p. 198). This comment by Jesus is the only record of the event.

13.6 *fig tree growing in his vineyard:* See the note at 6.44.

12.53 Mic 7.6.

I will have to suffer a lot of pain until it is over. [51]Do you think that I came to bring peace to earth? No indeed! I came to make people choose sides. [52]A family of five will be divided, with two of them against the other three. [53]Fathers and sons will turn against one another, and mothers and daughters will do the same. Mothers-in-law and daughters-in-law will also turn against each other.

Knowing What To Do
(Matthew 16.2, 3; 5.25, 26)

[54]Jesus said to all the people:

As soon as you see a cloud coming up in the west, you say, "It's going to rain," and it does. [55]When the south wind blows, you say, "It's going to get hot," and it does. [56]Are you trying to fool someone? You can predict the weather by looking at the earth and sky, but you don't really know what's going on right now. [57]Why don't you understand the right thing to do? [58]When someone accuses you of something, try to settle things before you are taken to court. If you don't, you will be dragged before the judge. Then the judge will hand you over to the jailer, and you will be locked up. [59]You won't get out until you have paid the last cent you owe.

TEACHINGS ABOUT GOD'S KINGDOM

Jesus teaches about living in God's kingdom and heals two more people on the Sabbath.

Turn Back to God

13 About this same time Jesus was told that Pilate had given orders for some people from Galilee to be killed while they were offering sacrifices. [2]Jesus replied:

Do you think that these people were worse sinners than everyone else in Galilee just because of what happened to them? [3]Not at all! But you can be sure that if you don't turn back to God, every one of you will also be killed. [4]What about those eighteen people who died when the tower in Siloam fell on them? Do you think they were worse than everyone else in Jerusalem? [5]Not at all! But you can be sure that if you don't turn back to God, every one of you will also die.

A Story about a Fig Tree

[6]Jesus then told them this story:

A man had a fig tree growing in his vineyard. One day he went out to pick some figs, but he didn't find any.

[7]So he said to the gardener, "For three years I have come looking for figs on this tree, and I haven't found any yet. Chop it down! Why should it take up space?"

[8]The gardener answered, "Master, leave it for another year. I'll dig around it and put some manure on it to make it grow. [9]Maybe it will have figs on it next year. If it doesn't, you can have it cut down."

Healing a Woman on the Sabbath

[10]One Sabbath, Jesus was teaching in a Jewish meeting place, [11]and a woman was there who had been crippled by an evil spirit for eighteen years. She was completely bent over and could not straighten up. [12]When Jesus saw the woman, he called her over and said, "You are now well." [13]He placed his hands on her, and right away she stood up straight and praised God.

[14]The man in charge of the meeting place was angry because Jesus had healed someone on the Sabbath. So he said to the people, "Each week has six days when we can work. Come and be healed on one of those days, but not on the Sabbath."

[15]The Lord replied, "Are you trying to fool someone? Won't any one of you untie your ox or donkey and lead it out to drink on a Sabbath? [16]This woman belongs to the family of Abraham, but Satan has kept her bound for eighteen years. Isn't it right to set her free on the Sabbath?" [17]Jesus' words made his enemies ashamed. But everyone else in the crowd was happy about the wonderful things he was doing.

A Mustard Seed and Yeast
(Matthew 13.31-33; Mark 4.30-32)

[18]Jesus said, "What is God's kingdom like? What can I compare it with? [19]It is like what happens when someone plants a mustard seed in a garden. The seed grows as big as a tree, and birds nest in its branches."

[20]Then Jesus said, "What can I compare God's kingdom with? [21]It is like what happens when a woman mixes yeast into three batches of flour. Finally, all the dough rises."

The Narrow Door
(Matthew 7.13,14,21-23)

[22]As Jesus was on his way to Jerusalem, he taught the people in the towns and villages. [23]Someone asked him, "Lord, are only a few people going to be saved?"

Jesus answered:

[24]Do all you can to go in by the narrow door! A lot of people will try to get in, but will not be able to. [25]Once the owner of the house gets up and locks the door, you will be left standing outside. You will knock on the door and say, "Sir, open the door for us!"

13.10 *Sabbath . . . Jewish meeting place:* See the notes at 4.15 (Jewish meeting place) and 4.16 (Sabbath).

13.14 *healed . . . on the Sabbath:* Doing any kind of work on the Sabbath, including healing someone, was against the Jewish Law. See the note at 6.9. See also Exod 20.9,10; Deut 5.13,14.

13.15 *ox or donkey:* Both animals were very valuable to the agricultural society of Jesus' day. The ox was used for work like plowing or pulling a stone to crush grain. Donkeys were used to carry and move things much more often than horses or camels were. Sometimes donkeys were also used to do farm work.

13.16 *Satan:* See the note at 4.3. In Jesus' day Satan and demons were often thought to be responsible for sickness and other physical and mental problems. See the article called "Miracles, Magic, and Medicine," p. 144.

13.18 *God's kingdom:* See the note at 4.43.

13.19 *mustard seed:* This tiny black seed was used to flavor food and to keep it fresh. It contained oil and was used in medicine. The mustard plant does not usually grow as tall as most trees, but it can grow taller than a human being. Sometimes the stem can be as thick as a person's arm.

13.21 *yeast:* Yeast is a tiny yellowish fungus. When it is mixed with water and flour, it causes the dough to rise, so the bread will not be flat when baked. Yeast is also called leavening. The three batches mentioned in this verse would have been a large amount, containing 144 cups of flour, enough for thirty-five to forty modern loaves of bread.

13.28 *Abraham, Isaac:* The Jewish people Jesus was talking to would have known that God made an agreement with Abraham, the ancestor of all Jewish people (Gen 12.1-3; 17.1-9). See also Matt 22.13; 25.30 and the mini-article called "Abraham," p. 155.

13.29 *feast in God's kingdom:* This feast refers to a future time when God will bring together faithful people not only from the people of Israel but from every nation. Jesus compares this time to a feast because a feast was a time of celebration. See also Matt 8.11,12.

13.31 *Pharisees:* See the note at 5.17.

13.31 *Herod:* See the notes at 3.1 and 9.7 (Herod Antipas). The Pharisees may have been trying to scare Jesus into leaving for Judea.

13.32 *fox:* The Greeks, like many people throughout the ages, thought of foxes as sly or clever animals.

13.33 *Jerusalem:* See the note at 9.51 (Jerusalem). A number of the prophets had also been killed when they brought unpopular messages to Jerusalem.

13.35 *temple:* This is the temple that Herod the Great built in Jerusalem. Work began in 20 B.C. and continued in Jesus' day (see John 2.20). The temple sat on a huge stone platform that was nearly a mile around at the base. Some of the huge blocks of stone in Herod's original foundation wall are still in place, but the temple itself was completely destroyed when the Romans, headed by Titus, captured Jerusalem in A.D. 70. See also the article called "People of the Law: The Religion of Israel," p. 109, which includes diagrams of the Jewish temple.

13.27 Ps 6.8. **13.30** Matt 19.30; 20.16; Mark 10.31. **13.35** Ps 118.26; Luke 19.38. **14.5** Luke 13.14; Matt 12.11.

But the owner will answer, "I don't know a thing about you!"

[26]Then you will start saying, "We dined with you, and you taught in our streets."

[27]But he will say, "I really don't know who you are! Get away from me, you evil people!"

[28]Then when you have been thrown outside, you will weep and grit your teeth because you will see Abraham, Isaac, Jacob, and all the prophets in God's kingdom. [29]People will come from all directions and sit down to feast in God's kingdom. [30]There the ones who are now least important will be the most important, and those who are now most important will be least important.

Jesus and Herod

[31]At that time some Pharisees came to Jesus and said, "You had better get away from here! Herod wants to kill you."

[32]Jesus said to them:

Go tell that fox, "I am going to force out demons and heal people today and tomorrow, and three days later I'll be through." [33]But I am going on my way today and tomorrow and the next day. After all, Jerusalem is the place where prophets are killed.

Jesus Loves Jerusalem
(Matthew 23.37-39)

[34]Jerusalem, Jerusalem! Your people have killed the prophets and have stoned the messengers who were sent to you. I have often wanted to gather your people, as a hen gathers her chicks under her wings. But you wouldn't let me. [35]Now your temple will be deserted. You won't see me again until the time when you say,

"Blessed is the one who comes in the name of the Lord."

Jesus Heals a Sick Man

14 One Sabbath, Jesus was having dinner in the home of an important Pharisee, and everyone was carefully watching Jesus. [2]All of a sudden a man with swollen legs stood up in front of him. [3]Jesus turned and asked the Pharisees and the teachers of the Law of Moses, "Is it right to heal on the Sabbath?" [4]But they did not say a word.

Jesus took hold of the man. Then he healed him and sent him away. [5]Afterwards, Jesus asked the people, "If your son or ox falls into a well, wouldn't you pull him out right away, even on the Sabbath?" [6]There was nothing they could say.

How To Be a Guest

[7]Jesus saw how the guests had tried to take the best seats. So he told them:

[8]When you are invited to a wedding feast, don't sit in the best place. Someone more important may have been invited. [9]Then the one who invited you will come and say, "Give your place to this other guest!" You will be embarrassed and will have to sit in the worst place.

[10]When you are invited to be a guest, go and sit in the worst place. Then the one who invited you may come and say, "My friend, take a better seat!" You will then be honored in front of all the other guests. [11]If you put yourself above others, you will be put down. But if you humble yourself, you will be honored.

[12]Then Jesus said to the man who had invited him:

When you give a dinner or a banquet, don't invite your friends and family and relatives and rich neighbors. If you do, they will invite you in return, and you will be paid back. [13]When you give a feast, invite the poor, the crippled, the lame, and the blind. [14]They cannot pay you back. But God will bless you and reward you when his people rise from death.

The Great Banquet
(Matthew 22.1-10)

[15]After Jesus had finished speaking, one of the guests said, "The greatest blessing of all is to be at the banquet in God's kingdom!"

[16]Jesus told him:

A man once gave a great banquet and invited a lot of guests. [17]When the banquet was ready, he sent a servant to tell the guests, "Everything is ready! Please come."

[18]One guest after another started making excuses. The first one said, "I bought some land, and I've got to look it over. Please excuse me."

[19]Another guest said, "I bought five teams of oxen, and I need to try them out. Please excuse me."

[20]Still another guest said, "I have just gotten married, and I can't be there."

[21]The servant told his master what happened, and the master became so angry that he said, "Go as fast as you can to every street and alley in town! Bring in everyone who is poor or crippled or blind or lame."

[22]When the servant returned, he said, "Master, I've done what you told me, and there is still plenty of room for more people."

[23]His master then told him, "Go out along the back roads and fence rows and make people come in, so that

Jesus said,
"The greatest blessing of all is to be at the banquet in God's kingdom!"
Luke 14.15

14.1-3 *Pharisee . . . teachers of the Law:* See the note at 5.17.

14.3 *heal on the Sabbath:* See the notes at 4.16 (Sabbath) and 6.9.

14.8 *wedding feast:* In Jesus' day, wedding feasts could be elaborate affairs, sometimes lasting for an entire week. Before marriage, couples had a betrothal (agreement to marry in the future), and there was a celebration to recognize the betrothal. A document called a *tena'im* was also drawn up. This document spelled out the time, place, and size of the wedding to come. The wedding itself was a very important ceremony and celebration. Both the bride and the bridegroom were beautifully dressed and ornamented. There was a procession from the house of the bride to the bridegroom's house, and this was followed by dancing, music, and poetry in which the whole community took part.

14.14 *when his people rise from death:* Jesus is talking about the future time when God will bring his faithful followers back from death to live under God's everlasting rule (Dan 12.2; John 5.28,29; 1 Thes 4.16; Rev 20.11-15). See also the mini-article called "Resurrection," p. 184.

14.15 *the banquet in God's kingdom:* See the note at 13.29.

14.19 *teams of oxen:* A team of oxen could be as few as two oxen tied or yoked together. See also note at 13.15.

14.8-10 Prov 25.6,7. **14.11** Matt 23.12; Luke 18.14.

14.34 *salt:* Salt was used to flavor food. It was also used to preserve food, especially meat and fish. Salt that has lost its taste was no longer useful.

15.1 *Tax collectors and sinners:* See the notes at 3.12 (tax collectors) and 13.2 (sinners). "Sinners" was the name given to people who are unclean or disobedient according to the Law of Moses. Jesus wanted to show how much God cared for sinners and wanted to welcome them into the community of God's people.

15.2 *Pharisees and the teachers of the Law of Moses:* See the note at 5.17.

14.26 Matt 10.37.   15.1,2 Luke 5.29,30.

my house will be full. [24]Not one of the guests I first invited will get even a bite of my food!"

Being a Disciple
(Matthew 10.37,38)

[25]Large crowds were walking along with Jesus, when he turned and said:
[26]You cannot be my disciple, unless you love me more than you love your father and mother, your wife and children, and your brothers and sisters. You cannot come with me unless you love me more than you love your own life. [27]You cannot be my disciple unless you carry your own cross and come with me.

[28]Suppose one of you wants to build a tower. What is the first thing you will do? Won't you sit down and figure out how much it will cost and if you have enough money to pay for it? [29]Otherwise, you will start building the tower, but not be able to finish. Then everyone who sees what is happening will laugh at you. [30]They will say, "You started building, but could not finish the job."

[31]What will a king do if he has only ten thousand soldiers to defend himself against a king who is about to attack him with twenty thousand soldiers? Before he goes out to battle, won't he first sit down and decide if he can win? [32]If he thinks he won't be able to defend himself, he will send messengers and ask for peace while the other king is still a long way off. [33]So then, you cannot be my disciple unless you give away everything you own.

Salt and Light
(Matthew 5.13; Mark 9.50)

[34]Salt is good, but if it no longer tastes like salt, how can it be made to taste salty again? [35]It is no longer good for the soil or even for the manure pile. People simply throw it out. If you have ears, pay attention!

THE LOST ARE FOUND

This chapter includes three stories about how God cares for people who are lost. In the book of LUKE, the "lost" are sinners and tax collectors who were considered to be outcasts by some in the Jewish community in Jesus' day.

One Sheep
(Matthew 18.12-14)

15 Tax collectors and sinners were all crowding around to listen to Jesus. [2]So the Pharisees and the teachers of the Law of Moses

started grumbling, "This man is friendly with sinners. He even eats with them."

[3]Then Jesus told them this story:

[4]If any of you has a hundred sheep, and one of them gets lost, what will you do? Won't you leave the ninety-nine in the field and go look for the lost sheep until you find it? [5]And when you find it, you will be so glad that you will put it on your shoulder [6]and carry it home. Then you will call in your friends and neighbors and say, "Let's celebrate! I've found my lost sheep."

[7]Jesus said, "In the same way there is more happiness in heaven because of one sinner who turns to God than over ninety-nine good people who don't need to."

One Coin

[8]Jesus told the people another story:

What will a woman do if she has ten silver coins and loses one of them? Won't she light a lamp, sweep the floor, and look carefully until she finds it? [9]Then she will call in her friends and neighbors and say, "Let's celebrate! I've found the coin I lost."

[10]Jesus said, "In the same way God's angels are happy when even one person turns to him."

Two Sons

[11]Jesus also told them another story:

Once a man had two sons. [12]The younger son said to his father, "Give me my share of the property." So the father divided his property between his two sons.

[13]Not long after that, the younger son packed up everything he owned and left for a foreign country, where he wasted all his money in wild living. [14]He had spent everything, when a bad famine spread through that whole land. Soon he had nothing to eat.

[15]He went to work for a man in that country, and the man sent him out to take care of his pigs. [16]He would have been glad to eat what the pigs were eating, but no one gave him a thing.

[17]Finally, he came to his senses and said, "My father's workers have plenty to eat, and here I am, starving to death! [18]I will go to my father and say to him, 'Father, I have sinned against God in heaven and against you. [19]I am no longer good enough to be called your son. Treat me like one of your workers.'"

[20]The younger son got up and started back to his father. But when he was still a long way off, his father saw

15.4 *go look for the lost sheep:* A good shepherd in Jesus' time would not have been likely to leave his whole herd unattended in order to go search for one lost sheep.

15.7 *heaven:* See the note at 10.20.

15.8 *ten silver coins:* The coins mentioned here are Greek *drachmas*. One drachma was worth the price of one sheep. And it would take five drachmas to buy an ox.

15.12 *my share of the property:* In a Jewish family, the sons inherited the family's goods and property from their father. Usually the older son received a greater share, often twice as much as his younger brothers.

15.15 *take care of his pigs:* The Law of Moses taught that pigs were not fit to eat or even to touch (Deut 14.8). A Jewish man would have felt terribly insulted if he had to feed pigs, much less eat with them. See also the mini-article called "Purity (Clean and Unclean)," p. 183.

15.16 *what the pigs were eating:* The Greek text has "(bean) pods," which came from a tree in Palestine called the carob tree. Ripe carob pods have a rich syrup-like juice that is very nourishing. Carob pods are still used to feed animals today, and many poor people continue to rely on them for nourishment.

The Prodigal Son by Marc Chagall, around 1975. When the religious leaders grumbled because Jesus was friendly with tax collectors and sinners, Jesus told them three stories about things that had been lost but were then found. (See chapter 15.) The third story tells of a son who asked his father for his inheritance. After he spent it all and was desperate, he returned to his father's estate. The father rejoiced at his son's return, saying, "This son of mine was dead, but has now come back to life. He was lost and has now been found." (Luke 15.24.)

15.22 *ring for his finger and sandals for his feet:* These show that the young man's father fully accepted him as his son. A ring was a sign of high position in the family. Sandals showed that he was a son instead of a slave, since slaves did not usually wear sandals.

him and felt sorry for him. He ran to his son and hugged and kissed him.

²¹The son said, "Father, I have sinned against God in heaven and against you. I am no longer good enough to be called your son."

²²But his father said to the servants, "Hurry and bring the best clothes and put them on him. Give him a ring for his finger and sandals for his feet. ²³Get the best calf and prepare it, so we can eat and celebrate. ²⁴This son of mine was dead, but has now come back to life. He was lost and has now been found." And they began to celebrate.

²⁵The older son had been out in the field. But when he came near the house, he heard the music and dancing. ²⁶So he called one of the servants over and asked, "What's going on here?"

²⁷The servant answered, "Your brother has come home safe and sound, and your father ordered us to kill the best calf." ²⁸The older brother got so angry that he would not even go into the house.

His father came out and begged him to go in. ²⁹But he said to his father, "For years I have worked for you like a slave and have always obeyed you. But you have never even given me a little goat, so that I could give a dinner for my friends. ³⁰This other son of yours wasted your money on prostitutes. And now that he has come home, you ordered the best calf to be killed for a feast."

³¹His father replied, "My son, you are always with me, and everything I have is yours. ³²But we should be glad and celebrate! Your brother was dead, but he is now alive. He was lost and has now been found."

> The father said, *Get the best calf and prepare it, so we can eat and celebrate. This son of mine was dead, but has now come back to life. He was lost and has now been found.* Luke 15.23,24

16.6 *hundred barrels of olive oil:* One of these barrels was called a *batos* in Greek (from the Hebrew word *bath*). Each batos held about eight or nine gallons.

FAITHFUL SERVANTS

As Jesus continues his journey toward Jerusalem, he healsmore people and talks to his disciples and others aboutwhat it means to be faithful servants of God.

A Dishonest Manager

16 Jesus said to his disciples:

A rich man once had a manager to take care of his business. But he was told that his manager was wasting money. ²So the rich man called him in and said, "What is this I hear about you? Tell me what you have done! You are no longer going to work for me."

³The manager said to himself, "What shall I do now that my master is going to fire me? I can't dig ditches, and I'm ashamed to beg. ⁴I know what I'll do, so that people will welcome me into their homes after I've lost my job."

⁵Then one by one he called in the people who were in debt to his master. He asked the first one, "How much do you owe my master?"

⁶"A hundred barrels of olive oil," the man answered.

So the manager said, "Take your bill and sit down and quickly write 'fifty.'"

⁷The manager asked someone else who was in debt to his master, "How much do you owe?"

16.8 *people of this world ... people who belong to the light:* The "people of this world" do not follow God or are opposed to God's purposes. In some parts of the New Testament, the "world" is often pictured as evil and as God's enemy (Rom 12.2; Gal 4.3; Jas 1.27). In the Bible, light is used to describe those people or things that reveal God's truth (see Isa 49.6; John 1.3,4). The followers of Jesus are also called "children of light" (Rom 12.36; Eph 5.8).

16.9 *wicked wealth:* Jesus is not saying that money is evil, but that people sometimes get money by cheating others. Money and possessions can also be used to make friends and to serve others. Money can run out, but God offers something more valuable: an eternal home (living with God forever).

16.14 *Pharisees:* See the note at 5.17.

16.16 *John the Baptist:* See Luke 3.

16.16 *the Law of Moses and the Books of the Prophets:* See the mini-article called "Law," p. 175. The Law of Moses refers to the first five books of the Bible. The Law gives the early history of God's people and lists the rules that God gave the people through Moses about how to live right.

The Books of the Prophets include those books written by God's special messengers. See the articles called "Prophets and Prophecy," p. 129, and "What Books Belong in the Bible," p. 7. See also Matt 11.12,13.

16.13 Matt 6.24. **16.17** Matt 5.18. **16.18** Matt 5.32; 1 Cor 7.10,11.

"A thousand bushels[c] of wheat," the man replied.

The manager said, "Take your bill and write 'eight hundred'."

[8]The master praised his dishonest manager for looking out for himself so well. That's how it is! The people of this world look out for themselves better than the people who belong to the light.

[9]My disciples, I tell you to use wicked wealth to make friends for yourselves. Then when it is gone, you will be welcomed into an eternal home. [10]Anyone who can be trusted in little matters can also be trusted in important matters. But anyone who is dishonest in little matters will be dishonest in important matters. [11]If you cannot be trusted with this wicked wealth, who will trust you with true wealth? [12]And if you cannot be trusted with what belongs to someone else, who will give you something that will be your own? [13]You cannot be the slave of two masters. You will like one more than the other or be more loyal to one than to the other. You cannot serve God and money.

Some Sayings of Jesus
(Matthew 11.12,13;5.31,32; Mark 10.11,12)

[14]The Pharisees really loved money. So when they heard what Jesus said, they made fun of him. [15]But Jesus told them:

You are always making yourselves look good, but God sees what is in your heart. The things that most people think are important are worthless as far as God is concerned.

[16]Until the time of John the Baptist, people had to obey the Law of Moses and the Books of the Prophets. But since God's kingdom has been preached, everyone is trying hard to get in. [17]Heaven and earth will disappear before the smallest letter of the Law does.

[18]It is a terrible sin[d] for a man to divorce his wife and marry another woman. It is also a terrible sin for a man to marry a divorced woman.

Lazarus and the Rich Man

[19]There was once a rich man who wore expensive clothes and every day ate the best food. [20]But a poor beggar named Lazarus was brought to the gate of the rich man's house. [21]He was happy just to eat the scraps that fell from the rich man's table. His body was covered with sores, and dogs kept coming up to lick them. [22]The poor

---

[c]**16.7** *A thousand bushels:* The Greek text has "a hundred measures," and each measure is about ten or twelve bushels. [d]**16.18** *terrible sin:* The Greek text uses a word that means the sin of being unfaithful in marriage (adultery).

The Rich Man and Lazarus, portal of Abbey Church, Moissac, France. Only Luke, of all the Gospel writers, tells the story of the poor man Lazarus who sat outside the gate of a rich man's house. Dogs licked his sores, but he was happy to eat the scraps that fell from the rich man's table. When he died he received a place of honor next to Abraham (shown here as being cradled in Abraham's lap like a baby), but the rich man went to hell and suffered terribly. (See 16.19-31.)

man died, and angels took him to the place of honor next to Abraham.

The rich man also died and was buried. [23]He went to hell [e] and was suffering terribly. When he looked up and saw Abraham far off and Lazarus at his side, [24]he said to Abraham, "Have pity on me! Send Lazarus to dip his finger in water and touch my tongue. I'm suffering terribly in this fire."

[25]Abraham answered, "My friend, remember that while you lived, you had everything good, and Lazarus had everything bad. Now he is happy, and you are in pain. [26]And besides, there is a deep ditch between us, and no one from either side can cross over."

[27]But the rich man said, "Abraham, then please send Lazarus to my father's home. [28]Let him warn my five brothers, so they won't come to this horrible place."

[29]Abraham answered, "Your brothers can read what Moses and the prophets wrote. They should pay attention to that."

[30]Then the rich man said, "No, that's not enough! If only someone from the dead would go to them, they would listen and turn to God."

[31]So Abraham said, "If they won't pay attention to Moses and the prophets, they won't listen even to someone who comes back from the dead."

16.22 *the place of honor next to Abraham:* Some Jewish people thought that the life to come would be like a banquet that God would give for them. Abraham would be the most important person there, and the guest of honor would sit next to him. See also the mini-article called "Eternal Life," p. 163.

16.23 *hell:* The Jewish people often thought of hell as the place where the dead wait for final punishment. See also the note at 12.5 and the mini-article called "Hell," p. 168.

16.29 *what Moses and the prophets wrote:* See the note at 16.16.

16.31 *they won't listen:* Jesus is saying that some people, including many of the Pharisees he is talking to, will not be convinced by his message even after he is raised from death.

Faith and Service
(Matthew 18.6,7,21,22; Mark 9.42)

17 Jesus said to his disciples:

There will always be something that causes people to

---

[e]**16.23** *hell:* The Greek text has "hades."

> Jesus said,
> *"If you had faith no bigger than a tiny mustard seed, you could tell this mulberry tree to pull itself up, roots and all, and to plant itself in the ocean. And it would!"*
> Luke 17.6

sin. But anyone who causes them to sin is in for trouble. A person who causes even one of my little followers to sin ²would be better off thrown into the ocean with a heavy stone tied around their neck. ³So be careful what you do.

Correct any followers[f] of mine who sin, and forgive the ones who say they are sorry. ⁴Even if one of them mistreats you seven times in one day and says, "I am sorry," you should still forgive that person.

⁵The apostles said to the Lord, "Make our faith stronger!" ⁶Jesus replied:

> If you had faith no bigger than a tiny mustard seed, you could tell this mulberry tree to pull itself up, roots and all, and to plant itself in the ocean. And it would!

⁷If your servant comes in from plowing or from taking care of the sheep, would you say, "Welcome! Come on in and have something to eat"? ⁸No, you wouldn't say that. You would say, "Fix me something to eat. Get ready to serve me, so I can have my meal. Then later on you can eat and drink." ⁹Servants don't deserve special thanks for doing what they are supposed to do. ¹⁰And that's how it should be with you. When you've done all you should, then say, "We are merely servants, and we have simply done our duty."

Ten Men with Leprosy

¹¹On his way to Jerusalem, Jesus went along the border between Samaria and Galilee. ¹²As he was going into a village, ten men with leprosy came toward him. They stood at a distance ¹³and shouted, "Jesus, Master, have pity on us!"

¹⁴Jesus looked at them and said, "Go show yourselves to the priests."

On their way they were healed. ¹⁵When one of them discovered that he was healed, he came back, shouting praises to God. ¹⁶He bowed down at the feet of Jesus and thanked him. The man was from the country of Samaria.

¹⁷Jesus asked, "Weren't ten men healed? Where are the other nine? ¹⁸Why was this foreigner the only one who came back to thank God?" ¹⁹Then Jesus told the man, "You may get up and go. Your faith has made you well."

God's Kingdom
(Matthew 24.23-28, 37-41)

²⁰Some Pharisees asked Jesus when God's kingdom would come. He answered, "God's kingdom isn't something you can see. ²¹There is no use saying, 'Look! Here it is' or 'Look! There it is.' God's kingdom is here with you."[g]

17.1 *sin:* See the note at 11.4.

17.6 *mustard seed . . . mulberry tree:* See the note at 13.19 (mustard seed). The mulberry tree was first grown in Persia. It can grow to a height of about 20 feet and is usually very wide at the top. Its berries turn black when ripe and contain a sweet red juice.

17.11 *Jerusalem . . . Samaria and Galilee:* See the notes at 9.51 (Jerusalem), 9.52 (Samaria), and 1.26 (Galilee). See also map on p. 197.

17.12 *leprosy:* See the note at 4.27.

17.14 *show yourselves to the priests:* See the note at 5.14.

17.16 *man was from the country of Samaria:* See the note at 9.52 (Samaritans). Those who heard this story may have been surprised that it was the Samaritan who thanked Jesus. But like other non-Jews ("foreigners") in Luke, he is healed because of his faith (see also 7.1-17).

17.20 *Pharisees:* See the note at 5.17.

17.20 *God's kingdom:* See the note at 4.43.

17.3 Matt 18.15. **17.14** Lev 14.1-32.

---

[f] **17.3** *followers:* The Greek text has "brothers," which is often used in the New Testament for followers of Jesus.   [g] **17.21** *here with you:* Or "in your hearts."

Christ Healing the Sick, stone roof carving from Norwich Cathedral, England, around 1500. Like the other Gospel writers, the author of LUKE tells of the many people Jesus healed as he traveled through Galilee and Judea preaching the good news (4.38-41). He healed a crippled man (4.17-26), a dying girl and a sick woman (8.40-56), ten men with leprosy (17.11-19), a blind beggar (18.35-43), and many others.

²²Jesus said to his disciples:

The time will come when you will long to see one of the days of the Son of Man, but you will not. ²³When people say to you, "Look there," or "Look here," don't go looking for him. ²⁴The day of the Son of Man will be like lightning flashing across the sky. ²⁵But first he must suffer terribly and be rejected by the people of today. ²⁶When the Son of Man comes, things will be just as they were when Noah lived. ²⁷People were eating, drinking, and getting married right up to the day when Noah went into the big boat. Then the flood came and drowned everyone on earth.

²⁸When Lot lived, people were also eating and drinking. They were buying, selling, planting, and building. ²⁹But on the very day Lot left Sodom, fiery flames poured down from the sky and killed everyone. ³⁰The same will happen on the day when the Son of Man appears.

³¹At that time no one on a rooftop should go down into the house to get anything. No one in a field should

17.22 *Son of Man:* See the mini-article called "Son of Man," p. 190.

17.26,27 *Noah:* God chose the good and faithful Noah to build a big boat (ark) that would save his family and other living things from the flood (see Gen 6–9).

17.28,29 *Lot . . . Sodom:* Lot, the nephew of Abraham, ran into trouble in Sodom, which was a very evil city (see Gen 18.16—19.29). God destroyed the evil people who lived there, but rescued Lot and his family. The location of Sodom is not known, but it may have been near the south end of the Dead Sea.

17.30 *Son of Man:* See the mini-article called "Son of Man," p. 190.

17.31 *rooftop:* See the note at 5.19.

17.26,27 Gen 6.5-8; Gen 7.6-24. **17.31** Matt 24.17,18; Mark 13.15,16.

17.32 *what happened to Lot's wife:* She turned into a block of salt when she disobeyed God by turning around to look at the destruction of Sodom (see Gen 19.26).

17.35-36 *grinding wheat:* Usually women sifted the harvested wheat grains and crushed (ground) them in a mill to make flour. A simple mill would have had a flat rock surface where grain could be pounded or rolled with a rock or wooden tool.

17.37 *Where there is a corpse . . . buzzards:* Buzzards are birds that feed on dead flesh. They will quickly surround the body of a dead animal and eat it. This saying may mean that when anything bad happens, people soon know about it, and curious people gather around and stare. But the word translated "buzzard" also means "eagle" and may refer to the Roman army, which had an eagle as its symbol.

18.3 *widow . . . fair treatment in court:* In Jewish culture, a woman who had lost her husband sometimes had no one else to stand up for her or to take care of her.

18.8 *Son of Man:* See the mini-article called "Son of Man," p. 190.

18.10 *into the temple to pray:* People usually went to the temple for prayer early in the morning and about three o'clock in the afternoon.

18.10 *Pharisee and . . . tax collector:* See the notes at 5.17 (Pharisees and experts in the Law of Moses) and 3.12 (tax collector).

18.12 *go without eating . . . give you one tenth of all I earn:* To go without eating is also called "fasting" (see the note at 2.37). Giving a tenth of everything you earn is called "tithing" (see the note at 11.42).

17.33 Matt 10.39; 16.25; Mark 8.35; Luke 9.24; John 12.25.

go back to the house for anything. [32]Remember what happened to Lot's wife.

[33]People who try to save their lives will lose them, and those who lose their lives will save them. [34]On that night two people will be sleeping in the same bed, but only one will be taken. The other will be left. [35-36]Two women will be together grinding wheat, but only one will be taken. The other will be left.[h]

[37]Then Jesus' disciples spoke up, "But where will this happen, Lord?"

Jesus said, "Where there is a corpse, there will always be buzzards."

A Widow and a Judge

18 Jesus told his disciples a story about how they should keep on praying and never give up:

[2]In a town there was once a judge who didn't fear God or care about people. [3]In that same town there was a widow who kept going to the judge and saying, "Make sure that I get fair treatment in court."

[4]For a while the judge refused to do anything. Finally, he said to himself, "Even though I don't fear God or care about people, [5]I will help this widow because she keeps on bothering me. If I don't help her, she will wear me out."

[6]The Lord said:

Think about what that crooked judge said. [7]Won't God protect his chosen ones who pray to him day and night? Won't he be concerned for them? [8]He will surely hurry and help them. But when the Son of Man comes, will he find on this earth anyone with faith?

A Pharisee and a Tax Collector

[9]Jesus told a story to some people who thought they were better than others and who looked down on everyone else:

[10]Two men went into the temple to pray. One was a Pharisee and the other a tax collector. [11]The Pharisee stood over by himself and prayed,[i] "God, I thank you that I am not greedy, dishonest, and unfaithful in marriage like other people. And I am really glad that I am not like that tax collector over there. [12]I go without eating for two days a week, and I give you one tenth of all I earn."

[13]The tax collector stood off at a distance and did not think he was good enough even to look up toward

---

[h]**17.35,36** *will be left:* Some manuscripts add, "Two men will be in the same field, but only one will be taken. The other will be left." [i]**18.11** *stood over by himself and prayed:* Some manuscripts have "stood up and prayed to himself."

heaven. He was so sorry for what he had done that he pounded his chest and prayed, "God, have pity on me! I am such a sinner."

[14]Then Jesus said, "When the two men went home, it was the tax collector and not the Pharisee who was pleasing to God. If you put yourself above others, you will be put down. But if you humble yourself, you will be honored."

Jesus Blesses Little Children
(Matthew 19.13-15; Mark 10.13-16)

[15]Some people brought their little children for Jesus to bless. But when his disciples saw them doing this, they told the people to stop bothering him. [16]So Jesus called the children over to him and said, "Let the children come to me! Don't try to stop them. People who are like these children belong to God's kingdom.[j] [17]You will never get into God's kingdom unless you enter it like a child!"

A Rich and Important Man
(Matthew 19.16-30; Mark 10.17-31)

[18]An important man asked Jesus, "Good Teacher, what must I do to have eternal life?"

[19]Jesus said, "Why do you call me good? Only God is good. [20]You know the commandments: 'Be faithful in marriage. Do not murder. Do not steal. Do not tell lies about others. Respect your father and mother.'"

[21]He told Jesus, "I have obeyed all these commandments since I was a young man."

[22]When Jesus heard this, he said, "There is one thing you still need to do. Go and sell everything you own! Give the money to the poor, and you will have riches in heaven. Then come and be my follower." [23]When the man heard this, he was sad, because he was very rich.

[24]Jesus saw how sad the man was. So he said, "It's terribly hard for rich people to get into God's kingdom! [25]In fact, it's easier for a camel to go through the eye of a needle than for a rich person to get into God's kingdom."

[26]When the crowd heard this, they asked, "How can anyone ever be saved?"

[27]Jesus replied, "There are some things that people cannot do, but God can do anything."

[28]Peter said, "Remember, we left everything to be your followers!"

[29]Jesus answered, "You can be sure that anyone who gives up home or wife or brothers or family or children because of God's

18.13 *sinner:* See the note at 13.2.

18.16,17 *God's kingdom:* See the note at 4.43.

18.18 *eternal life:* See the note at 10.25.

18.19,20 *the commandments:* The five commandments Jesus recites here are part of the Ten Commandments that God gave to Moses on Mount Sinai. See Exod 20.1-17 and Deut 5.1-21.

 18.25 *camel:* Camels are large animals that can be very nasty and stubborn. Jesus used such a bold statement to emphasize the truth of what he was saying.

18.28 *Peter:* See the note at 5.8 (Simon Peter).

18.29,30 *God's kingdom ... eternal life:* See the notes at 4.43 (kingdom) and 10.25 (eternal life).

18.14 Matt 23.12; Luke 14.11. **18.20** Exod 20.14; Deut 5.18; Exod 20.13; Deut 5.17; Exod 20.15; Deut 5.19; Exod 20.16; Deut 5.20; Exod 20.12; Deut 5.16. **18.28** Luke 5.1-11.

---

[j]**18.16** *People who are like these children belong to God's kingdom:* Or "God's kingdom belongs to people who are like these children."

18.31 *Son of Man:* See the note at 5.24.

18.32 *foreigners:* The Romans, who ruled Judea at this time.

18.35 *Jericho:* See the note at 10.30. Joshua 5.13—6.26 describes how the people of Israel destroyed Jericho after crossing the Jordan River into the land of Canaan.

18.35 *blind man:* He is called Bartimaeus in Mark 10.46.

18.37 *Jesus from Nazareth:* Jesus was often identified by adding his hometown to his name, since many Jewish men were named Jesus at the time he lived.

18.38 *Son of David:* The Jewish people expected the Messiah to be from the family of Jesse, King David's father (Isa 11.1-11). For this reason the Messiah was often called the "Son of David." See also the note at 3.15.

19.1 *Jericho:* See the note at 18.35.

19.2 *Zacchaeus . . . collecting taxes:* Zacchaeus is mentioned only here in all of the New Testament. See the note at 3.12 (tax collectors).

19.3-4 *sycamore tree:* The sycamore comes from the same family of trees as the mulberry and fig trees. It is a broad tree with strong branches. Its fruit doesn't taste very good but it was eaten by some poor people.

19.7 *sinner:* See the note at 13.2.

19.8 *pay back four times as much:* Both Jewish and Roman law said that a person must pay back anything taken by theft or cheating, plus a penalty. Four times was about the most that Jewish law would have required a thief to repay (Exod 22.1; 2 Sam 12.6).

18.31 Ps 22; Isa 53; Zech 13.7.
19.11-27 Matt 25.14-30.

---

kingdom [30]will be given much more in this life. And in the future world they will have eternal life."

Jesus Again Tells about His Death
(Matthew 20.17-19; Mark 10.32-34)

[31]Jesus took the twelve apostles aside and said:

We are now on our way to Jerusalem. Everything that the prophets wrote about the Son of Man will happen there. [32]He will be handed over to foreigners, who will make fun of him, mistreat him, and spit on him. [33]They will beat him and kill him, but three days later he will rise to life.

[34]The apostles did not understand what Jesus was talking about. They could not understand, because the meaning of what he said was hidden from them.

Jesus Heals a Blind Beggar
(Matthew 20.29-34; Mark 10.46-52)

[35]When Jesus was coming close to Jericho, a blind man sat begging beside the road. [36]The man heard the crowd walking by and asked what was happening. [37]Some people told him that Jesus from Nazareth was passing by. [38]So the blind man shouted, "Jesus, Son of David, have pity on me!" [39]The people who were going along with Jesus told the man to be quiet. But he shouted even louder, "Son of David, have pity on me!"

[40]Jesus stopped and told some people to bring the blind man over to him. When the blind man was getting near, Jesus asked, [41]"What do you want me to do for you?"

"Lord, I want to see!" he answered.

[42]Jesus replied, "Look and you will see! Your eyes are healed because of your faith." [43]Right away the man could see, and he went with Jesus and started thanking God. When the crowds saw what happened, they praised God.

Zacchaeus

19 Jesus was going through Jericho, [2]where a man named Zacchaeus lived. He was in charge of collecting taxes and was very rich. [3-4]Jesus was heading his way, and Zacchaeus wanted to see what he was like. But Zacchaeus was a short man and could not see over the crowd. So he ran ahead and climbed up into a sycamore tree.

[5]When Jesus got there, he looked up and said, "Zacchaeus, hurry down! I want to stay with you today." [6]Zacchaeus hurried down and gladly welcomed Jesus.

[7]Everyone who saw this started grumbling, "This man Zacchaeus is a sinner! And Jesus is going home to eat with him."

[8]Later that day Zacchaeus stood up and said to the Lord, "I will give half of my property to the poor. And I will now pay back four times as much to everyone I have ever cheated."

⁹Jesus said to Zacchaeus, "Today you and your family have been saved, because you are a true son of Abraham. ¹⁰The Son of Man came to look for and to save people who are lost."

A Story about Ten Servants
(Matthew 25.14-30)

¹¹The crowd was still listening to Jesus as he was getting close to Jerusalem. Many of them thought that God's kingdom would soon appear, ¹²and Jesus told them this story:

A prince once went to a foreign country to be crowned king and then to return. ¹³But before leaving, he called in ten servants and gave each of them some money. He told them, "Use this to earn more money until I get back."

¹⁴But the people of his country hated him, and they sent messengers to the foreign country to say, "We don't want this man to be our king."

19.9 *saved:* After admitting his sin, he is rescued and placed under God's care. See the mini-article below called "God's Saving Love (Salvation)."

19.9 *true son of Abraham:* The Jewish people were also called the sons and daughters of Abraham. Here, Jesus says Zacchaeus is truly one of God's special people.

19.10 *Son of Man:* See the note at 5.24. See also Matt 18.10,11.

19.11 *God's kingdom:* See the note at 4.43. Some thought a great earthly king like David would defeat the Romans and get back Israel's land and freedom. Others thought the whole world would be changed when God's kingdom came.

GOD'S SAVING LOVE (SALVATION)

In the Bible the term "salvation" refers to what God has done and is still doing to free humans from sin, sorrow, sickness, death, and the powers of evil. God wants human beings to live as God created them to live in the beginning (Gen 1,2). When sin entered the world (Gen 3), people needed to "be saved" from the power that death now had over them.

The people of Israel knew that God acted to save them (Exod 12.17; Ps 44.1-8; 78; Deut 6.20-24). God saved the Israelites from slavery in Egypt, and then helped them defeat their enemies and settle in the land of Canaan. God also saved some of them many centuries later after they had been forced to go and live in Babylonia (Isa 43.14-16). For a full description of these events read the articles called "From Joshua to the Exile: The People of Israel in the Promised Land," p. 118, and "After the Exile: God's People Return to Judea," p. 125.

Israel's worship also centers on what God has done to save them from the suffering they had to face (Deut 26.6-10). They offered sacrifices in the temple to show that they were sorry for breaking God's laws and to ask for God's saving help, so they could continue to be God's holy people.

God also promised to give new life to them and to the whole earth, bringing peace and taking care of all their needs (Isa 65.17-25). The prophets of Israel said that someone called a savior would bring good news to those who were sad or imprisoned or poor. This savior would also make a new agreement with God's people in the presence of all the nations of the world (Isa 61.1-11). And God would overcome the powers of evil and make his rule over the world last forever (Dan 7.27).

The New Testament describes Jesus as the one who "will save his people from their sins" (Matt 1.21). He is the one who has been sent "to look for and save people who are lost" (Luke 19.10). His healings and his telling about God's forgiveness are signs that he is bringing salvation (Luke 7.50; 19.9; Mark 5.34). Jesus' death saves human beings and sets them free from their sins (Mark 10.45). By rising from death, he saves and frees people from the power of death (Rom 4.25; 5.10).

> *"That's fine, my good servant!" the king said. "Since you have shown that you can be trusted with a small amount, you will be given ten cities to rule."*
> Luke 19.17

19.23 *interest:* Bankers used the money given to them to make more money by buying and selling. Some of the bankers' profits were returned as interest to the people who gave the banker money to invest.

19.26 Matt 13.12; Mark 4.25; Luke 8.18.

[15]After the prince had been made king, he returned and called in his servants. He asked them how much they had earned with the money they had been given.

[16]The first servant came and said, "Sir, with the money you gave me I have earned ten times as much."

[17]"That's fine, my good servant!" the king said. "Since you have shown that you can be trusted with a small amount, you will be given ten cities to rule."

[18]The second one came and said, "Sir, with the money you gave me, I have earned five times as much."

[19]The king said, "You will be given five cities."

[20]Another servant came and said, "Sir, here is your money. I kept it safe in a handkerchief. [21]You are a hard man, and I was afraid of you. You take what isn't yours, and you harvest crops you didn't plant."

[22]"You worthless servant!" the king told him. "You have condemned yourself by what you have just said. You knew that I am a hard man, taking what isn't mine and harvesting what I've not planted. [23]Why didn't you put my money in the bank? On my return, I could have had the money together with interest."

[24]Then he said to some other servants standing there, "Take the money away from him and give it to the servant who earned ten times as much."

[25]But they said, "Sir, he already has ten times as much!"

[26]The king replied, "Those who have something will be given more. But everything will be taken away from those who don't have anything. [27]Now bring me the enemies who didn't want me to be their king. Kill them while I watch!"

QUESTIONS ABOUT LUKE 9.51—19.27

1. How is love expressed in the story about the good Samaritan? (10.25-37) How do you respond to Jesus' question, "Who is my neighbor?"
2. Describe what Jesus says about being his disciple (14.25-31). What do you think this means for the way you live your life?
3. What do you see as the main point in Jesus' stories about the lost sheep, the lost coin, and the lost son? (15.1-32)
4. Jesus healed ten men with leprosy (17.11-19). What are your thoughts about the nine who did not return to thank Jesus?

Why is it important to say thank you to people who help us? What people in society today might be considered "lepers" or outcasts? What is your attitude toward such persons? Why?
5. Compare the story of the rich and important man (18.18-30) with the story of Zacchaeus (19.1-10). What strikes you about each man and his meeting with Jesus?
6. Choose one verse or passage from this section of LUKE that has special meaning for you and explain why you chose it.

Jesus' Final Week in Jerusalem

After a long journey, Jesus is finally ready to enter Jerusalem. He knows that he must face his enemies in order to fulfill God's plan. Before he is arrested and put on trial, he has a few days to teach in the temple and to prepare his disciples for what will happen after he dies.

JESUS TEACHES IN JERUSALEM

Jesus Enters Jerusalem
(Matthew 21.1-11; Mark 11.1-11; John 12.12-19)

²⁸When Jesus had finished saying all this, he went on toward Jerusalem. ²⁹As he was getting near Bethphage and Bethany on the Mount of Olives, he sent two of his disciples on ahead. ³⁰He told them, "Go into the next village, where you will find a young donkey that has never been ridden. Untie the donkey and bring it here. ³¹If anyone asks why you are doing that, just say, 'The Lord[k] needs it.'"

³²They went off and found everything just as Jesus had said. ³³While they were untying the donkey, its owners asked, "Why are you doing that?"

³⁴They answered, "The Lord needs it."

³⁵Then they led the donkey to Jesus. They put some of their clothes on its back and helped Jesus get on. ³⁶And as he rode along, the people spread clothes on the road in front of him. ³⁷When Jesus was starting down the Mount of Olives, his large crowd of disciples were happy and praised God because of all the miracles they had seen. ³⁸They shouted,

"Blessed is the king who comes in the name of the Lord!
Peace in heaven and glory to God."

³⁹Some Pharisees in the crowd said to Jesus, "Teacher, make your disciples stop shouting!"

⁴⁰But Jesus answered, "If they keep quiet, these stones will start shouting."

⁴¹When Jesus came closer and could see Jerusalem, he cried ⁴²and said:

It is too bad that today your people don't know what will bring them peace! Now it is hidden from them. ⁴³Jerusalem, the time will come when your enemies will build walls around you to attack you. Armies will surround you and close in on you from every side. ⁴⁴They will level you to the ground and kill your people. Not one

---

[k] **19.31** *The Lord:* Or "The master of the donkey."

19.28,29 *Jerusalem … Bethphage and Bethany on the Mount of Olives:* See the note at 9.51 (Jerusalem). Bethphage, which means "house of figs," was a little village on the road between Jericho and Jerusalem. Bethany is on the slopes of the Mount of Olives. Luke 24.50 suggests that Bethany was the place where Jesus went up to heaven. The Mount of Olives is a ridge about two and a half miles long to the east of the Kidron Valley and Jerusalem. It rises about 300 to 500 feet above the temple area in Jerusalem. See the map on p. 198 and the mini-article called "Jerusalem," p. 172.

19.36 *spread clothes on the road:* This is one way that people welcomed a famous person (2 Kgs 9.13).

19.37 *starting down the Mount of Olives:* See the note at 19.28,29. If Jesus entered the city by way of the temple gate (see the map on p. 198) crowds could have been lined up for over a mile. People in the temple area could have watched Jesus ride down from the Mount of Olives, across the Kidron Valley, and back up the road that led to the temple gate.

19.43 *Jerusalem, the time will come:* Jesus' predictions came true. In A.D. 70, the Romans put down a Jewish revolt in Jerusalem. In the process, they destroyed many of the city walls and ruined the temple.

19.38 Ps 118.26.

19.44 *that God had come to save you:* The Jewish people looked for the time when God would rescue them from their enemies. But when Jesus came, many did not recognize him as their "savior." See also the mini-article called "God's Saving Love (Salvation)," p. 85.

19.47 *chief priests, the teachers . . . and some other important people:* See the note at 9.22. These groups had the most to lose if the people accepted Jesus and his teachings. Jesus challenged their authority and power, which made them mad enough to want to kill Jesus (19.47). See also the articles called "The People of the Law: The Religion of Israel," p. 109, and "The World of Jesus: Peoples, Powers, and Politics," p. 133.

20.1 *good news:* See the note at 4.43.

20.4 *John:* John the Baptist. See the note at 1.13.

20.9 *vineyard:* The place where grapes are grown, often on a hillside. Grapevines need lots of special care. Many workers were needed to care for and protect the grape vines. A vineyard was a very valuable possession, and many vineyards had walls around them and a watchtower where someone could keep an eye out for robbers or stray animals that might eat or damage the vines.

19.46 Isa 56.7; Jer 7.11. **20.9** Isa 5.1.

stone in your buildings will be left on top of another. This will happen because you did not see that God had come to save you."

Jesus in the Temple
(Matthew 21.12-17; Mark 11.15-19; John 2.13-22)

⁴⁵When Jesus entered the temple, he started chasing out the people who were selling things. ⁴⁶He told them, "The Scriptures say, 'My house should be a place of worship.' But you have made it a place where robbers hide!"

⁴⁷Each day, Jesus kept on teaching in the temple. So the chief priests, the teachers of the Law of Moses, and some other important people tried to have him killed. ⁴⁸But they could not find a way to do it, because everyone else was eager to listen to him.

A Question about Jesus' Authority
(Matthew 21.23-27; Mark 11.27-33)

20 One day, Jesus was teaching in the temple and telling the good news. So the chief priests, the teachers, and the nation's leaders ²asked him, "What right do you have to do these things? Who gave you this authority?"

³Jesus replied, "I want to ask you a question. ⁴Who gave John the right to baptize? Was it God in heaven or merely some human being?"

⁵They talked this over and said to each other, "We can't say that God gave John this right. Jesus will ask us why we didn't believe John. ⁶And we can't say that it was merely some human who gave John the right to baptize. The crowd will stone us to death, because they think John was a prophet."

⁷So they told Jesus, "We don't know who gave John the right to baptize."

⁸Jesus replied, "Then I won't tell you who gave me the right to do what I do."

Renters of a Vineyard
(Matthew 21.33-46; Mark 12.1-12)

⁹Jesus told the people this story:

A man once planted a vineyard and rented it out. Then he left the country for a long time. ¹⁰When it was time to harvest the crop, he sent a servant to ask the renters for his share of the grapes. But they beat up the servant and sent him away without anything. ¹¹So the owner sent another servant. The renters also beat him up. They insulted him terribly and sent him away without a thing. ¹²The owner sent a third servant. He was also beaten terribly and thrown out of the vineyard.

¹³The owner then said to himself, "What am I going

to do? I know what. I'll send my son, the one I love so much. They will surely respect him!"

[14]When the renters saw the owner's son, they said to one another, "Someday he will own the vineyard. Let's kill him! Then we can have it all for ourselves." [15]So they threw him out of the vineyard and killed him.

Jesus asked, "What do you think the owner of the vineyard will do? [16]I'll tell you what. He will come and kill those renters and let someone else have his vineyard."

When the people heard this, they said, "This must never happen!"

[17]But Jesus looked straight at them and said, "Then what do the Scriptures mean when they say, 'The stone that the builders tossed aside is now the most important stone of all'? [18]Anyone who stumbles over this stone will get hurt, and anyone it falls on will be smashed to pieces."

[19]The chief priests and the teachers of the Law of Moses knew that Jesus was talking about them when he was telling this story. They wanted to arrest him right then, but they were afraid of the people.

Paying Taxes
(Matthew 22.15-22; Mark 12.13-17)

[20]Jesus' enemies kept watching him closely, because they wanted to hand him over to the Roman governor. So they sent some men who pretended to be good. But they were really spies trying to catch Jesus saying something wrong. [21]The spies said to him, "Teacher, we know that you teach the truth about what God wants people to do. And you treat everyone with the same respect, no matter who they are. [22]Tell us, should we pay taxes to the Emperor or not?"

[23]Jesus knew that they were trying to trick him. So he told them, [24]"Show me a coin." Then he asked, "Whose picture and name are on it?"

"The Emperor's," they answered.

[25]Then he told them, "Give the Emperor what belongs to him and give God what belongs to God." [26]Jesus' enemies could not catch him saying anything wrong there in front of the people. They were amazed at his answer and kept quiet.

Life in the Future World
(Matthew 22.23-33; Mark 12.18-27)

[27]The Sadducees did not believe that people would rise to life after death. So some of them came to Jesus [28]and said:

> Teacher, Moses wrote that if a married man dies and has no children, his brother should marry the widow. Their first son would then be thought of as the son of the dead brother.

> Then [Jesus] told them, *"Give the Emperor what belongs to him and give God what belongs to God."*
> Luke 20.25

20.18 *this stone:* Jesus was describing himself as this important stone.

20.19 *chief priests and the teachers of the law of Moses:* See the note at 9.22.

20.20 *Roman governor:* See the note at 13.1 (Pontius Pilate).

20.22 *pay taxes to the Emperor:* In Jesus' time, Judea was part of the Roman Empire, so the people in Judea had to pay taxes to the Roman government. The highest Roman leader was called the Emperor, who ruled from Rome.

20.24 *coin:* This coin was probably a denarius, which was roughly the amount paid to a laborer for a day's work. In the time of Jesus, a denarius had a picture of Emperor Tiberius on one side. On the other side were the words: "Tiberius Caesar Augustus, son of the divine Augustus."

20.27 *Sadducees:* The Sadducees were a wealthy group of Jews who worked closely with the priests in the temple. They taught that the most important thing in life was going to the temple and offering sacrifices there. The Sadducees didn't believe that God brought people back to life from death, because it was not directly taught in the Law of Moses. See also the article called "The World of Jesus: Peoples, Powers, and Politics," p. 133.

20.17 Ps 118.22. **20.28** Deut 25.5,6.

20.36 *will be like the angels and ... God's children:* Jesus taught that people will be raised to life and will live forever like angels do. Those who are worthy to be God's children won't have to worry about something like who they are married to.

20.37 *The Lord is the God worshiped by Abraham, Isaac, and Jacob:* See the note at 1.55. Jesus argues that if God is worshiped by Abraham, Isaac, and Jacob, who entered into an agreement (covenant) with God in ancient times, then they must still be alive, because God is the God of the living.

20.41 *son of King David:* See the note at 18.38.

20.41 *right side:* The place of power and honor.

20.44 *David ... Messiah:* See the notes at 1.27 (Mary), 2.11 (Savior), and the mini-article called "Messiah," p. 176. The Jewish leaders argued about how the people would be saved. Some said the work of the priests to purify the nation would do this. Others stressed the power of the king. Jesus asks how a person could be both David's son and David's Lord.

20.46,47 *Guard against the teachers ... pray long prayers just to show off:* See the note at 11.46.

21.1 *offering box:* These funnel-shaped boxes were located in the court of women in the temple area.

21.2 *two pennies:* The Greek has *lepton,* which was the smallest Greek coin. It was worth only half of the smallest Roman coin.

20.37 Exod 3.6. **20.42,43** Ps 110.1.

---

²⁹There were once seven brothers. The first one married, but died without having any children. ³⁰The second one married his brother's widow, and he also died without having any children. ³¹The same thing happened to the third one. Finally, all seven brothers married that woman and died without having any children. ³²At last the woman died. ³³When God raises people from death, whose wife will this woman be? All seven brothers had married her.

³⁴Jesus answered:

The people in this world get married. ³⁵But in the future world no one who is worthy to rise from death will either marry ³⁶or die. They will be like the angels and will be God's children, because they have been raised to life.

³⁷In the story about the burning bush, Moses clearly shows that people will live again. He said, "The Lord is the God worshiped by Abraham, Isaac, and Jacob." ³⁸So the Lord isn't the God of the dead, but of the living. This means that everyone is alive as far as God is concerned.

³⁹Some of the teachers of the Law of Moses said, "Teacher, you have given a good answer!" ⁴⁰From then on, no one dared to ask Jesus any questions.

About David's Son
(Matthew 22.41-46; Mark 12.35-37)

⁴¹Jesus asked, "Why do people say that the Messiah will be the son of King David? ⁴²In the book of Psalms, David himself says,

'The Lord said to my Lord,
Sit at my right side
⁴³   until I make your enemies into a footstool for you.'

⁴⁴David spoke of the Messiah as his Lord, so how can the Messiah be his son?"

Jesus and the Teachers of the Law of Moses
(Matthew 23.1-36; Mark 12.38-40; Luke 11.37-54)

⁴⁵While everyone was listening to Jesus, he said to his disciples: ⁴⁶Guard against the teachers of the Law of Moses! They love to walk around in long robes, and they like to be greeted in the market. They want the front seats in the meeting places and the best seats at banquets. ⁴⁷But they cheat widows out of their homes and then pray long prayers just to show off. These teachers will be punished most of all.

A Widow's Offering
(Mark 12.41-44)

21 Jesus looked up and saw some rich people tossing their gifts into the offering box. ²He also saw a poor widow putting in two

pennies. ³And he said, "I tell you that this poor woman has put in more than all the others. ⁴Everyone else gave what they didn't need. But she is very poor and gave everything she had."

The Temple Will Be Destroyed
(Matthew 24.1, 2; Mark 13.1, 2)

⁵Some people were talking about the beautiful stones used to build the temple and about the gifts that had been placed in it. Jesus said, ⁶"Do you see these stones? The time is coming when not one of them will be left in place. They will all be knocked down."

Warning about Trouble
(Matthew 24.3-14; Mark 13.3-13)

⁷Some people asked, "Teacher, when will all this happen? How can we know when these things are about to take place?"
⁸Jesus replied:

> Don't be fooled by those who will come and claim to be me. They will say, "I am Christ!" and "Now is the time!" But don't follow them. ⁹When you hear about wars and riots, don't be afraid. These things will have to happen first, but that isn't the end.

21.6 *The time is coming:* See the note at 19.43.

21.8 *Christ:* This comes from the Greek word *christos*, which means "anointed one." See the note at 2.11.

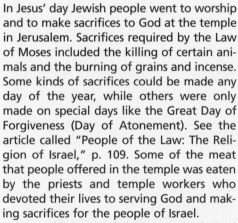

TEMPLE OFFERINGS

In Jesus' day Jewish people went to worship and to make sacrifices to God at the temple in Jerusalem. Sacrifices required by the Law of Moses included the killing of certain animals and the burning of grains and incense. Some kinds of sacrifices could be made any day of the year, while others were only made on special days like the Great Day of Forgiveness (Day of Atonement). See the article called "People of the Law: The Religion of Israel," p. 109. Some of the meat that people offered in the temple was eaten by the priests and temple workers who devoted their lives to serving God and making sacrifices for the people of Israel.

In addition to bringing animals and grain to be sacrificed for the forgiveness of sin, the Jewish people also gave vegetables they had grown, valuable items, and money to help with the cost of running the temple and providing for the needs of the priests and temple workers. The Law of Moses also stated that the people should give to the LORD one-tenth of what they grew or earned (Lev 27.30-33; Num 18.21-32). This practice was called tithing.

The Jewish people believed that God was present among them in the most holy place in the temple. Offerings were given to God each day in the same way servants might bring gifts or food to their masters. The size of the gift offered was based on who offered the gift. Poor people, for example, were not expected to offer as much as someone who was wealthy.

Some offerings were presented to God in order to confess guilt and to ask for forgiveness of sins (Lev 4.1—6.7; 6.24-30; 7.1-6; 8.14-17; 16.3-22). Other offerings were presented as a way of worshiping God, giving thanks to God, and showing commitment to God (Lev 1–3; 6.8-23; 7.11-34). Compare the praise Jesus had for the poor widow who gave her last two pennies (Luke 21.1-4) with the warning he has for people who make a big show of their generosity while neglecting important matters of the Law, such as justice, mercy, and faithfulness (Matt 23.23, 24).

21.12 *your meeting places:* See the note at 4.15. What Jesus said later came true. The book of Acts tells about how some of Jesus' disciples are put on trial in the Jewish meeting places and at the temple (see Acts 4.1-22; 5.17-42; 6.8—8.2; 17.1-9; 21.27—26.32).

21.20 *When you see Jerusalem surrounded:* See the note at 19.43.

21.21 *Judea:* Hills can be found in various parts of Judea, especially north and southeast of Jerusalem. See the map on p. 197, and the note at 1.39.

21.26 *Every power in the sky will be shaken:* In ancient times, some thought that the stars were spiritual powers. Others compared the stars to nations on earth. So this verse may mean that God would shake earthly powers (nations) or the spiritual powers that opposed God.

21.14,15 Luke 12.11,12. **21.22-24** Isa 63.4; Jer 5.29; Hos 9.7. **21.25** Isa 13.10; Ezek 32.7; Joel 2.31; Rev 6.12,13. **21.27** Dan 7.13; Rev 1.7.

[10]Nations will go to war against one another, and kingdoms will attack each other. [11]There will be great earthquakes, and in many places people will starve to death and suffer terrible diseases. All sorts of frightening things will be seen in the sky.

[12]Before all this happens, you will be arrested and punished. You will be tried in your meeting places and put in jail. Because of me you will be placed on trial before kings and governors. [13]But this will be your chance to tell about your faith.

[14]Don't worry about what you will say to defend yourselves. [15]I will give you the wisdom to know what to say. None of your enemies will be able to oppose you or to say that you are wrong. [16]You will be betrayed by your own parents, brothers, family, and friends. Some of you will even be killed. [17]Because of me, you will be hated by everyone. [18]But don't worry![1] [19]You will be saved by being faithful to me.

Jerusalem Will Be Destroyed
(Matthew 24.15-21; Mark 13.14-19)

[20]When you see Jerusalem surrounded by soldiers, you will know that it will soon be destroyed. [21]If you are living in Judea at that time, run to the mountains. If you are in the city, leave it. And if you are out in the country, don't go back into the city. [22]This time of punishment is what is written about in the Scriptures. [23]It will be an awful time for women who are expecting babies or nursing young children! Everywhere in the land people will suffer horribly and be punished. [24]Some of them will be killed by swords. Others will be carried off to foreign countries. Jerusalem will be overrun by foreign nations until their time comes to an end.

When the Son of Man Appears
(Matthew 24.29-31; Mark 13.24-27)

[25]Strange things will happen to the sun, moon, and stars. The nations on earth will be afraid of the roaring sea and tides, and they won't know what to do. [26]People will be so frightened that they will faint because of what is happening to the world. Every power in the sky will be shaken. [27]Then the Son of Man will be seen, coming in a cloud with great power and glory. [28]When all of this starts happening, stand up straight and be brave. You will soon be set free.

---

[1]**21.18** *But don't worry:* The Greek text has "Not a hair of your head will be lost," which means, "There's no need to worry."

A Lesson from a Fig Tree
(Matthew 24.32-35; Mark 13.28-31)

[29]Then Jesus told them a story:

When you see a fig tree or any other tree [30]putting out leaves, you know that summer will soon come. [31]So, when you see these things happening, you know that God's kingdom will soon be here. [32]You can be sure that some of the people of this generation will still be alive when all of this takes place. [33]The sky and the earth won't last forever, but my words will.

A Warning

[34]Don't spend all of your time thinking about eating or drinking or worrying about life. If you do, the final day will suddenly catch you [35]like a trap. That day will surprise everyone on earth. [36]Watch out and keep praying that you can escape all that is going to happen and that the Son of Man will be pleased with you.

[37]Jesus taught in the temple each day, and he spent each night on the Mount of Olives. [38]Everyone got up early and came to the temple to hear him teach.

THE LAST DAYS OF JESUS: HIS TRIAL AND DEATH

During the Festival of Thin Bread, some of the chief priests and teachers of the Law plot to arrest Jesus. Jesus is betrayed by his disciple Judas after Jesus and the other disciples share a Passover meal. His arrest is followed by a trial in front of the Jewish leaders. Later, the Roman governor Pilate sentences Jesus to die on a cross.

A Plot To Kill Jesus
(Matthew 26.1-5,14,16; Mark 14.1,2,10,11; John 11.45-53)

22 The Festival of Thin Bread, also called Passover, was near. [2]The chief priests and the teachers of the Law of Moses were looking for a way to get rid of Jesus, because they were afraid of what the people might do. [3]Then Satan entered the heart of Judas Iscariot,[m] who was one of the twelve apostles.

[4]Judas went to talk with the chief priests and the officers of the temple police about how he could help them arrest Jesus. [5]They were very pleased and offered to pay Judas some money. [6]He agreed and started looking for a good chance to betray Jesus when the crowds were not around.

---

[m] 22.3 *Iscariot:* See the footnote at 6.16.

21.29 *fig tree:* See the note at 6.44.

21.36 *Son of Man:* See the mini-article "The Son of Man," p. 190.

21.37 *temple ... Mount of Olives:* See 19.47 and the notes at 19.28,29 and 19.37.

22.1 *Festival of Thin Bread ... Passover:* Two special festivals celebrated by the Jewish people. See the mini-article called "Passover and the Festival of Thin Bread," p. 94.

22.2 *chief priests and the teachers of the Law of Moses:* See the note at 19.47.

22.3 *Satan entered the heart of Judas Iscariot:* See the note at 4.3 (devil).

22.3 *Then Satan entered ... Judas Iscariot:* Judas is the Greek spelling of the Hebrew name "Judah," which could mean that he was from Judea. There are many possible meanings of his second name, "Iscariot." It may mean "a man from Kerioth" (a place in Judea) or it may mean "a man who was a betrayer" or "a man who was a liar." Some scholars believe "Iscariot" comes from "Sicarii," a group of assassins who used knives, and that Judas was a member of a group called Zealots who fought against the Romans. Judas acted as treasurer for Jesus and the twelve (John 12.5,6). Luke says here that Satan has entered Judas' heart. Having left Jesus for a while (Luke 4.13), the devil is now back, and will lead Judas to betray Jesus.

22.4 *chief priests and the officers of the temple police:* The chief priests and other leaders formed a council, which the Romans allowed to make some decisions about local matters. These men are not to be confused with the high priest (see the notes at 3.2; 22.54). The temple police were Jewish men who guarded the temple and helped keep order in the temple area.

22.7 *Festival of Thin Bread . . . Passover lambs:* See the note at 22.1 and mini-article below called "Passover and the Festival of Thin Bread."

22.10 *man carrying a jar of water:* Usually this kind of work was done by a woman, so the man would have been easy to spot. He may have been a slave, which probably meant that the family he worked for was rich.

22.13 *Peter and John:* Two of Jesus' disciples. See the notes at 5.8 (Simon Peter), 5.10 (James and John), 8.51 and 9.28 (Peter, James, and John).

22.16 *God's kingdom:* See the note at 4.43.

Jesus Eats with His Disciples
(Matthew 26.17-25; Mark 14.12-21; John 13.21-30)

[7]The day had come for the Festival of Thin Bread, and it was time to kill the Passover lambs. [8]So Jesus said to Peter and John, "Go and prepare the Passover meal for us to eat."

[9]But they asked, "Where do you want us to prepare it?"

[10]Jesus told them, "As you go into the city, you will meet a man carrying a jar of water. Follow him into the house [11]and say to the owner, 'Our teacher wants to know where he can eat the Passover meal with his disciples.' [12]The owner will take you upstairs and show you a large room ready for you to use. Prepare the meal there."

[13]Peter and John left. They found everything just as Jesus had told them, and they prepared the Passover meal.

The Lord's Supper
(Matthew 26.26-30; Mark 14.22-26; 1 Corinthians 11.23-25)

[14]When the time came for Jesus and the apostles to eat, [15]he

---

PASSOVER AND THE FESTIVAL OF THIN BREAD

These two special spring festivals were brought together in the Jewish calendar long before the time of Jesus. Passover was celebrated to remind the people of Israel how God rescued them from slavery in Egypt (Exod 12,13). It was to be celebrated on the fourteenth day of the first month, Nisan, a month that overlaps March and April on modern calendars. Passover started at sunset. The Festival of Thin Bread began the next day, the fifteenth day of the first month, and lasted for seven days (Lev 23.4-8; Num 28.17-25).

During the Passover Festival, a lamb was to be killed, roasted, and eaten. The blood of the lamb was a reminder of the blood that the Israelites put on their doorposts before God sent a final plague on Egypt. God's angel of death "passed over" the Israelite homes that were marked by the blood, but the death angel killed the first-born in the families of Egypt (Exod 12.1-27). The thin bread (unleavened bread) that was to be eaten during Passover and during the seven days of the Festival of Thin Bread was a reminder of how quickly the people had to leave Egypt. They did not have time to let the dough for their bread rise, so they made bread without using yeast. Bread made this way will always be flat, like a cracker.

The Festival of Thin Bread also became a time to give thanks to God for the annual harvest of grain, which provided food for all the people. Later, these two feasts were joined and celebrated partly at the temple in Jerusalem and partly in people's homes. Jewish people came from all over the world to be in Jerusalem to take part in these yearly feasts. Here they recalled with thanks what God had done for them in the past and celebrated their life together in the present.

The reports of the celebration of these meals in the time of Jesus includes both the offering and eating of the sacrificial lamb, eating thin (unleavened) bread and drinking wine. Children were taught the meaning of the meal as they ate it. Jews throughout the world continue to celebrate these important festivals in much the same manner.

See also the chart called "Jewish Calendar and Festivals" in the article called "People of the Law: The Religion of Israel." p. 109.

Family gathered to celebrate the Passover meal. In Jesus' day, only men had to take part in this ritual pilgrimage festival. On the first day of the festival, a passover meal was celebrated in which the men reclined around a low table. Today, men and women alike take part in the ritual, called a Seder. The photograph shows a Seder plate, a later addition to the ritual dinner, with foods that have symbolic meanings connected to the story of Exodus.

said to them, "I have very much wanted to eat this Passover meal with you before I suffer. [16]I tell you that I will not eat another Passover meal until it is finally eaten in God's kingdom."

[17]Jesus took a cup of wine in his hands and gave thanks to God. Then he told the apostles, "Take this wine and share it with each other. [18]I tell you that I will not drink any more wine until God's kingdom comes."

[19]Jesus took some bread in his hands and gave thanks for it. He broke the bread and handed it to his apostles. Then he said, "This is my body, which is given for you. Eat this as a way of remembering me!"

[20]After the meal he took another cup of wine in his hands. Then he said, "This is my blood. It is poured out for you, and with it God makes his new agreement. [21]The one who will betray me is here at the table with me! [22]The Son of Man will die in the way that has been decided for him, but it will be terrible for the one who betrays him!"

[23]Then the apostles started arguing about who would ever do such a thing.

22.19 *bread:* This probably would have been the thin bread that was made for the Passover meal and the Festival of Thin Bread.

22.20 *God makes his new agreement:* God made an agreement with Moses when God gave him the laws the Israelites were to live by. Here Jesus is saying that God is about to create a new agreement (see Jer 31.31-34; Exod 24.8). This new agreement is for all people. See also the mini-articles called "God's Saving Love (Salvation)," p. 85, and "Agreements (Covenants)," p. 156.

22.22 *Son of Man:* See the mini-article called "Son of Man," p. 190.

22.21 Ps 41.9.

22.30 *my kingdom:* See the note at 4.43.

22.30 *twelve tribes of Israel:* Originally the twelve tribes of Israel referred to the Hebrew descendants of Jacob's twelve sons (see Gen 32.20-32; 35.23-26). Because the priestly line of Levi did not hold land (Num 1.47-53), it was no longer considered one of the twelve tribes. Joseph's descendants formed two separate tribes (Ephraim and Manasseh). See also the article called "From Joshua to the Exile: The People of Israel in the Promised Land," p. 118.

22.31 *Simon:* See the notes at 4.38 and 5.8.

22.31 *separates wheat from the husks:* See the note at 3.17.

22.36 *moneybag . . . traveling bag . . . sword:* Things that someone would take on a dangerous journey. Jesus was telling his disciples to be ready for anything that might happen. They must have understood what he meant (see 22.49-51).

22.39 *Mount of Olives:* See the note at 19.28,29.

22.24 Matt 18.1; Mark 9.34; Luke 9.46. **22.26** Matt 23.11; Mark 9.35. **22.25,26** Matt 20.25-27; Mark 10.42-44. **22.27** John 13.12-15. **22.35** Matt 10.9,10; Mark 6.8,9; Luke 9.3; 10.4. **22.37** Isa 53.12.

An Argument about Greatness

[24]The apostles got into an argument about which one of them was the greatest. [25]So Jesus told them:

Foreign kings order their people around, and powerful rulers call themselves everyone's friends.[n] [26]But don't be like them. The most important one of you should be like the least important, and your leader should be like a servant. [27]Who do people think is the greatest, a person who is served or one who serves? Isn't it the one who is served? But I have been with you as a servant.

[28]You have stayed with me in all my troubles. [29]So I will give you the right to rule as kings, just as my Father has given me the right to rule as a king. [30]You will eat and drink with me in my kingdom, and you will each sit on a throne to judge the twelve tribes of Israel.

Jesus' Disciples Will Be Tested
(Matthew 26.31-35; Mark 14.27-31; John 13.36-38)

[31]Jesus said, "Simon, listen to me! Satan has demanded the right to test each one of you, as a farmer does when he separates wheat from the husks. [32]But Simon, I have prayed that your faith will be strong. And when you have come back to me, help the others."

[33]Peter said, "Lord, I am ready to go with you to jail and even to die with you."

[34]Jesus replied, "Peter, I tell you that before a rooster crows tomorrow morning, you will say three times that you don't know me."

Moneybags, Traveling Bags, and Swords

[35]Jesus asked his disciples, "When I sent you out without a moneybag or a traveling bag or sandals, did you need anything?"

"No!" they answered.

[36]Jesus told them, "But now, if you have a moneybag, take it with you. Also take a traveling bag, and if you don't have a sword, sell some of your clothes and buy one. [37]Do this because the Scriptures say, 'He was considered a criminal.' This was written about me, and it will soon come true."

[38]The disciples said, "Lord, here are two swords!"

"Enough of that!" Jesus replied.

Jesus Prays
(Matthew 26.36-46; Mark 14.32-42)

[39]Jesus went out to the Mount of Olives, as he often did, and his disciples went with him. [40]When they got there, he told them, "Pray that you won't be tested."

---

[n] **22.25** *everyone's friends:* This translates a Greek word that rulers sometimes used as a title for themselves or for special friends.

[41]Jesus walked on a little way before he knelt down and prayed, [42]"Father, if you will, please don't make me suffer by having me drink from this cup. But do what you want, and not what I want."

[43]Then an angel from heaven came to help him. [44]Jesus was in great pain and prayed so sincerely that his sweat fell to the ground like drops of blood.°

[45]Jesus got up from praying and went over to his disciples. They were asleep and worn out from being so sad. [46]He said to them, "Why are you asleep? Wake up and pray that you won't be tested."

Jesus Is Arrested
(Matthew 26.47-56; Mark 14.43-50; John 18.3-11)

[47]While Jesus was still speaking, a crowd came up. It was led by Judas, one of the twelve apostles. He went over to Jesus and greeted him with a kiss.

[48]Jesus asked Judas, "Are you betraying the Son of Man with a kiss?"

[49]When Jesus' disciples saw what was about to happen, they asked, "Lord, should we attack them with a sword?" [50]One of the disciples even struck at the high priest's servant with his sword and cut off the servant's right ear.

[51]"Enough of that!" Jesus said. Then he touched the servant's ear and healed it.

[52]Jesus spoke to the chief priests, the temple police, and the leaders who had come to arrest him. He said, "Why do you come out with swords and clubs and treat me like a criminal? [53]I was with you every day in the temple, and you didn't arrest me. But this is your time, and darkness is in control."

Peter Says He Doesn't Know Jesus
(Matthew 26.57, 58, 67-75; Mark 14.53, 54, 66-72;
John 18.12-18, 25-27)

[54]Jesus was arrested and led away to the house of the high priest, while Peter followed at a distance. [55]Some people built a fire in the middle of the courtyard and were sitting around it. Peter sat there with them, [56]and a servant girl saw him. Then after she had looked at him carefully, she said, "This man was with Jesus!"

[57]Peter said, "Woman, I don't even know that man!"

[58]A little later someone else saw Peter and said, "You are one of them!"

"No, I'm not!" Peter replied.

[59]About an hour later another man insisted, "This man must have been with Jesus. They both come from Galilee."

[60]Peter replied, "I don't know what you are talking about!" Right then, while Peter was still speaking, a rooster crowed.

 22.42 *drink from this cup:* Here to "drink from this cup" means to suffer. Jesus knew that God had planned that he would have to suffer and die to fulfill God's purposes (see 9.22; 18.31-33; 22.20-22).

22.43 *an angel from heaven:* See the note at 2.13-15.

22.47 *Judas:* See the note at 22.3.

22.52 *chief priests, the temple police, and the leaders:* See the notes at 22.4 and 19.47.

22.53 *darkness:* Darkness stands for the power of the devil and evil. See also 16.8.

22.54 *house of the high priest:* See the note at 3.2 (Caiaphas). The council of Jewish leaders who questioned Jesus (22.66-71) may have met at the house of Caiaphas See also the article called "People of the Law: The Religion of Israel," p. 109.

22.59 *Galilee:* See the note at 1.26 (Galilee). Peter came from Galilee, where people probably spoke with an accent that was different from people around Jerusalem. That is how these people could tell where Peter was from.

 22.53 Luke 19.47; 21.37.

°**22.43, 44** *Then an angel...like drops of blood:* Verses 43, 44 are not in some manuscripts.

Peter Repentant, Mary and John, a in illuminated page from an early fifteenth century Ethiopian book containing the Pentateuch, JOSHUA, JUDGES, RUTH, and the four Gospels. At the Last Supper, Jesus warned Peter that he would be tested by Satan, told him to be strong, and instructed him to help others. Peter assured Jesus that he would be willing to die for him, but Jesus told him "that before a rooster crows tomorrow morning, you will say three times that you don't know me" (22.34). When what Jesus predicted happened Peter "went out and cried hard." (See 22.54-62.)

22.66 *At daybreak ... brought Jesus before their council:* The council mentioned here was made up of representatives of various Jewish groups (see the notes at 19.47; 22.4; 22.54). The Romans allowed this council to hear cases that involved crimes against Jewish religious laws. Since the Jewish laws did not allow the officials to do any business at night, Jesus was brought before them first thing in the morning. The Law of Moses taught that two witnesses were needed before a person could be put to death (Deut 19.15).

22.67 *Messiah:* See the notes at 2.11.

22.69 *Son of Man:* See the mini-article "Son of Man," p. 190.

22.70 *Son of God:* See the mini-article called "Son of God," p. 189.

23.1 *Pilate:* See the note at 13.1.

⁶¹The Lord turned and looked at Peter. And Peter remembered that the Lord had said, "Before a rooster crows tomorrow morning, you will say three times that you don't know me." ⁶²Then Peter went out and cried hard.

⁶³The men who were guarding Jesus made fun of him and beat him. ⁶⁴They put a blindfold on him and said, "Tell us who struck you!" ⁶⁵They kept on insulting Jesus in many other ways.

Jesus Is Questioned by the Council
(Matthew 26.59-66; Mark 14.55-64; John 18.19-24)

⁶⁶At daybreak the nation's leaders, the chief priests, and the teachers of the Law of Moses got together and brought Jesus before their council. ⁶⁷They said, "Tell us! Are you the Messiah?"

Jesus replied, "If I said so, you wouldn't believe me. ⁶⁸And if I asked you a question, you wouldn't answer. ⁶⁹But from now on, the Son of Man will be seated at the right side of God All-Powerful."

⁷⁰Then they asked, "Are you the Son of God?"

Jesus answered, "You say I am!" [P]

[71]They replied, "Why do we need more witnesses? He said it himself!"

Pilate Questions Jesus
(Matthew 27.1, 2, 11-14; Mark 15.1-5;
John 18.28-38)

23 Everyone in the council got up and led Jesus off to Pilate. [2]They started accusing him and said, "We caught this man trying to get our people to riot and to stop paying taxes to the Emperor. He also claims that he is the Messiah, our king."

[3]Pilate asked Jesus, "Are you the king of the Jews?"

"Those are your words," Jesus answered.

[4]Pilate told the chief priests and the crowd, "I don't find him guilty of anything."

[5]But they all kept on saying, "He has been teaching and causing trouble all over Judea. He started in Galilee and has now come all the way here."

Jesus Is Brought before Herod

[6]When Pilate heard this, he asked, "Is this man from Galilee?" [7]After Pilate learned that Jesus came from the region ruled by Herod, he sent him to Herod, who was in Jerusalem at that time.

[8]For a long time Herod had wanted to see Jesus and was very happy because he finally had this chance. He had heard many things about Jesus and hoped to see him work a miracle. [9]Herod asked him a lot of questions, but Jesus did not answer. [10]Then the chief priests and the teachers of the Law of Moses stood up and accused him of all kinds of bad things.

[11]Herod and his soldiers made fun of Jesus and insulted him. They put a fine robe on him and sent him back to Pilate. [12]That same day Herod and Pilate became friends, even though they had been enemies before this.

The Death Sentence
(Matthew 27.15-26; Mark 15.6-15;
John 18.39—19.16)

[13]Pilate called together the chief priests, the leaders, and the people. [14]He told them, "You brought Jesus to me and said he was a troublemaker. But I have questioned him here in front of you, and I have not found him guilty of anything that you say he has done. [15]Herod didn't find him guilty either and sent him back. This man doesn't deserve to be put to death! [16-17]I will just have him beaten with a whip and set free." [q]

23.2 *stop paying taxes to the Emperor:* See the note at 20.22. Jesus had not done what the council accused him of doing, but they were trying to get him in trouble with the Roman rulers.

23.2 *Messiah:* See the notes 2.11. Because the Romans were in charge of the land, no one could declare himself to be a king. Only the Roman authorities could give someone such a powerful position.

23.5 *Judea . . . Galilee:* See the notes at 4.44 (Judea) and 1.26 (Galilee).

23.6,7 *Galilee . . . region ruled by Herod:* Herod Antipas, the son of King Herod the Great, ruled Galilee at this time. See the notes at 3.1 and 9.7. Pilate didn't really want to handle this case, so he sent Jesus to Herod. Although Herod's main headquarters were in the city of Tiberias by Lake Galilee, he was in Jerusalem because of the Passover celebration.

23.13 *chief priests, the leaders, and the people:* See the note at 22.4 (chief priests and leaders). The "people" here may simply refer to the crowd, or even to a small mob that had gathered. It does not mean everyone in Jerusalem or all the Jewish people. In the narrow streets of Jerusalem it probably didn't take many to make a crowd.

---

¹⁸But the whole crowd shouted, "Kill Jesus! Give us Barabbas!" ¹⁹Now Barabbas was in jail because he had started a riot in the city and had murdered someone.

²⁰Pilate wanted to set Jesus free, so he spoke again to the crowds. ²¹But they kept shouting, "Nail him to a cross! Nail him to a cross!"

²²Pilate spoke to them a third time, "But what crime has he done? I have not found him guilty of anything for which he should be put to death. I will have him beaten with a whip and set free."

²³The people kept on shouting as loud as they could for Jesus to be put to death. ²⁴Finally, Pilate gave in. ²⁵He freed the man who was in jail for rioting and murder, because he was the one the crowd wanted to be set free. Then Pilate handed Jesus over for them to do what they wanted with him.

Jesus Is Nailed to a Cross
(Matthew 27.31-44; Mark 15.21-32;
John 19.17-27)

²⁶As Jesus was being led away, some soldiers grabbed hold of a man from Cyrene named Simon. He was coming in from the fields, but they put the cross on him and made him carry it behind Jesus.

²⁷A large crowd was following Jesus, and in the crowd a lot of women were crying and weeping for him. ²⁸Jesus turned to the women and said:

Women of Jerusalem, don't cry for me! Cry for yourselves and for your children. ²⁹Someday people will say, "Women who never had children are really fortunate!" ³⁰At that time everyone will say to the mountains, "Fall on us!" They will say to the hills, "Hide us!" ³¹If this can happen when the wood is green, what do you think will happen when it is dry?

³²Two criminals were led out to be put to death with Jesus. ³³When the soldiers came to the place called "The Skull," they nailed Jesus to a cross. They also nailed the two criminals to crosses, one on each side of Jesus.

³⁴⁻³⁵Jesus said, "Father, forgive these people! They don't know what they're doing." ^r

While the crowd stood there watching Jesus, the soldiers gambled for his clothes. The leaders insulted him by saying, "He saved others. Now he should save himself, if he really is God's chosen Messiah!"

³⁶The soldiers made fun of Jesus and brought him some wine. ³⁷They said, "If you are the king of the Jews, save yourself!"

³⁸Above him was a sign that said, "This is the King of the Jews."

³⁹One of the criminals hanging there also insulted Jesus by saying, "Aren't you the Messiah? Save yourself and save us!"

^r *23.34,35 Jesus said, "Father, forgive these people! They don't know what they're doing.":* These words are not in some manuscripts.

Mount Calvary by William H. Johnson, 1939. In Luke's version of the death of Jesus, the Gospel writer tells how two criminals were nailed to crosses next to Jesus. One criminal insulted Jesus, but the other answered him saying, "Don't you fear God? . . . We got what was coming to us, but he didn't do anything wrong." Jesus then said to the criminal who feared God, "I promise that today you will be with me in paradise." (See 23.26-43.)

⁴⁰But the other criminal told the first one off, "Don't you fear God? Aren't you getting the same punishment as this man? ⁴¹We got what was coming to us, but he didn't do anything wrong." ⁴²Then he said to Jesus, "Remember me when you come into power!"

⁴³Jesus replied, "I promise that today you will be with me in paradise."

The Death of Jesus
(Matthew 27.45-56; Mark 15.33-41;
John 19.28-30)

⁴⁴Around noon the sky turned dark and stayed that way until the middle of the afternoon. ⁴⁵The sun stopped shining, and the curtain in the temple split down the middle. ⁴⁶Jesus shouted, "Father, I put myself in your hands!" Then he died.

⁴⁷When the Roman officer saw what had happened, he praised God and said, "Jesus must really have been a good man!"

23.43 *paradise:* In the Greek translation of the Old Testament (the Septuagint), this word is used for the Garden of Eden. See also the mini-article called "Paradise," p. 181.

23.45 *curtain in the temple:* The curtain referred to here was the one that separated the holy place from the most holy place (Exod 26.31-33). Only the high priest could go past this curtain. See the diagram of the temple on p. 112.

23.46 *Father:* See the note at 9.26. See also Ps 31.5.

23.50-51 *Joseph . . . from Ari-mathea in Judea:* Arimathea was a small village about twenty miles from Jerusalem, in the hilly area called Ephraim. Because Joseph was rich (see Matt 27.57), he probably had money to pay off Pilate and the guards, so he could take the body. Joseph risked his reputation as a member of the Jewish council by giving Jesus a decent burial.

23.53 *wrapped it in fine cloth . . . put it in a tomb:* The cloth was a kind of linen. Some of the Jewish people buried their dead in rooms carved into soft limestone rock. These tombs had a small square entrance about a yard high and a yard wide. A groove was cut on the outside of the tomb, and a large round stone that looked like a millstone was rolled down to cover the entrance. See the mini-article called "Burial," p. 58.

23.54 *Friday, and the Sabbath was about to begin:* The Jewish day of rest. The Sabbath begins at sunset on Friday. No work was to be done on the Sabbath, including burying a body. See the note at 4.16 (Sabbath).

23.56 *sweet-smelling spices:* These were probably spices called myrrh and aloes (see John 19.39). Many cultures in the Middle East used aloe for medicine and for embalming the dead. Since myrrh and aloes do not grow in Palestine they had to be imported, which made them expensive.

23.56 *on the Sabbath they rest-ed:* After preparing the spices, the women could not actually walk to the tomb and prepare the body because the Law of Moses would not allow them to do this kind of work on the Sabbath (see Exod 20.10; Deut 5.14). They waited until the next morning, which was Sunday.

24.1 *early on Sunday morning:* The Sabbath ended at sunset on Saturday evening, so they went to the tomb early on Sunday morning when it was light.

 **23.49** Luke 8.2,3. **24.6,7** Matt 16.21; 17.22,23; 20.18,19; Mark 8.31; 9.31; 10.33,34; Luke 9.22; 18.31-33.

[48]A crowd had gathered to see the terrible sight. Then after they had seen it, they felt brokenhearted and went home. [49]All of Jesus' close friends and the women who had come with him from Galilee stood at a distance and watched.

Jesus Is Buried
(Matthew 27.57-61; Mark 15.42-47;
John 19.38-42)

[50-51]There was a man named Joseph, who was from Ari-mathea in Judea. Joseph was a good and honest man, and he was eager for God's kingdom to come. He was also a member of the council, but he did not agree with what they had decided.

[52]Joseph went to Pilate and asked for Jesus' body. [53]He took the body down from the cross and wrapped it in fine cloth. Then he put it in a tomb that had been cut out of solid rock and had never been used. [54]It was Friday, and the Sabbath was about to begin.

[55]The women who had come with Jesus from Galilee fol-lowed Joseph and watched how Jesus' body was placed in the tomb. [56]Then they went to prepare some sweet-smelling spices for his bur-ial. But on the Sabbath they rested, as the Law of Moses commands.

Jesus Rises from Death and Appears to the Disciples

The women discover that Jesus has risen from the dead and tell the apostles. Later, two male disciples meet Jesus on the road. After sharing a meal with him they realize that he is Jesus raised from death and go to share this good news with the others.

Jesus Is Alive
(Matthew 28.1-10; Mark 16.1-8;
John 20.1-10)

24 Very early on Sunday morning the women went to the tomb, carrying the spices that they had prepared. [2]When they found the stone rolled away from the entrance, [3]they went in. But they did not find the body of the Lord[s] Jesus, [4]and they did not know what to think.

Suddenly two men in shining white clothes stood beside them. [5]The women were afraid and bowed to the ground. But the men said, "Why are you looking in the place of the dead for someone who is alive? [6]Jesus isn't here! He has been raised from death. Remember that while he was still in Galilee, he told you, [7]'The Son of Man will be handed over to sinners who will nail him to a cross. But three days later he will rise to life.' " [8]Then they remembered what Jesus had said.

[9-10]Mary Magdalene, Joanna, Mary the mother of James, and

---
[s] **24.3** *the Lord:* These words are not in some manuscripts.

Road to Emmaus by Karl Schmidt-Rottluff, 1918, woodcut. On the same day that Jesus was raised to life, two of his disciples were going to the town of Emmaus, not far from Jerusalem. As they made their way, Jesus began walking with them. He talked with them and they told him about how Jesus had been put to death and how the women had found his tomb empty that morning. But they did not recognize Jesus. Only later, when they sat down to eat with Jesus did they realize that he was their risen Lord. (See Luke 24.13-35.)

24.7 *Son of Man:* See the mini-article called "Son of Man," p. 190. Jesus had predicted his death (9.22).

24.9-10 *Mary Magdalene, Joanna, Mary the mother of James:* See the notes at 8.2 (Mary Magdalene) and 8.3 (Joanna). Mary the mother of James is also mentioned in Mark 16.1. Who she was, or which James was her son, is not clear. She may have been the mother of one of the two disciples whose names were James.

24.9-10 *eleven apostles:* These are Jesus' hand-picked followers (see 6.12-16). There are only eleven because Judas, who betrayed Jesus, is no longer with them. Matthew 27.3-5 reports that Judas committed suicide.

24.13 *two of Jesus' disciples:* These were followers of Jesus but not two of Jesus' twelve closest apostles.

24.13 *Emmaus:* Emmaus was a small village in Judea. Its exact location is not certain. Archaeologists think that Emmaus could be one of three different places. One of the most likely is Amwas, which is about twenty miles from Jerusalem.

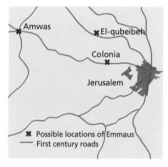

some other women were the ones who had gone to the tomb. When they returned, they told the eleven apostles and the others what had happened. [11]The apostles thought it was all nonsense, and they would not believe.

[12]But Peter ran to the tomb. And when he stooped down and looked in, he saw only the burial clothes. Then he returned, wondering what had happened.[t]

Jesus Appears to Two Disciples
(Mark 16.12,13)

[13]That same day two of Jesus' disciples were going to the village of Emmaus, which was about seven miles from Jerusalem. [14]As they were talking and thinking about what had happened, [15]Jesus came near and started walking along beside them. [16]But they did not know who he was.

[17]Jesus asked them, "What were you talking about as you walked along?"

The two of them stood there looking sad and gloomy. [18]Then the one named Cleopas asked Jesus, "Are you the only person from

---

[t]**24.12** *But Peter ran to the tomb…what had happened:* Verse 12 is not in some manuscripts.

24.18 *Cleopas:* He was a follower of Jesus mentioned only here in Luke, and nothing else is known about him.

24.26 *Messiah:* See the notes 2.11.

24.27 *the Law of Moses and the Books of the Prophets:* See the note at 16.16 (the Law of Moses and the Books of the Prophets).

24.32 *Scriptures:* These are the Jewish Scriptures, which Christians call the Old Testament.

24.39 *my hands and my feet:* Sometimes large nails were driven through the wrists and feet of a person who was being put to death on a cross. Jesus wanted them to see his wounds so that they would realize who he was.

Jerusalem who didn't know what was happening there these last few days?"

[19]"What do you mean?" Jesus asked.

They answered:

Those things that happened to Jesus from Nazareth. By what he did and said he showed that he was a powerful prophet, who pleased God and all the people. [20]Then the chief priests and our leaders had him arrested and sentenced to die on a cross. [21]We had hoped that he would be the one to set Israel free! But it has already been three days since all this happened.

[22]Some women in our group surprised us. They had gone to the tomb early in the morning, [23]but did not find the body of Jesus. They came back, saying that they had seen a vision of angels who told them that he is alive. [24]Some men from our group went to the tomb and found it just as the women had said. But they didn't see Jesus either.

[25]Then Jesus asked the two disciples, "Why can't you understand? How can you be so slow to believe all that the prophets said? [26]Didn't you know that the Messiah would have to suffer before he was given his glory?" [27]Jesus then explained everything written about himself in the Scriptures, beginning with the Law of Moses and the Books of the Prophets.

[28]When the two of them came near the village where they were going, Jesus seemed to be going farther. [29]They begged him, "Stay with us! It's already late, and the sun is going down." So Jesus went into the house to stay with them.

[30]After Jesus sat down to eat, he took some bread. He blessed it and broke it. Then he gave it to them. [31]At once they knew who he was, but he disappeared. [32]They said to each other, "When he talked with us along the road and explained the Scriptures to us, didn't it warm our hearts?" [33]So they got right up and returned to Jerusalem.

The two disciples found the eleven apostles and the others gathered together. [34]And they learned from the group that the Lord was really alive and had appeared to Peter. [35]Then the disciples from Emmaus told what happened on the road and how they knew he was the Lord when he broke the bread.

What Jesus' Followers Must Do
(Matthew 28.16-20; Mark 16.14-18; John 20.19-23; Acts 1.6-8)

[36]While Jesus' disciples were talking about what had happened, Jesus appeared and greeted them. [37]They were frightened and terrified because they thought they were seeing a ghost.

[38]But Jesus said, "Why are you so frightened? Why do you doubt? [39]Look at my hands and my feet and see who I am! Touch me and find out for yourselves. Ghosts don't have flesh and bones as you see I have."

⁴⁰After Jesus said this, he showed them his hands and his feet. ⁴¹The disciples were so glad and amazed that they could not believe it. Jesus then asked them, "Do you have something to eat?" ⁴²They gave him a piece of baked fish. ⁴³He took it and ate it as they watched.

⁴⁴Jesus said to them, "While I was still with you, I told you that everything written about me in the Law of Moses, the Books of the Prophets, and in the Psalms had to happen."

⁴⁵Then he helped them understand the Scriptures. ⁴⁶He told them:

The Scriptures say that the Messiah must suffer, then three days later he will rise from death. ⁴⁷They also say that all people of every nation must be told in my name to turn to God, in order to be forgiven. So beginning in Jerusalem, ⁴⁸you must tell everything that has happened. ⁴⁹I will send you the one my Father has promised, but you must stay in the city until you are given power from heaven.

Jesus Returns to Heaven
(Mark 16.19, 20; Acts 1.9-11)

⁵⁰Jesus led his disciples out to Bethany, where he raised his hands and blessed them. ⁵¹As he was doing this, he left and was taken up to heaven.ᵘ ⁵²After his disciples had worshiped him,ᵛ they returned to Jerusalem and were very happy. ⁵³They spent their time in the temple, praising God.

ᵘ **24.51** *and was taken up to heaven:* These words are not in some manuscripts.
ᵛ **24.52** *After his disciples had worshiped him:* These words are not in some manuscripts.

24.43 *ate it as they watched:* This was another way he showed them that he was not a ghost.

24.44 *Law of Moses . . . Psalms:* The Jewish Scriptures are made up of three parts: 1) the Law of Moses, 2) the Books of the Prophets, 3) and the Writings, which include the Psalms. See the article called "Different Kinds of Literature in the Bible," p. 13.

24.49 *the one my Father has promised:* Jesus is talking about the Holy Spirit. Acts 2 tells how this promise came true on the day of Pentecost. See also Acts 1.1-11 and the note on p. 24 (Holy Spirit).

24.50 *Bethany:* See the note at 19.28,29.

24.53 *temple:* The temple in Jerusalem (see the note at 13.35).

24.46,47 Ps 22; Isa 53; 50.6; Hos 6.2. **24.50,51** Acts 1.9-11.

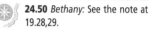

QUESTIONS ABOUT LUKE 19.28—24.53

1. Why did Jesus cry when he approached Jerusalem? (19.41-44) Compare this passage with 21.1-4, 20-24. What does Jesus say is going to happen?
2. Jesus tells about things that will happen when he comes again (21.25-38). What warning does he give? How does this warning affect the way you live your life?
3. How did Jesus settle the argument among the disciples who were discussing which one of them was the greatest? (22.24-30) Think of situations today where people want to be "Number 1." What can be learned from Jesus' teachings about power and service? (See also 9.46-48.)
4. Jesus asked God to forgive his enemies while he was on the cross (23.34,35). Why is it difficult to forgive those who hurt or make fun of us? Someone I need to forgive or to ask for forgiveness is . . .
5. How did the disciples react to what they were told by the women who had gone to the tomb? (24.1-12) Why do you think they acted that way? Do you find the women's story hard to believe or not? Why?
6. Why didn't the two disciples who met Jesus on the road to Emmaus recognize him right away? At what point do they recognize him? Why? (24.13-35) How does one recognize Jesus today? Explain.
7. What does Jesus tells his followers to do? What does he promise will happen? (24.45-48)
8. Complete this sentence: I think being a follower of Jesus means . . .

FEATURE ARTICLES
·
MINI-ARTICLES
·
CHARTS
·
ILLUSTRATIONS
·
MINI-ATLAS
·
CREDITS

The faith of Israel, now more commonly known as the Jewish faith, did not begin as a set of religious practices or system of beliefs. Rather, it began when God commanded Abraham to leave his home and take his wife Sarah and family to a new land called Canaan. Along with this command, God promised Abraham three things: (1) he would have many descendants who would become a great nation; (2) his descendants would be famous and have a land they could call their own; and (3) God would bless Abraham's descendants, and everyone on earth would be blessed because of them (Gen 12.1-3; 15.1-6; 17.1-8).

In return for these promises, Abraham and his descendants were to trust in God alone and obey what God told them to do. A special agreement (also known as a "covenant") had been formed. Abraham confirmed this agreement with God by having his son and all his male descendants circumcised (Gen 17.9-27). Having male children circumcised became an important sign of belonging to God's special people. See also the mini-article called "Agreements (Covenants)," p. 156, and the note on circumcision at Gen 17.10,11.

The following things made the faith of Israel unique among the religions of the ancient world:

1. They believed that God (*Yahweh*) had selected them to be God's special (chosen) people.
2. They believed God acted in history and was involved in the life of the whole community. God's relationship was with all the people, not just with a few individuals or the community's leaders.
3. They believed only in *Yahweh* and did not worship any other gods.

The LORD Gives His Chosen People the Law

The Bible describes how God was at work in the history of the Hebrew people (later called Israelites). When they went to Egypt to escape a famine (Gen 42), God took care of them. Later, God helped them escape, led by Moses, from slavery in Egypt (Exod 12-14). The festival called Passover commemorates this important event, and is observed by Jewish people today. Remembering God's blessings and guidance has been an important part of their worship life as God's people.

God made an important agreement with the Israelite people at Mount Sinai, a place in the desert where Moses and the Israelites arrived after escaping from Egypt (Exod 19.1,2). This happened before they entered Canaan, the land God promised to give them. At Sinai, God gave the Law to Moses and the people. This Law includes the Ten Commandments (Exod 20.2-17; Deut 5.6-21) and other instructions about how the Israelite people should live together and worship God. Other sections of this Law of Moses are given in Exodus 19–34, LEVITICUS, and DEUTERONOMY. The Law includes rules about making sacrifices to God, about how to treat others, and about who would be in charge of Israel's worship. It also included instructions about observing special festivals and holy days and explained what should happen if someone broke a law. At this point in their history, the people of Israel did not need a system of government or a constitution because they were supposed to live according to the Law of Moses. God promised that if the people followed the Law they would be rewarded. But if they were unfaithful to God and did not live according to the Law, they could expect to be punished (Exod 20.5,6; Lev 25.14-46).

The People Enter the Land God Promised Them

In addition to the Law, God also gave Moses instructions for making a sacred tent (also known as the Tabernacle). The people would gather to worship God and offer sacrifices (Exod 25–30). This tent had three sections:

1. **The outer area.** This is where animals were sacrificed and burned on an altar. There was also a bronze bowl in this area for the priests to wash their hands (Exod 27.1-19; 30.17-21).

2. **A holy place.** This area had a table, a golden candlestick, and an altar where incense was burned. The altar and table were made of acacia wood and covered with gold. A special kind of bread called Sacred Bread, or the Bread of the Presence was kept on the table. Twelve loaves of bread, one for each of Israel's tribes, were to be set out on the table every Sabbath (the day of rest), and only the priests were permitted to eat it (Lev 24.5-9). The lampstand was made of gold and had seven branches that curved upward. An oil-burning lamp was placed on each of the seven branches (Exod 25.31-40). The lampstand had seven branches probably because seven was a holy number that symbolized the Sabbath, the seventh day of the week (the day God rested after creating the world; see Gen 2.1,2).

3. **The most holy place (holy of holies).** This is where God was said to be present and where the sacred chest (or ark) containing the stone tablets of the Law was kept. The sacred chest was covered with gold and measured about 4-feet long and was just over 2-feet wide and high. Gold rings were put on each side, so the people could carry the chest with them when they moved from place to place (Exod 25.10-22). The lid of the box was called the place of mercy (or mercy seat; see Exod 26.34), because this is where God "sat" (was present) to be among the people, to receive their sacrifices, and to meet a representative of the people. Only Moses, and later the high priest, were allowed to enter the most holy place. It was separated from the rest of the tent by a curtain (Exod 27.21) and inside the most holy place was a lamp that was to be kept burning (Exod 27.20).

Each of the areas of the sacred tent was separated from the others by curtains. A frame made of forty-eight acacia wood planks supported the whole tent, and it measured about 150-feet by 75-feet. The people carried the sacred tent and sacred chest with them as they journeyed. When they finally entered the land of Canaan, they divided it among Israel's twelve tribes. At this point, there was no single leader and no government in charge of the people. What the people shared in common was their faith in *Yahweh,* which their tribal leaders renewed at the central place of worship at Shechem in Canaan (Josh 24.1-28).

The agreement God had made with Abraham and Sarah was beginning to take shape. *Yahweh* had led the people of Israel out of slavery in Egypt and had helped them get their own land. With each new generation, the people of Israel grew in number and began to enjoy the blessings of living in the promised land. But the people had a difficult time being completely loyal to God, so problems arose.

JUDGES describes how God raised up special leaders, called judges, to help the people in times of crisis. Israelites lived in this way for many years, until the people begged the judge and prophet named Samuel to give them a king like the ones who ruled neighboring countries. Samuel thought the people's request showed a lack of faith, but God eventually told Samuel to choose Saul as Israel's first king (1 Sam 8–10). Later, a shepherd named David was made king (1 Sam 16). David captured Jerusalem and made it the capital of Israel and the single place of worship for all the tribes (2 Sam 5,6). He even set up the sacred tent in Jerusalem on a hill that was known as Zion.

David's son Solomon built the first temple to take the place of the sacred tent. Solomon asked King Hiram of Tyre to supply some materials and skilled builders to help the Israelites construct the temple. In exchange for grain and olive oil from Israel, King Hiram gave Solomon lumber for the temple. People from both kingdoms worked together and the two nations were at peace with one another (1 Kgs 5). The temple was built using cedar, olive wood, and brick, with beautiful decorations made of gold and ivory. Like the sacred tent, the temple had three areas, but in the temple a large olive wood door, instead of a curtain, separated the holy place from the most holy place (1 Kgs 6.1-38; 7.13—8.13). It took seven years to build Solomon's temple, which was dedicated sometime between 960 and 950 B.C. during the Festival of Shelters (1 Kgs 8.62-65).

After King Solomon died, the ten northern tribes of Israel broke away and made Shechem and then Tirzah their capital. They created several places of worship (1 Kgs 12.25-33), and some of the northern leaders, such as Ahab and Jezebel, encouraged the people to worship the Canaanite god Baal (1 Kgs 18). They also built idols to worship the local gods (1 Kgs 14.15). This was one of the things God and God's prophets had warned the people not to do. Because the people did not remain loyal to *Yahweh* alone, they were punished. In 722 B.C. the Assyrians invaded (Israel) the northern kingdom and took most of the people from their homeland to live in Assyria (2 Kgs 17). The people of the southern kingdom (Judah) saw this as God's punishment for the northern tribes' disobedience to their agreement with God.

Later the people of Judah also disobeyed God and were invaded by the Babylonians, who destroyed Jerusalem and the temple in 586 B.C. Solomon's temple had stood for nearly 400 years, but the Babylonian invasion put a temporary end to worship at the temple. Israel's priests and prophets were forced to discover how Israel's faith could survive in exile, far away from Jerusalem in captivity in Babylon.

Israel Returns and Rebuilds the Temple

The people of Israel lived in exile in Babylon for about 50 years, but the priests and teachers of Israel did not let their faith die. Although the temple was destroyed, and they were far from home, they still had God's Word in the Scriptures and in their hearts. Some scholars believe that the time of exile marked a renewed commitment to God and to studying Scripture. The Jewish people probably continued to meet for worship, but they had to do so in private homes.

In 540 B.C. the Persians defeated the Babylonians. The Persian ruler, Cyrus, followed the Persian custom of allowing captured people to return to their homelands and to worship freely, as long as they promised not to start a revolt against the Persians. Many, but not all Israelites, did return to Judah beginning in 539 B.C. They completed work on a new, smaller temple ("the second temple") in 515 B.C. (Ezra 3–5). The prophet Haggai said it could not compare with Solomon's temple (Hag 2.3), but it was used for more than 400 years, somewhat longer than Solomon's temple was used.

Two men, Ezra and Nehemiah, were especially important leaders during the first hundred years after the people returned to Judah from exile. Ezra, a Jewish priest and scribe, studied the Law of Moses and taught it to the people (Neh 8). Copies of the Law of Moses and the historical records were recovered, edited, and again became the basic guidelines for the relationship between the God and the people of Israel. Nehemiah, who was appointed by the Persian king to be governor of Judah, supervised the reconstruction of the walls of Jerusalem (Neh 2,3).

During the centuries after the second temple was built and before Jesus was born, the people of Israel were often under the rule of foreign powers. This caused them to start thinking of themselves more

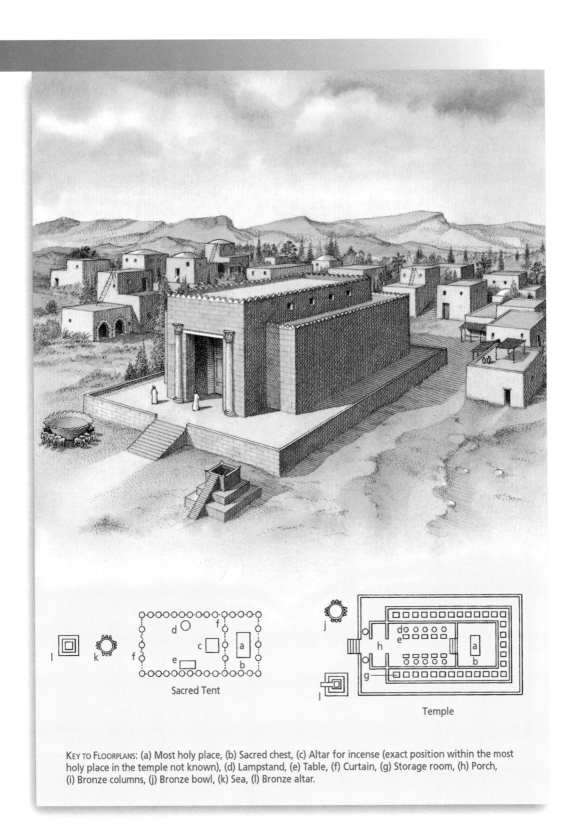

KEY TO FLOORPLANS: (a) Most holy place, (b) Sacred chest, (c) Altar for incense (exact position within the most holy place in the temple not known), (d) Lampstand, (e) Table, (f) Curtain, (g) Storage room, (h) Porch, (i) Bronze columns, (j) Bronze bowl, (k) Sea, (l) Bronze altar.

as a religious group than as a nation with physical boundaries and a political leadership of its own. At this time, the most important feature of Israel's religion, which had come to be known as Judaism, was its stress on keeping the Law of Moses. To be a Jew meant following the Law of Moses. This included observing all the religious festivals as well as the special rules for priests and worship in the temple.

The second temple was at the center of an important event in Israel's history in the second century B.C. The Syrian king Antiochus IV Epiphanes set up an altar to the Greek god Zeus in the temple in 168 B.C. This was a horrible offense against God and the Jewish people, so the Jewish people revolted against Antiochus and restored the temple in 164 B.C. The Maccabean priests who led the revolt to free the Jews from Syrian rule set up a Jewish state with themselves as kings. It lasted until the Romans invaded in 63 B.C. For more about this period in Israel's history, see the article "After the Exile: God's People Return to Judea," p. 125.

Herod Rebuilds and Enlarges the Temple

In 37 B.C., the Romans named a local leader ruler of Judah. In 20 B.C., Herod received permission to rebuild and expand the temple. Most of the building was completed in a year and a half, but work continued on the temple for another forty to fifty years, into the time when Jesus began his teaching (John 2.20). This expanded second temple, sometimes called "Herod's temple," was built on a huge four-sided platform that was almost a mile around its base. Its largest stones were as big as 40-feet long and 6-feet high. Some of these stones are still in place today on the temple site in Jerusalem. What is left of this "temple mount" can be seen clearly at the site called the "Western Wall" (or "Wailing Wall"), where many Jews still go to pray. The temple itself was surrounded by a large wall that had many different entrances. The outer area of the temple grounds included a court of the Gentiles, where anyone was allowed to visit. In this outer area, birds and animals suitable for sacrifice were sold to pilgrims, and foreign money was exchanged so pilgrims could pay their temple tax. In addition to the traditional sections discussed earlier—an altar area where burnt offerings were sacrificed by the priests, a holy area, where only priests were allowed, and the most holy place (or holy of holies), where only the high priest was allowed to go—the second temple also included a woman's court.

The religious life of the temple went on in clear view of the Romans, who occupied the Antonia Fortress built right outside the northwest corner of the wall surrounding the temple area. This fortress was the living quarters for a large number of Roman soldiers, whose job was to keep peace in Jerusalem (Acts 21.34-37). The Roman governor's official residence was in Caesarea, but he usually stayed at this fortress while in Jerusalem.

During the time of Herod's temple, the Romans were in charge of Jerusalem and Judea. They did, however, allow a council of local Jewish leaders, including the high priest and other important religious and business leaders, to have some control over settling local matters, especially those having to do with the temple and religious issues. For example, no Gentile (non-Jew) was allowed in the inner parts of the temple. If someone broke this law, the Jewish leaders could call upon the Roman authorities to put the offender to death.

In Jesus' day, the temple continued to be the center of the Jewish faith. Jewish men and many of their family members traveled to Jerusalem to celebrate yearly festivals such as Passover and the Harvest Festival. The temple priests and the rituals surrounding the temple were important to the Jewish people. Some Jews, such as the Pharisees, also emphasized the importance of studying and interpreting the Jewish Scriptures. This means that there were a number of different and important ways

JEWISH CALENDAR AND FESTIVALS

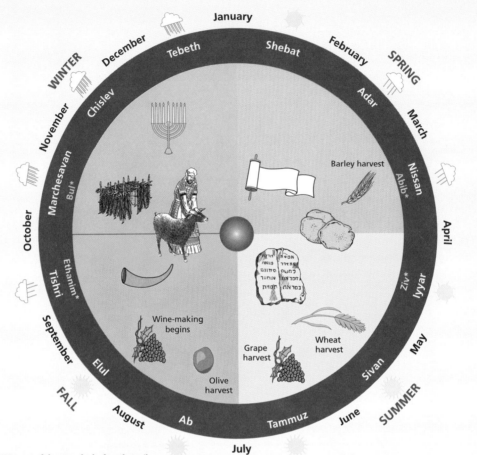

*Names of the months before the exile.

THE CALENDAR IN THE ANCIENT WORLD

As in other parts of the ancient Near East, the people of Israel developed a calendar that was based on the yearly movement of the sun and on the phases of the moon. The year was divided into twelve months, based on the observation that the moon's phases changed about twelve times in the period of days that made up a year. The number of days in the lunar (moon-based) year was about eleven days shorter than the solar (sun-based) year, so the Israelites periodically added an extra month to the calendar to make sure that the festivals they celebrated would continue to fall at their expected times in relation to the weather patterns (seasons) and agricultural cycles (planting and harvesting).

Early in Israelite history the year was considered to begin in the seventh month (around the fall fruit harvest). Later, it began in the spring on the first new moon after the vernal equinox (one of two times in the year when day and night are equal in length).

Time was measured, however, more often by season than by names of months. The year was divided into the dry season (April to September) and the rainy season (October to March). These, in turn, were divided into times for planting grain (November to December) and times for harvesting (April to June). Time was also measured by the agricultural activities that were undertaken in specific months. For example, wheat was harvested in March and April, grapes matured in June and July, and summer fruit was picked in August and September.

The months themselves had religious significance for the people of Israel. The beginning of each month (when the moon is "new") was considered a holy time and a time when the New Moon Festivals were celebrated (Num 28.11-15). Most of the yearly religious festivals had traditional associations with agricultural events, as well as to the events in Jewish history they commemorated.

FALL FESTIVALS

FESTIVAL OF TRUMPETS
(ROSH HASHANAH, FIRST DAY OF TISHRI, THE SEVENTH MONTH)

A day to celebrate the New Year and to remember the agreement God made with the people at Mount Sinai. This holiday marks the beginning of the festival year.
Lev 23.23-25; Num 29.2-6.

GREAT DAY OF FORGIVENESS
(YOM KIPPUR, TENTH DAY OF TISHRI)

The day of the year when the people expressed their sorrow for their sins by going without eating (fasting) and the priest purified the most holy place by sacrificing a bull for his own sins and a goat for the sins ofthe people. A second goat (called a scapegoat) wasreleased into the desert to show that the people'ssins were being taken away.
Lev 16.1-34; Num 29.7-11.

FESTIVAL OF SHELTERS
(SUCCOTH, FIFTEENTH DAY OF TISHRI)

A week-long celebration to remember how the people wandered for forty years in the desert before entering into the land God promised to them.
Lev 23.33-43.

TEMPLE FESTIVAL
(HANUKKAH, TWENTY-FIFTH DAY OF CHISLEV)

A week-long celebration to remember the rededication of the temple by Judas Maccabeus in 164 B.C. The story of Judas and his brothers is told in a book called *1 Maccabees*, which describes events in Jewish history from 175 to 134 B.C.

1 Maccabees 4.36-59; John 10.22.

SPRING FESTIVALS

PASSOVER AND FESTIVAL OF THIN BREAD
(FIFTEENTH DAY OF NISAN)

A week-long festival to recall how God delivered the people from slavery in Egypt and to give thanks for the yearly production of food crops and flocks.
Exod 12.23-25.

HARVEST FESTIVAL
(SHAVUOTH, SIXTH DAY OF SILVAN)

A day to celebrate the grain harvest and the beginning of the season when the first fruits were offered. It was also a day to recall how God delivered the nation from Egypt and provided a land that could supply the needs of the people.
Lev 23.15-21; Deut 16.9-12.

PURIM
(THIRTEENTH DAY OF ADAR)

A day to celebrate how Queen Esther helped stop Haman's plot against the Jews in the time of King Xerxes of Persia.
Esth 9.20-32.

PILGRIMAGE FESTIVALS

Three times a year, Jewish men were required to go to Jerusalem to celebrate these special festivals:

FESTIVAL OF SHELTERS

PASSOVER AND THE FESTIVAL OF THIN BREAD

HARVEST FESTIVAL

SABBATH: A WEEKLY FESTIVAL

The word Sabbath comes from the Hebrew verb *shabbat*, to "stop" or to "rest," and refers to the seventh day of the week, from sunset on Friday to sunset on Saturday. The ancient Israelites, like modern Jews, worshiped on the Sabbath and rested from their work.

The Bible's description of the Sabbath's origin is found in Genesis 2.1-3. These verses at the end of the creation story tell how God rested from the work of creation on the seventh day and made it a special, holy day. In EXODUS a connection is made between God's resting from creation and commanding Israel to rest from work on the Sabbath and worship the LORD (Exod 20.8-11; 31.17). This resting was not only for Israelites, but for their animals, servants (including slaves), and any foreigners living in Israel, as well (Exod 23.12; Deut 5.14,15).

Related to the weekly Sabbath observance is the biblical command that every seven years the land must be allowed to rest for a full year. During this Seventh Year (or "sabbatical year") the land was not to be plowed or planted. This was done to honor the LORD, the one who the land truly belonged to (Exod 23.10,11; Lev 25.1-7). Any crops that grew on their own were to be left in the fields for the poor and for work animals. The Seventh Year was also a time when debts were cancelled (Deut 15.1-3).

In addition, the Bible speaks of a Year of Celebration (sometimes called the "Jubilee Year"). Each seventh Sabbatical Year (that is, every forty-nine years), land that had been sold was to be returned to its original owner, and all slaves were to be freed to their families (Lev 25.8-34). This year began on the "Great Day of Forgiveness" with the blowing of the ram's horn.

The Sabbath observance was one of the most important elements in Israelite religion. It reminded people of their special status as God's chosen people and that God was the Creator of the world. The three Sabbath observances of rest and freedom point to God's desire to free all of creation. Celebrating them reminds people of their own need for continual re-creation.

that Jewish people expressed their faith. If this had not been true, the Jewish faith might have died out when the temple was destroyed in A.D. 70.

Jesus' prediction that the temple would be destroyed (Mark 13.1,2) came to pass when the Romans destroyed Herod's temple while putting down a Jewish revolt that lasted between A.D. 64-70. The Roman emperor Hadrian (A.D. 117-138) crushed a second Jewish revolt about A.D. 131. In 132, Hadrian built a temple to honor the Roman god Jupiter on the same site, and in the seventh century A.D., Muslims built a mosque called the Dome of the Rock on the temple site. The shrine and mosque are still standing today, as are a few parts of Herod's original temple area.

The Role of Israel's Priests

According to the agreement God made with Moses, all the people of Israel were to serve God as priests (Exod 19.5,6). They would be God's holy nation among all the other nations. The Law of Moses also set aside special priests to represent the whole people in their relationship with God. The priests of Israel were to be from the tribe of Levi. Those who were not born into this tribe could not serve as priests.

The priesthood of Israel appears to fall into three levels. In the lowest level were those Levites who were not direct descendants of Moses' brother Aaron (see Num 3.5-13). They were to help the priests and take care of the furnishings in the sacred tent (and later, in the temple). At the next level were the priests who were responsible for offering sacrifices and leading the worship. These priests were also from the Levite tribe, but had to be direct descendants of Aaron. The Levites and the priests were divided into twenty-four groups or shifts. Each group served in the temple for one week on a rotating basis. With twenty-four groups, a particular priest might serve for a total of two or, very occasionally, three weeks each year. At the head of the priesthood was the high priest. He was in charge of the other priests, and was the only priest

The Arch of Titus. *Rome, built in A.D. 81, celebrates how this Roman general put down the Jewish Rebellion in Palestine eleven years earlier. This relief from the Arch shows how Titus brought the temple treasures, including the gold lampstand (menorah), to the emperor and paraded them through the streets of Rome.*

who could enter the most holy place to offer sacrifices on the Great Day of Forgiveness (Lev 16.1-25). For more about the role of priests in the religious life of Israel, see the mini-article called "Israel's Priests," p. 171.

The priests wore special clothes made of linen and other fine materials. For a description of these, see Exodus 28.1–29.31. The high priest wore a special vest and breastpiece. The breastpiece was made partly of metal (gold) and partly of cloth (fine linen) and was to have four rows of precious stones with three in each row, representing the twelve tribes of Israel. In the early days of the priesthood, the breastpiece had a pouch in it that contained the "Urim and Thummim," objects the high priest could use to get a "yes" or "no" answer from God (Exod 28.30). Most likely, by the time the time the Jewish people returned from their exile in Babylonia the use of the Urim and Thummim had been discontinued. Another distinctive part of the high priest's attire was a turban. It had a gold rosette with the words "Dedicated to the Lord" engraved on it (Exod 28.36; 39.30).

When the Jewish people returned to Jerusalem after exile in Babylon, the Persian king would not allow them to have their own king. Because they could not have a king, the high priest became an even more significant person in the life of the people. In the centuries before Jesus and during Jesus' lifetime, the high priest was the head of the temple and of the Jewish people.

Worship and Festivals

The worship practices of Israel included the offering of sacrifices, prayers, and Scripture reading. Selected texts were read for certain occasions, and sometimes songs were sung. Psalms includes prayers and songs that were sung or said in worship by the whole people or used by individuals in private prayer. The text of Deuteronomy 6.4 ("Hear, O Israel," called the *Shema*) was to be said in prayer every morning and evening.

One of the most important aspects of the religious life of the Jewish people, both before and after the exile, was the keeping of the Sabbath (Exod 20.8-11; Exod 31.12-17). On the Sabbath, the seventh day of the week, Jews are commanded not to do any work and to rest, just as God rested after creating the world in six days (Gen 1.1—2.4). The Sabbath is also devoted to prayer and to remembering how God brought the Israelite people out of slavery in Egypt. On this day, they and their children, their servants, their visitors, and even their livestock should rest and not work (Deut 5.12-15).

The festival celebrations that were commanded in the Law of Moses and established by Jewish tradition greatly influenced Israel's life of faith. These celebrations can be grouped according to the time they were to take place as well as by purpose. See the chart on the previous page for an explanation of the major festivals in the Jewish calendar.

JOSHUA. Like the biblical books that tell about how Moses led the people (Exod, Num, Deut), JOSHUA is full of miracles. Before the people of Israel could enter Canaan, they had to cross the Jordan River. Once again, God was with them and helped them in a miraculous way. Just as God had helped Moses by opening up the waters of the Red Sea (Exod 14), so God made the waters of the Jordan River stop flowing when the priests of Israel stepped into the river (Josh 3.15-17). After they crossed the river and came to Gilgal, the people made a monument using twelve rocks, one rock for each tribe of Israel. Then they set up camp there.

Moses led the people of Israel in the desert for forty years after they escaped from slavery in Egypt. But when the people were camped in the lowlands of Moab on the east side of the Jordan River, Moses died, and Joshua became their new leader. The promise God made more than five hundred years earlier to Abraham (Gen 12.1,2; 15.7-21) and repeated to Joshua (Josh 1.1-8) was about to be fulfilled. Abraham's descendants, the people of Israel, were ready to take over the land of Canaan. But this would not be easy. Other people had lived in Canaan for thousands of years. They had built walled cities and farmed the land, and they were not simply going to give their land to the people of Israel.

Here the people of Israel prepared to capture Jericho, a nearby walled city that stood on a mound along an important east-west trade route in the fertile Jordan River valley. The conquest of Jericho is another miraculous story. After the Israelite priests and army marched around the city for

The People of Israel
Enter the Promised Land

The story of how the people of Israel conquered the people of Canaan is told in

ABOVE: *The land promised to the people of Israel as it looks today. The Jezreel Valley at the foot of Mount Gilboa is rich and productive farmland.*
RIGHT: *Jericho, sometimes called "the oldest walled settlement in the world," dates back to around 9000 B.C. Shown here are the remains of a fortification wall.*

seven days as the LORD had instructed, the priests blew their trumpets and the people shouted. The walls of the city fell flat and the Israelites captured the city (Josh 6). From Jericho, Joshua and the people moved into other parts of Canaan, capturing other cities in battle or making agreements with the people who already lived in the land.

The Tribes of Israel and Their Lands

Eventually Joshua gave different parts of the land of Canaan to each of Israel's twelve tribes (Josh 13–21; see also the map on p. 210). These tribes were like big extended families, with the oldest male (father) serving as the center of authority. As the tribes took ownership of their pieces of land, they settled down to build towns, grow crops, and raise herds of sheep and goats. The land these tribes owned was believed to have been assigned by God, and so no one was to sell or give their property to anyone else. If that did happen, the land was to eventually be given back to the tribe God first gave it to. This would happen during the Year of the Celebration which was celebrated approximately every fifty years (Lev 25.8-17, 23-28; see also the chart called "Jewish Calendar and Festivals," p. 114).

The tribe of Levi did not get their own land, because they were given a special task and would not be farmers or herders. The Law of Moses said they would be in charge of offering sacrifices to God (Deut 18.1). The other tribes were to provide these sacrifices, and the Levites were allowed to keep some of the food sacrifices for themselves. Thus, the Levites (priests from the tribe of Levi) had an important place as the religious leaders of the other tribes: they would be the priests for all Israel.

Even though the twelve tribes were scattered in different areas around Canaan, they shared a common history and followed the Law of Moses. Just before Joshua died,

he called all the tribes together for a meeting at Shechem. He challenged them to remain faithful to God and never to worship other gods (Josh 24.14-24). The people promised to remain faithful, and Joshua set up a stone as a witness to their promises (Josh 24.25-27).

Judges Are Chosen To Rule the People of Israel

After Joshua died, the tribes of Israel continued to fight against the Canaanites (Judg 1), but they did not drive out all the people who had lived in the land. In addition, the tribes of Israel were surrounded by other peoples who were not friendly.

At this time, the Israelites began to forget the promises they had made to the LORD while Joshua was still alive. Some of them worshiped the Canaanite gods, Baal and Astarte, as well as idols of other gods from nearby lands. The LORD was so angry that he let the surrounding nations raid Israel's lands and steal their crops and possessions (Judg 2.6-15).

When the people cried out for help, God felt sorry for them. Help came from special leaders known as judges. The "judges" sometimes settled legal cases (see Judg 4.4,5), but most of them were more well known as military leaders chosen by God to lead the Israelites in battle against their enemies. The lives of these judges are described in JUDGES, chapters 3–16.

Samuel: Prophet, Priest, and Leader

Near the end of the period of the judges, a boy named Samuel was born to Hannah and Elkanah (1 Sam 1). They took him to Shiloh, where he was dedicated to the LORD by the priest Eli. Samuel stayed with Eli in Shiloh and helped Eli serve the LORD. While Samuel was still very young (1 Sam 3), the LORD chose him to be his special servant and he grew up to be the LORD's prophet (1 Sam

THE JUDGES OF ISRAEL

JUDGE	YEARS OF SERVICE	CHIEF ENEMY	ACCOMPLISHMENTS	SCRIPTURE PASSAGE
Othniel	40	Northern Syria	Helped Israel defeat King Cushan Rishathaim of Northern Syria and brought Israel forty years of peace.	Judg 3.7-11
Ehud	80	Moabites and Amalekites	Killed King Eglon of Moab and defeated the Moabites, who had joined with the Amalekites to attack Israel.	Judg 3.12-30
Shamgar	10	Philistines	Rescued Israel by killing 600 Philistines.	Judg 3.31
Deborah and Barak	40	Canaanites	Defeated the army of Canaanite King Jabin of Hazor and his commander Sisera.	Judg 4.1—5.31
Gideon	40	Midianites and Amalekites	Built an altar for worshiping the LORD and pulled down the altar where his father had worshiped the Canaanite god Baal. Defeated the Midianites who had joined with the Amalekites to steal Israel's livestock and crops. Honored the LORD by refusing to be made king.	Judg 6.1—8.35
Tola	23	Not stated in the Bible	The Bible says he rescued Israel but gives very little information about this judge.	Judg 10.1,2
Jair	22	Not stated in the Bible	The Bible says little about this judge's accomplishments, but it does say he had thirty sons, each one in charge of a town in Gilead.	Judg 10.3-5
Jephthah	6	Ammonites and Ephraimites	Defeated the Ammonites who had invaded Gilead. Battled the army of the Israelite tribe of Ephraim.	Judg 11.1—12.7
Ibzan	7	Not stated in the Bible	The Bible says little about this judge's accomplishments, but it does say he had thirty daughters and thirty sons.	Judg 12.8-10
Elon	10	Not stated in the Bible	The Bible gives no specific information about this judge's accomplishments.	Judg 12.11,12
Abdon	8	Not stated in the Bible	The Bible says little about this judge's accomplishments, but it does say he had forty sons and thirty grandsons.	Judg 12.13-15
Samson	20	Philistines	Took revenge on the Philistine leaders and people who burned his wife and family.	Judg 13.1—16.31

3.19—4.1; 7.3-5). Samuel also served as a priest (1 Sam 7.9,10) and was a leader in Israel all his life (1 Sam 7.15). Because his time as Israel's leader immediately followed the period of judges, he is sometimes called the last of Israel's judges.

Kings and Kingdoms

When Samuel was getting old, the leaders of Israel's tribes asked him to choose a king to rule over them, because all the lands around them were ruled by kings. Samuel did not really like this idea. He believed that a king would not treat the people well (1 Sam 8.9-18), and he thought that the people's request for a king showed their lack of trust in the LORD as their leader (1 Sam 10.17-19). But when Samuel prayed about the situation, the LORD told him to go ahead and give the people a king (1 Sam 8.1-22). This was a major change in the history of the Israelite people. For a long time they had been a loose-ly connected group of tribes with one God but separate leaders. Now, they were about to become a single nation made up of tribes united not only by one God, but also under a king.

The people of ancient Israel were ruled by kings from the time of Saul (about 1030 to 1010 B.C.) and David (1010 to 970 B.C.) to the reign of Zedekiah (597 to 587 B.C.). Some of the kings were strong rulers who remained faithful to God. But other kings actually led the people away from worshiping God, made bad agreements with Israel's enemies, and treated the people cruelly and unfairly. The history of the kings is told in 1 and 2 SAMUEL, 1 and 2 KINGS, and is retold in 1 and 2 CHRONICLES. See the chart called, "The Kings of Israel," p. 123, for the names of all of the kings of Israel mentioned in the Bible.

Saul: Israel's First King

The period of the kings is divided into two main parts. The first part is known as the time of the United Israelite Kingdom, when there was just one king for all of the Israelite people and tribes. Samuel chose Saul to be the first king of Israel (1 Sam 9,10) and he was accepted by the tribal leaders because of his courage and military abilities (1 Sam 11). He ruled for about twenty years and did much to bring the tribes together and to defeat some of Israel's enemies. But Saul was also a troubled man who was unfaithful to God at times (1 Sam 13; 15).

David Becomes Israel's King

While Saul was still king the LORD told Samuel to go to Bethlehem to find the next king. This turned out to be David, the youngest son of Jesse (1 Sam 16.1-13). David soon entered Saul's court as a special servant who played the harp to console the troubled king (1 Sam 16.14-23). Another account

Ashurnasirpal, the king of Assyria from 883 to 859 B.C., shown in a royal procession. After settling in the land God had promised to them, the people of Israel wanted to have a king like the ones that ruled Israel's neighbors.

of David's life shows him to be an amazingly brave soldier who trusted in the LORD. David killed the giant Philistine Goliath (1 Sam 17.1-54) and impressed the king so much that Saul made him a high officer in the army (1 Sam 18.5). Eventually, the king became suspicious of David and jealous of his military successes. Saul tried several times to have David killed, but was never successful. Eventually, Saul committed suicide after being injured in battle against the Philistines (1 Sam 31.1-13).

After Saul's death, there was a short period when the people of Israel were divided between loyalty to Saul's only living son, Ishbosheth, and to David, the powerful military leader. David became king of the people of Judah at Hebron (2 Sam 2.4), and then king of all of Israel after the murder of Saul's son (2 Sam 5.1-3). He then conquered the Jebusite city Jerusalem and made it the capital of the United Israelite Kingdom (2 Sam 5.6-12). He put the sacred chest on the hilltop where the temple would later be built (2 Sam 6.1-19). The prophet Nathan told David that God would dwell in the great temple in Jerusalem some day. But he said that David's son would build it, not David (2 Sam 7.1-17).

One of greatest things David did was to defeat the Philistines in battle and take control of all the land east of the Jordan River and north of Damascus in Syria as far as the Euphrates River (2 Sam 8). PSALMS and books of the prophets describe David as a model king who had a close relationship with God. In many ways, he became a symbol of new life for God's people and of God's rule in the world (2 Sam 23.5; Ps 89.3,4; Isa 9.1-7; Jer 33.14-26; Mic 5.2-5). However, David also had his faults; he was not always perfect (2 Sam 11;12). See also the mini-article called "David," p. 160.

Solomon: Israel's Wisest King

David's son, Solomon, became king after David died and ruled from about 970 to 931 B.C. Solomon was known as a wise man (1 Kgs 2.9; 3.12,28; 4.29-34), and he was in charge of building Israel's first temple in Jerusalem (1 Kgs 5–8). He expanded his father David's kingdom, built an enormous palace (1 Kgs 7.1-12) and many fortresses, established store cities, and made Israel a very rich country (1 Kgs 4.20-28). But in doing this he married foreign wives and allowed them to set up shrines and monuments to other gods (1 Kgs 11.1-13), things which were certainly not pleasing to the LORD.

The Kingdom Is Divided

When Solomon died around 922 B.C., his son Rehoboam became king. Shortly after that, the ten northern tribes rebelled against the king and formed their own kingdom. This period of Israel's history became known as the Divided Kingdom.

The tribes of Judah and Benjamin in the south became known as the kingdom of Judah (or the southern kingdom). The rest of the tribes to the north formed the kingdom of Israel (or the northern kingdom). See the map called "The Kingdoms of Israel and Judah," p. 204. Each kingdom

ISRAELITE KINGDOM UNDER DAVID AND SOLOMON
◉ Solomon's fortifications

MEDITERRANEAN SEA

Hazor
Megiddo ◉

Gezer Beth-Horan
Baalath? ◉ ◉
David's Kingdom   Jerusalem
around 1010 B.C.

Tamar

David's expansion around 970 B.C.

THE KINGS OF ISRAEL

This chart lists all of the kings of Israel starting with the three who ruled the United Israelite Kingdom. After Solomon's death the northern tribes broke away from the southern tribes and continued to call themselves Israel. From that time on the southern tribes came to be known as Judah. The prophets, shown in *italic*, sometimes spoke to the people of the northern or southern kingdoms, and sometimes to both.

DATE	THE UNITED ISRAELITE KINGDOM
1050 B.C.	Saul (1030–1010) — *Eli* / *Samuel*
1000 B.C.	David (1010–970)
950 B.C.	*Nathan* — Solomon (970–931)

DATE	JUDAH (SOUTHERN KINGDOM)	THE KINGDOM DIVIDES *Prophets*	ISRAEL (NORTHERN KINGDOM)
950 B.C.	Rehoboam (931–913) Abijah (913–911) Asa (911–870)		Jeroboam (931–910) Nadab (910–909) Baasha (909–886)
900 B.C.	Jehoshaphat (870–848)	*Elijah*	Elah (886–885) Zimri (7 days in 885) Omri (885–874) Ahab (874–853) Ahaziah (853–852)
850 B.C.	Jehoram (848–841) Ahaziah (of Judah, 841) Queen Athaliah (841–835) Joash (835–796)	*Elisha*	Joram (852–841) Jehu (841–814) Jehoahaz (814–798)
800 B.C.	Amaziah (796–781) Uzziah (781–740)	*Jonah* *Amos*	Jehoash (798–783) Jeroboam II (783–743)
750 B.C.	Jotham (740–736) Ahaz (736–716) Hezekiah (716 – 687)	*Isaiah* *Micah* *Hosea*	Zechariah (6 mos. in 743) Shallum (1 mo. in 743) Menahem (743–738) Pekah (737–732) Hoshea (732–723)
700 B.C.	Manasseh (687 – 642)		Assyrians defeat Israel and capture its capital, Samaria, 722. **Kingdom of Israel ends.**
650 B.C.	Amon (642 – 640) Josiah (640 – 609) Joahaz (3 mos. in 609) Jehoiakim (609 – 598) Jehoiachin (3 mos. in 598) Zedekiah (598 – 587)	*Zephaniah (640-609)* *Nahum (663-612)* *Jeremiah* *Habakkuk* *(620-597)* *Ezekiel*	
600 B.C.	**Babylonians defeat Judah and destroy Jerusulem, 587 or 586.** **The exile in Babylon, 586-538.**		*All dates are approximate.* *Kings who ruled for one year or less are in smaller type.*

had its own king. In Judah, the kings continued to be descendants of King David, but in Israel the tribal and military leaders had to fight to become king. Sometimes a family would reign for a period of years, only to be defeated by an opponent who then ruled for a time.

The capital of Judah was still Jerusalem where the people of Judah continued to worship the LORD in the temple. But in Israel, King Jeroboam I made a shrine in Bethel so that people could offer sacrifices there instead of going to the temple in Jerusalem (1 Kgs 12.25-33). Later, Samaria became the capital city of Israel (1 Kgs 16.24-29).

Israel: The Northern Kingdom

In the northern kingdom of Israel, some rulers allowed the people to worship idols such as the Canaanite god Baal. This practice was condemned by a number of the prophets who preached in Israel during this time. For example, the prophet Elijah spoke out against King Ahab and his wife Queen Jezebel, who openly encouraged the worship of Baal and supported Baal's prophets (see 1 Kings 18.1—19.18).

The practice of allowing the people to worship other gods led to Israel's downfall. They fought civil wars with Judah and battled with neighbors like Syria and Moab. Eventually, the Assyrians invaded Israel and attacked the capital city of Samaria. In 722 B.C. the city was conquered and many of the Israelites were captured and taken away to Assyria as prisoners. Others stayed in the area, lived with, and sometimes married the people the Assyrians brought in to settle the land. The northern kingdom of Israel never regained its power as a nation.

Judah: The Southern Kingdom

Meanwhile, Judah in the south had its own problems. Though many of its kings, such as Hezekiah and especially Josiah, were faithful to God and followed the teachings of the Law of Moses (2 Kgs 18.1-8; 2 Kgs 22.1—23.25), other kings, like Manasseh, did things to make the LORD angry (2 Kgs 21.1-18). Eventually Judah could no longer hold out against the attacks of its powerful neighbors. The kingdom of Babylon finally invaded and destroyed Jerusalem and its temple in 587 B.C. Many of the people of Judah were taken to Babylon as prisoners. During the next fifty years this group of Israelites remained in Babylon and could not return to their own land. This period of time is known as "the exile." To learn about how the people of Israel were allowed to return to their homeland, read the next article, "After the Exile: God's People Return to Judea."

The Hanging Gardens of Babylon, *one of the "Seven Wonders of the Ancient World." The Gardens were built during the time of King Nebuchadnezzar, who ruled Babylonia from around 605 to 562 B.C.. It was during this period that the Babylonians conquered Jerusalem and took the people of Judah into captivity.*

In Babylon

The Bible provides little information about the years in the sixth century B.C. when many of the Israelite people lived in exile in Babylon. Though the people could no longer worship God in the temple in Jerusalem, the Babylonians allowed them to gather and practice their religion. The Israelites told the stories of their ancestors, heard the words of prophets, and studied the Law of Moses. Some believe that it was during the time of the exile that some of Israel's priests added to the old Scriptures and wrote new ones, so the people would not forget who they were and where they came from.

Back Home in Judea

Many of the Jewish people had been sent into exile between the years 597 to 582 B.C. In 539 B.C., Cyrus of Persia conquered Babylonia. About one year later he gave the Jewish people permission to return to their homeland of Judea. The books of EZRA and

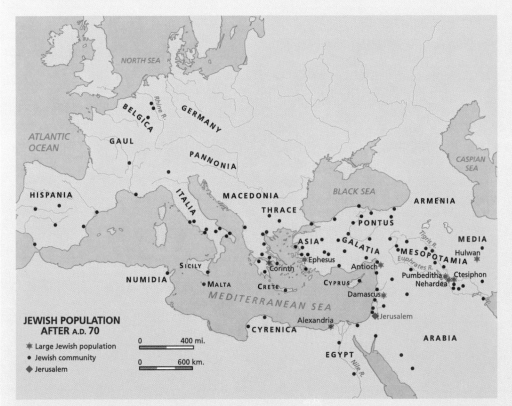

Jewish Communities in the Mediterranean World. By the time of Jesus there were far more Jews living outside Palestine than in Palestine. This was due to both negative causes (war and exile) and to positive ones (commerce, improved travel, and Roman tolerance of the Jewish religion). After the destruction of the temple in Jerusalem in A.D. 70, the Jewish communities outside Palestine, called the "Diaspora" (meaning "scattered abroad"), would become increasingly important. When the first followers of Jesus left Judea to take the good news to other parts of the Roman Empire, they usually went first to cities with large Jewish populations. This map shows how far from Jerusalem many Jews lived in the first century.

NEHEMIAH in the Old Testament tell about the hundred-year period that followed the time of the exile. The books of the prophets Haggai and Zechariah also come from this time. Sometime between 500 and 425 B.C. the priest named Ezra encouraged the people to return to their Jewish traditions and to obey the Law of Moses. He went so far as to force Jewish men to give up their foreign wives (Ezra 9,10).

Two religious issues were most important to the people who had returned from exile: (1) worship of the God of Israel in the rebuilt temple in Jerusalem, and (2) study of the Law of Moses to see how God's people were to live in the present situation. Also in this period, Nehemiah served for a time as governor of Judea and helped supervise the rebuilding of Jerusalem's walls. Though the people had the freedom to worship as they wished, their land was still under control of the Persians.

Outside of Judea

While some of the Jewish people were settling back in Jerusalem, others stayed in the lands ruled by Persia or moved on to other major cities in the eastern Mediterranean world. Some of these groups developed their own collections of the Jewish Scriptures and their own methods of interpreting them. Jewish groups also appeared in Syria and Asia Minor, in North Africa, and on islands in the Mediterranean. Many Jewish writings of the period after the exile come from Alexandria in Egypt, where Jewish teachers read their Scriptures along with Greek philosophy. These teachers believed that this approach would help people to understand the basic truths of the Bible.

The Influence of Alexander the Great

Between 336 B.C. and 323 B.C., Alexander the Great of Macedonia conquered much of the eastern Mediterranean world, including Egypt, Palestine (where Jerusalem was located), and much of Persia. After Alexan-

Antiochus IV, called "Epiphanes" ("the manifested one"), ruled Judea from 175 to 164 B.C. His cruelty toward his Jewish subjects and his enactment of laws that prohibited many customs that were required by the Law of Moses led to Jewish rebellion. The military capture, purification, and rededication of the temple by Jewish soldiers led by Judas Maccabeus is commemorated in the Jewish festival of Hanukkah.

der died, these lands were ruled for over a century by his generals or those who followed them. The most important of these rulers were the Seleucids, who controlled Syria, and the Ptolemies, who controlled Egypt. One or the other of these royal families ruled Palestine, the land of the Jewish people, for much of this time. However, in 168 B.C. the Seleucid king, Antiochus IV, began to try to stop people from practicing the Jewish religion. He declared that it was forbidden to study the Law of Moses, observe the Sabbath, or practice circumcision. Antiochus IV also set up a statue of the Greek god Zeus in the Jewish temple. His actions deeply offended the Jewish people.

Most Jews continued to worship in Jerusalem and to pay yearly fees to support the temple and its priests. From the time of their captivity in Babylon, Jews had met informally in homes or in public halls to study the Scriptures. The moral teachings and the understanding of God contained in the Jewish Scriptures attracted many non-Jews (Gentiles) to these meetings. Some non-Jewish men were circumcised in order to become full members of the Jewish com-

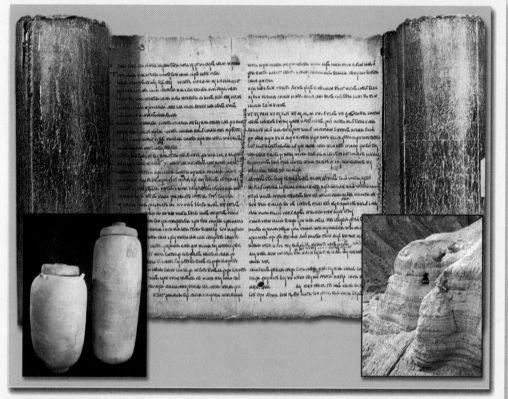

Dead Sea Scrolls. *The most important archaeological find of the twentieth century was the discovery beginning in 1947 of over eight hundred documents from a Jewish group (most likely Essenes) who lived near the Dead Sea from the middle of the second century B.C. until their defeat by the Romans around A.D. 68. Many of these leather or papyrus scrolls were stored in clay jars and hidden away in caves to keep them safe. Although most of the documents are mere scraps, a nearly complete version of ISAIAH was found. This important manuscript is older than any other copy of ISAIAH that exists.*

munity (see Acts 2.11; 16.1-3; see also the note on circumcision at Gen 17.10,11).

Greek, Roman, and Persian philosophies and ideas influenced Jewish writings of the time. This influence is apparent in many of the books that are included in some editions of the Bible and known as "deuterocanonical" or "apocryphal." (See the article called "What Books Belong in the Bible?," p. 7). Jewish writers also copied the style and form of a kind of popular Roman literature called "sibylline oracles," which told of prophecies concerning Caesar and the Roman people. The Jewish Sibylline Oracles told about God's plan for the future of his people.

The religion of the Jewish people after the exile in Babylon did not move toward one single pattern or style. People were practicing Judaism and living as Jews in a variety of ways. This was the situation when Jesus came to teach the people many new things about God and God's kingdom. For a description of this next phase in Jewish history see the articles called "People of the Law: The Religion of Israel," p. 109, and

"The World of Jesus: Peoples, Powers, and Politics," p. 133. See also the mini-article called "Synagogues," p. 191.

The Jewish People Reclaim Their Land

The Jewish people revolted against Antiochus. The rebellion broke out suddenly. Soon the rebellion had a leader named Judas Maccabeus. (One of the possible meanings for his last name is "the hammer.") Led by Judas Maccabeus, the small bands of Jewish fighters defeated the mighty army of Antiochus. This revolt is described *1* and *2 Maccabees* in the Apocrypha. (See the article "What Books Belong in the Bible?" p. 7.) Eventually the rebels purified the temple, an event still remembered by Jews today in the celebration of Hanukkah.

Finally, the Maccabees set up their own government. Those Maccabean rulers who came after Judas called themselves by the title of king, even though they were not descendants of King David or from the tribe of Judah. This upset many Jews, who did not like the Maccabeans' cruel style of control and the agreements they made with Rome in order to remain in power. The rule of the Maccabees lasted until the Roman general Pompey invaded Jerusalem and brought all the land under direct Roman control in 63 B.C.

Because they were bitterly disappointed over the Maccabean style of political rule, some of the Jewish people turned to other kinds of religions or philosophies. For example, one group of Jews became very disappointed with the temple priests in Jerusalem who seemed to love the wealth and power connected with running the temple. This group withdrew from Jewish society and lived as a separate community in a barren area near the Dead Sea. They remained there, living in complete obedience to God's Law as they understood it. They believed that God would help them drive out the present priests and rebuild the city of Jerusalem and the temple. In the middle of the twentieth century, many books and writings of this group were discovered in a place called Qumran near the Dead Sea. These writings are known as the Dead Sea Scrolls. Included in these scrolls is the oldest surviving copy of ISAIAH, as well as the rule books for this community.

PROPHETS AND PROPHECY

A prophet is someone who speaks God's message. The message the prophet speaks is called a "prophecy." And to speak as a prophet is to "prophesy." In general culture, prophets are sometimes compared with fortunetellers or those who predict future events. The prophets of the Old Testament, however, were somewhat different. Their task was to observe what was happening around them and then deliver God's message for that situation. Their messages were given both to God's people and to those who did not trust in Israel's God. Sometimes the message was a reminder to the people or their leaders that they were not obeying God, and that they should change their ways. This kind of message sometimes included strong warnings about God's judgment. At other times, the prophets brought words of hope in tough times, or said that even though things were bad in the present, God would cause things to change for the better in the future.

Prophets in the Old Testament

The Old Testament includes fifteen books written by or called by the names of different prophets, but these fifteen are not the only prophets who had an impact on the people of Israel. Some of the prophets mentioned in the Old Testament were not even part of God's chosen people, the Israelites. Some prophets were connected with other temples or kings, and some acted on their own. Using the very broad definition of prophet as one who speaks God's message, certain people from Israel's earliest history were called prophets: Abraham (Gen 20.7), Aaron (Exod 7.1), Miriam (Exod 15.20), Moses (Deut 18.18; 34.10), and Deborah (Judg 4.4). Moses certainly passed God's message to the people of Israel, but he also spoke to God for them. This was also the task of prophets. (See the mini-article called, "Moses," on p. 178.) Samuel, the last of Israel's judges, was known as a prophet (1 Sam 3.20). He heard and followed God's command to choose (anoint) Saul as Israel's first king (1 Sam 10.1).

Some prophets described in the Old Testament went into a kind of trance when they prophesied. They lost control over their speech and actions and were not aware of what was happening around them. Some of the prophets that Saul met were these sorts of prophets. Saul himself also got caught up by God's Spirit, and was therefore called a prophet (1 Sam 10.10-12). At one point some of these prophets had a contest with Israel's prophet, Elijah (875-845 B.C.), to try to prove who was stronger, Israel's God *Yahweh,* or the Canaanite god, Baal. The prophets of Baal acted like they were caught up in a trance. As they cried out to Baal they had what looked like a seizure and began to dance around. They even used their swords to cut themselves until blood poured out (1 Kgs 18.24-29). Elijah also opposed King Ahab of the northern kingdom of Israel and his wife Jezebel, who encouraged the people to worship the Canaanite god Baal (1 Kgs 17–21).

A few other examples of Old Testament prophets include Balaam of Pethor near the Euphrates River, who was hired by the king of Moab to put a curse on Israel (Num 22.2–24.25). The prophet Nathan gave King David the good news that his descendants would always rule the people of Israel (2 Sam 7.11-16), but Nathan also delivered God's angry message after David had arranged the death of a man named Uriah so that he could have Uriah's wife Bathsheba. Because of this evil action, Nathan told David that David and Bathsheba's son would die (2 Sam 12.1-14). Another prophet named Micaiah warned King Ahab that he would die in battle against the Syrian army (1 Kgs 22.5-38). Elisha became Elijah's assistant and eventually took his place (1 Kgs 19.19-21; 2 Kgs 2.1-18). He was the prophet who healed Naaman (2 Kgs 5.1-14). Another prophet, Huldah, gave advice to King Josiah (640-609 B.C.) when Josiah asked what he should do with *The*

King David and the Prophet Nathan from a Byzantine Psalter (around A.D. 950). The Bible tells of many prophets who brought difficult news to powerful rulers. Nathan told King David that David's son would die because of his sin.

Book of God's Law that had been found in the temple (2 Kgs 22.14-20).

The Writings of the Prophets

The kingdom of Israel split into two sections (northern and southern) around 931 B.C., after the death of King Solomon. Each of these kingdoms had its own temple and king, and prophets in both parts of Israel gave warnings and encouragement to the rulers and the people. The first books of the prophets probably date back to just after 800 B.C. The prophecies of Amos and Hosea were written for the rulers and the people of the northern kingdom (Israel). They warned the leaders and the people who had grown rich to care for the poor and stop worshiping idols. About the same time or a little later, the prophets Micah and Isaiah delivered their prophecies in the southern kingdom (Judah). Isaiah warned that a king would come from the east to take over the land and force the people to leave. He called the people to obey God in order to avoid the punishment that he predicted, but he also gave them the promise that God would help them triumph in the end. The suffering they would undergo was to be seen as punishment from God. Though Isaiah's message began in the 700s B.C., some of his followers continued writing prophecy in his name even after the Babylonian exile in 586 B.C. Jeremiah, Zephaniah, Nahum, and Habakkuk were prophets in Judah during the time just before it was defeated by Babylon and many of its people were taken off as captives in 586 B.C. About the time Jeremiah was finishing his work as a prophet, Ezekiel began to bring God's message to the people. His prophecies were given to the people of Judah before they were taken away from their homes and forced to live in exile, and continued into the period of the exile in Babylon, where Ezekiel was also taken as captive. The last part of his prophecy includes a great vision of the future when God would rebuild the temple in Jerusalem and bring a new day for God's people (Ezek 40–46).

After the people of Judah were allowed to leave Babylon and return home, the prophets Haggai and Zechariah delivered God's message. Speaking around 520 B.C., Haggai told the people that God wanted them to rebuild the temple. About the same time Zechariah told the people the LORD's chosen king would again rule in Jerusalem and that all people on earth would someday worship Israel's God. Still later came the prophecies of Malachi, who told the priests to be faithful to the agreement the LORD had made with Israel. The time of the prophet Obadiah is unclear, though he probably wrote some time after 587 B.C. when the country of Edom helped Babylon defeat Judah. It is not clear when the prophet Joel delivered his message of both judgment and hope, though it was most likely some time after the people returned from captivity in Babylon.

JONAH is different from the other prophetic books, because it gives only one sentence of what Jonah preached (3.4). The rest of the book tells about how Jonah tried to run away when God told him to preach to the people of Nineveh, the capital of Assyria, who were enemies of Israel. The first half of DANIEL tells about Daniel and what happened to him as he lived in exile in Babylon. The second half of DANIEL tells of Daniel's vision of the future when God would help bring victory to his people. Daniel's vision belongs to a kind of writing known as "apocalyptic." (See the article called "Different Kinds of Literature in the Bible," p. 13.

Prophecy and the New Testament

The New Testament focuses on the life and work of Jesus Christ. The New Testament writers used the Jewish Scriptures, especially the writings of the prophets, to show that Jesus was God's promised Messiah. For example, MATTHEW often uses the phrase, "just as the prophet had said" which is followed by a quote from one of the Old Testament prophets (Matt 1.22; 2.5-6,17-18; 4.14-16). Each quote is meant to show that Jesus' life fulfills what was said by one of the prophets hundreds of years earlier. In his letters, the apostle Paul quoted the Old Testament prophets to show that Jesus was God's chosen one who had come to save all people, Jews and Gentiles alike (Rom 9.25,26,33; 15.11,12).

The New Testament writers also used the words of the prophet Isaiah to show that John the Baptist was the one who had been sent to prepare the way for Jesus (Matt 3.1-3; Luke 3.3-6). And John preached like a prophet, telling the people to turn to

God and get ready for the one (Jesus) who was coming to baptize them with the Holy Spirit (Mark 1.7,8; Luke 3.15-17).

Jesus quoted the Old Testament prophets to show that he was the Son of Man who would come from heaven with power and great glory (Matt 24.29,30 quotes Joel 2.10; Matt 26.64 quotes Dan 7.13,14). Jesus also said that he was the shepherd who would be rejected and struck down (Matt 26.31 quotes Zech 13.7). He applied the writing of the prophet Isaiah to himself, explaining why he had come to earth (Luke 4.16-21 quotes Isa 61.1). Paul said it was because God's purpose for people and all creation was fulfilled in Jesus (1 Cor 15.20-28), who overcame the powers of evil.

St. John the Baptist by Sally Barton Elliott. John, like many of the prophets of the Old Testament, gave the people of his time strong warnings and told them to turn to God and get ready for the one God was sending to save them.

Prophecy and the Church

Some of the followers of Jesus received the special gift of prophecy from God's Spirit (Rom 12.6; 1 Cor 12.27-31). These New Testament prophets were to use this gift to speak God's messages of truth (1 Cor 14.29-32). God's followers are also warned in the New Testament to watch out for false prophets who would try to lead them away from the truth about God (1 Tim 6.2-10; 2 Pet 2.1-3). REVELATION warns of a false prophet who would perform fake miracles and make false predictions in an effort to trick God's people (Rev 13.11-15), and the faithful are told to be careful to listen only to the message of God's true prophets (Rev 22.18,19).

Jesus was born in the town of Bethlehem in the province of Judea during the reign of Augustus Caesar, the first Roman ruler called emperor. About sixty years earlier, the Romans had invaded Palestine as they continued expanding their great empire throughout the lands surrounding the Mediterranean Sea and beyond (see the map, p. 195). At the time of Augustus, the Roman Empire ruled over fifty million people from many different nationalities—from Palestine and Syria in the east to Spain in the west, including most of northern Africa and much of Europe. Because the Romans were well-organized and had a strong army, their empire was actually very stable. Travel and trade between areas was easier than it had ever been. Historians have observed that the international peace brought by Roman rule and the superior system of Roman roads helped disciples to spread a new religion based on Jesus' teachings.

Palestine before Roman Rule

The centuries leading up to Jesus' birth were not politically stable in the area known as Palestine. The Jewish people who returned to Judah from exile in Babylon had been allowed to rebuild their cities and the temple in Jerusalem, but they were ruled by the Persians. (See the article called "After the Exile: God's People Return to Judea," p. 125). Then the Greeks, led by Alexander the Great, defeated the Persians and drove them out of Palestine. Alexander's generals and their descendants ruled the land for many years, bringing with them Greek (Hellenistic) culture. One Greek ruler from the Seleucid family (Antiochus IV Epiphanes) tried to force the Hellenistic way of life on the Jewish people in Palestine. When he put up a statue of a pagan god in the holy Jewish temple in 168 B.C., Jewish people were enraged and rebelled. Led by Judas Maccabeus, the people defeated the Seleucids, reclaimed the temple, and created their own government.

When Jesus began preaching the good news of the kingdom of God to the people of Galilee and Judea in the first century A.D. the Romans were in control of the entire Mediterranean world.

For nearly one hundred years the Jewish people were again in charge of the land, led by members of Judas Maccabeus' family (the Hasmoneans), who took over as kings and priests of Israel. Yet many thought that the Hasmonean rulers were as selfish and cruel as the foreign kings who had ruled before them, so Jews did not fight back when the Romans invaded the country in 63 B.C.

During these two centuries before Jesus was born, a number of different Jewish religious groups were formed, each having different ideas about how to interpret the Scriptures and live the Jewish faith. These groups with their competing ideas appear in the New Testament and will be discussed individually later in this article.

Roman Rule in Palestine

Though many peoples and cultures contributed to the cultural life in Palestine in Jesus' day, the Romans were by far the most powerful. They controlled the land with strong, well-trained armies. The Roman emperor appointed a governor (procurator) who was in charge of collecting taxes and preventing the people from rebelling against Rome. The Romans placed heavy taxes on land, on goods and food that were bought and sold, and on inheritances. They also charged tolls for people traveling through the areas they controlled. The taxes went to support the Roman army and to maintain control of Palestine. Farmers and the poor suffered the most under this system of taxes.

The Romans made contracts with local people in order to collect taxes. These local tax collectors (publicans) would often collect much more than the amount they were supposed to turn over to the Romans. They kept the rest. In Palestine, this led to bad feelings between the Jewish people and their neighbors who agreed to collect taxes for the Romans. Tax collectors were often seen as traitors by the Jewish religious leaders. Some called them sinners, and said they were not welcome to be part of the Jewish people or to worship with them. When Jesus ate with tax collectors and welcomed them (Luke 5.27-32; 19.1-10), he offended those who wanted to keep the tax collectors apart from Jewish social life.

Roman policy was to respect local customs and the laws of the peoples they ruled. They let local people form councils to control local affairs. In Judea the local ruling council (Sanhedrin) was made up of the high priest and chief priests and wealthy supporters of the Roman government. Their participation in the work of the council made them become even wealthier.

The Romans also set up rulers in the areas that were under their control. These local kings and governors reported to the Roman senate or to the emperor's representatives. For example, in 37 B.C. the Romans appointed Herod the Great as king of Palestine, partly because Herod's father had helped the Romans take control of the region. Herod ruled until 4 B.C. and was responsible for rebuilding the temple in Jerusalem, which attracted many worshipers and visitors from all over the Roman Empire during the days of Jesus. The outer court of the temple, called the Court of the Gentiles, was a place where non-Jews (Gentiles) could come to see the beauty of this great building. They could also watch the temple priests offering sacrifices as representatives between God and the followers of Judaism. The high priest was the person in charge of the temple. He was able to hold this position because of the support of the Roman authorities. The income from gifts and offerings to the temple was the major source of money for the whole people of Israel.

When Herod died, his three sons were appointed by the Romans to rule Galilee and Perea, the land east of the Jordan River. The map on p. 196 shows the lands ruled by each son. Under the Herods, the priests and their supporters on the council gained greater power and wealth. Although John the Baptist and Jesus were born during the time of Herod the Great, it was Herod's son, Herod Antipas, who was in power when they came to trial. Herod Antipas ordered the death of John the Baptist (Matt 14.1-12). During Jesus' trial, the Roman governor, Pontius Pilate, sent Jesus to see Herod Antipas because Jesus was from Galilee, the area under this Herod's rule. Usually, the Roman governors did not want to get mixed up in local problems and arguments. This is why Pilate sentenced Jesus to death only after the leaders of the people almost started a riot and argued that Jesus claimed to be a king of the Jews. This claim meant Jesus was considered guilty of rebellion against Rome and could therefore be put to death according to Roman law.

Class and Rank in the Roman Empire

The Roman Empire had a class structure based on wealth, birth, and citizenship. At the very top of Roman society was the emperor, who was considered the empire's "first citizen." Some emperors even declared themselves to be equal with the gods. Below the emperor were six hundred senators, who were the empire's wealthiest citizens. Next came a group known as "knights," who had reached a certain level of wealth. They were well-educated and often were recruited to serve in the government of the empire. Beneath them were wealthy local citizens, known as "honorable men," who formed city councils. The upper classes in Roman society wore special clothes and got the best seats at special events.

Below these top groups came the large group of ordinary working people. They were divided into levels. First came those who were not wealthy but still had the privileges of Roman citizenship. Rome recognized only a small group of its subjects as full citizens. Citizens had the freedom and protection of their personal rights. For example, the apostle Paul was able to have his trial in Rome because he was a Roman citizen (Acts 16.37; 22.27). Jesus was not a Roman citizen, so he could be condemned to death without a formal trial by the personal decision of the Roman governor, Pontius Pilate.

Below citizens in the class structure was a large group of non-citizens who were free but did not have the special privileges allowed to Roman citizens. And beneath these non-citizens, at the very bottom of the class structure, were slaves, who could legally be bought or sold, beaten or tortured, as their owners saw fit. Slaves worked mostly as household servants for the rich. At the time of Jesus, almost one-third of the population of Italy were slaves. Slavery was very common and accepted throughout the Roman Empire in Jesus' day. For more, see the mini-article called "Slaves and Servants in the Time of Jesus," p. 69.

The Jewish people in Palestine had different opinions about the best way to deal with the Roman authorities who had control of their land. Even though they may have had different outlooks on these kinds of matters, they all turned to the Law of Moses and discussed it passionately in public and in their meeting places (synagogues).

Jewish Groups in Palestine

As mentioned above, the Romans allowed the various peoples in their empire to develop their own local councils. These councils usually included the wealthy and powerful people in a region, who were free to make laws and to force the people in that region to obey them. The chief priests and the rich people who worked with the Roman authorities formed the Jewish council based in Jerusalem. The Greek word for this council was the *synedrion*. After the Romans destroyed the temple in A.D. 70, the Jews began to use this name spelled in Hebrew (*Sanhedrin*) for the group that replaced the priests as the organizers and lawmakers of the Jewish people in Jerusalem. This group began to write down formulas for applying the Law of Moses. These interpretations developed into what today are known as the "Mishnah" and "Talmud."

The Jews in the time of Jesus had different opinions about what it meant to be the people of God. Here is a summary of some of the

EMPEROR

600 Senators

Wealthy Knights

Honorable Men

Common Workers (citizens)

Common Workers (non-citizens)

Slaves

key groups that formed and how each one interpreted the Law of Moses:

Zealots. The Maccabees, as discussed earlier, insisted that the Jewish people have their own king. They were defeated when the Romans took over the land in 63 B.C. Later attempts to win freedom and create an independent Jewish state failed in A.D. 70 and again in A.D. 135. The Jewish nationalists who tried to organize the revolt against the Romans were called Zealots. Scholars disagree about whether this term applies to a single, well-organized group or to any number of groups of dissatisfied Jews who wanted to be rid of their Roman rulers. At one time, this term also meant "someone who was strongly devoted to God and God's law." The *CEV* translates zealot as "Eager One." In the New Testament the term is even applied to one of the followers of Jesus (Luke 6.15; Acts 1.13).

Pharisees. By Jesus' day, it was common for Jewish people to meet in private homes for worship and to study the Scriptures. This practice had begun in the later second century B.C. and continued in the first century A.D. One group that did this would become very powerful within the Jewish community. They called themselves "Pharisees," which meant "The Separate Ones" in Hebrew. They wanted to renew and protect Judaism by having all Jewish people strictly follow the laws concerning the Sabbath, fasting, and the purity of food. Most Pharisees had regular jobs and were involved in the Roman culture of the day. But their special meetings and the strict way they followed the Sabbath law forbidding work on the seventh day of the week set them apart. As a result, they had a strong sense of group identity. There were also Pharisaic groups in cities outside Palestine. The apostle Paul, who was from Tarsus in southeastern Asia Minor, said he was once a Pharisee who strictly observed the law (Phil 3.5).

The Pharisees taught the Law of Moses as well as other traditional laws not found in the Scriptures. Their interpretation of traditional laws are included in the Mishnah and Talmud. The Pharisees were popular with the common people and established synagogues (Jewish meeting places) and schools. Unlike some other Jewish groups, they believed in life after death (resurrection) and future rewards and punishments (see Acts 23.6).

Sadducees. This group's name may come from Zadok, the high priest of Israel at the time of King David. The Sadducees also may have been descendants of the Zadokites, who had controlled the temple as high priests for many years until the middle of the second century B.C., when they were forced from power by Jonathan, the first Maccabean high priest. The Sadducees stayed close to the priestly families and tried to influence the business of the temple. They were willing to work with the Romans when they came to rule Palestine. Unlike the Pharisees, the Sadducees did not accept interpretations of the Law, but believed in following only the Law of Moses. They also did not believe that the dead were raised to life (Mark 12.18; Acts 23.8). As long as the Sadducees followed the main teachings of the Law and stayed friendly with the Romans, they expected to continue in positions of power and wealth among their people. After the Jewish revolt led to the destruction of the temple in A.D. 70, the Sadducees no longer existed as a group.

Essenes. The Essenes may have been formed as a group at about the same time as the Sadducees. Instead of trying to influence the priesthood and religion of Israel from the inside, they withdrew from Jewish society, met secretly to study, and had their own special interpretation of the Jewish Scriptures. As a group, they disagreed completely with the priests and other official leaders of the Jews, and like the Pharisees, they believed in life after death.

The Essene communities were very structured. Each group had a leader who controlled who was allowed into the group, decided how property and belongings would be shared among group members, and made rulings concerning the law. Some scholars think that the Dead Sea community was an Essene group. Whether they were or not, the Essenes' beliefs show how deeply disappointed many Jews were with their religious leaders. The Dead Sea group withdrew from Jewish society and lived on a bluff overlooking the Dead Sea until the Roman army invaded the land in A.D. 66 to put down the Jewish revolt and completely destroyed the community there.

Scribes. Those Jews who filled jobs set up by the Romans to help run the government in the land were called "scribes." Because they could read and write in a time when many people could not, they were very valuable to kings and governments. In the Jewish Scriptures (Old Testament) they are shown as having the authority to write legal papers. Scribes are identified as keepers of government records (2 Kgs 18.18). Like Jeremiah's scribe Baruch, they took dictation and then read it aloud for people to hear (Jer 36.4-18). Scribes also worked as secretaries of state and treasurers.

In the New Testament, scribes are described as working as lawyers (Luke 5.17) and judges (Matt 23.2). Because of their extensive learning, they knew about interpreting the law, and sometimes argued with Jesus about the meaning of traditional Jewish laws (Matt 9.3; 15.1; Mark 2.16; 7.1,2; Luke 5.30; 6.7). The scribes are not the same as the Pharisees, but Pharisees and chief priests paid the scribes for legal advice. The scribes saw Jesus as a threat to law and order as set up by the Romans, which the scribes were in charge of carrying out on the local level.

Samaritans. Another group mentioned a few times in the New Testament are the Samaritans. The ancestors of the Samaritans came from the ten Israelite tribes that rebelled against King Solomon's son Rehoboam and formed a separate kingdom known as Israel, or the northern kingdom. They had their own temple on Mount Gerizim near Shechem, and their own priests. They followed the laws about the Sabbath in a very strict way, and they said that their holy Mount Gerizim was more important than Mount Zion, where the temple in Jerusalem was located. The Jewish people did not like the Samaritans and believed they were not really part of God's chosen people. The writers of the Gospels, however, record that Jesus reached out to them (Luke 17.11-19; John 4.3-9), and used one as a positive example when explaining to an expert in the Law of Moses what it means to have compassion and be a neighbor (Luke 10.25-37).

Jesus faced this complicated situation as he tried to preach his message of good news. When he defended the poor and reached out to accept people such as tax collectors, Samaritans, and prostitutes, he offended the local religious leaders. The arguments described by the New Testament writers are mainly between different groups who have different ideas about who can or can not be part of God's people. The Romans controlled Palestine but were not very interested in getting involved in these local arguments, unless they led to rebellion against Roman authority.

The Bible describes a wide range of cultures and lifestyles. The time from Abraham to the time of the early church spans a period of about two thousand years. How people made a living varied depending on when and where they lived. Some people were "nomads," living in small groups, keeping flocks of sheep and goats, and traveling from place to place in order to feed and protect their animals. Others lived more settled lives, growing crops or providing services to people in towns and urban areas. Most of the "jobs" described in this article were still practiced by at least some part of the population of Palestine at the time of Jesus.

Living Off the Land:
Herding and Farming

The Bible describes the many different kinds of jobs people had in the ancient world, but caring for land and animals are two of the central jobs mentioned. GENESIS reports that one of Adam and Eve's sons herded sheep while the other farmed the land (Gen 4.2). The earliest ancestors of the people of Israel, including Abraham and Sarah, traveled from place to place and survived by keeping herds and flocks of animals (Gen 13.1-3). Another piece of evidence for the importance of herding and farming in ancient Israelite society is that the Bible gives special instructions about eating (Lev 11), sacrificing animals (Lev 1), and sacrificing grain (Lev 2).

Keeping herds of animals like sheep and goats was common among the many generations of the people of Israel. At first, these herders (shepherds) were wandering nomads who lived in tents and had very little personal property. They moved from place to place, always trying to find food and water for their animals. They survived by eating the meat and drinking the milk produced by their flocks. They used the animals' wool and hides to make clothes and other things, including the tents they lived in.

From the time of Abraham to the present day, the herding of sheep and goats has been an important occupation throughout much of the Near East.

Closer to the time of Jesus, when urban life was more developed, shepherds may also have lived in or near villages. They had the right to let their flocks feed in nearby pastures and would have been hired by landowners who needed help to harvest their fields. When food supplies got scarce near the villages, shepherds would move their herds to mountain pastures in the hot summer, or to warmer valleys in the winter.

A shepherd's life was not easy. Shepherds spent most of their time outside watching over the herd, no matter what the weather. They often slept near their flock to protect it from robbers or wild animals. The shepherd's tools and weapons were a rod, a staff, and a sling. Each night, the shepherds would gather their flocks into places called "sheepfolds." These could be stone walls made by the shepherds or natural enclosures, such as a cave. Shepherds used their rods to help count their animals each evening when they brought them into the fold and again in the morning when they left for the pastures. For more, see mini-article called "Shepherds," p. 32.

When the Israelites settled in Canaan after leaving their life of slavery in Egypt, farming became a more important way of making a living for them. Grains, such as wheat and barley, were used for making bread, and were the most important crop. Grains, as well as lentils and peas, are known to have been cultivated in Palestine since prehistoric times. Unlike farmers in Egypt and Mesopotamia, Israelite farmers did not need to depend on irrigation for water. Even though the rainy season in Palestine was rather short and the soil was often rocky, the farmers' know-how in clearing and fertilizing the land usually produced fine crops. The Israelite farmers learned how to grow crops according to the yearly cycle of

Planting and Growing Grain. Bread made from grains like wheat and barley was a daily food for people in Jesus' day. To grow grain, farmers had to first plow the soil to break it up and make it suitable for planting. Here, two yoked oxen pull a plow while the farmer guides it from behind. Next, seeds are scattered (sown) in the field, though sowing was sometimes done before plowing. Planting was done after the first rains in autumn. Barley was harvested in late April or early May, and wheat was harvested about a month later. At harvest time, the standing grain was cut with sickles that had flint or iron blades and was then tied into sheaves that could easily be gathered and carried to threshing place.

rainy and dry spells. They also learned to adjust the crops to what was best for the different kinds of land: fertile plains, rocky hills, and semi-barren areas. As time went on, their knowledge as farmers helped them to grow fruits, including melons, figs, dates, grapes, and olives.

Growing crops affected the economy and social life of the people. For example, some of the major religious festivals in Israel—the Harvest Festival and the Festival of Shelters—were coordinated with the farming cycle. The Harvest Festival, also called the Festival of Weeks, celebrated the wheat harvest in the spring (Exod 23.16; 34.22; Lev 23.15-22; Num 28.26-31; Deut 16.9). The Festival of Shelters (or Booths) is an autumn holiday for the occasion of the planting and gathering of crops, and the annual harvest (Exod 23.16; 34.22; Lev 23.33-43; Num 29.12-39; Deut 16.13-17; Ezek 45.25).

An amazing feature of the life of Israel was the sabbatical year, the one year in every seven when farmers would let the land rest. This followed the pattern of working only six days out of each week according to God's command to rest on seventh day, called the Sabbath (Exod 23.10-12). This sabbatical rest for fields also had practical benefits, since it increased the long-term fertility of the land.

The people may also have practiced crop rotation, further improving the soil (Isa 28.23-29). The orderly way in which the farmers grew their crops was to match God's plan for the Israelite people and for the good of creation. From a religious perspective, however, DEUTERONOMY makes it clear that a large harvest also depended on how the people of Israel obeyed God's commandments (Deut 11.10-17).

Fishing

Fishing was a far less important source of food and income for the people of Israel, since the Philistines and others controlled the seacoast. What fish were available usu-

ally came from Lake Galilee and the Jordan River. The most common fish was a type of sardine. According to the Law of Moses, the Israelite people were not to eat fish that lacked fins or scales (Deut 14.9), but the Bible does not mention specific kinds of fish. Since fishing is mentioned so little in the Jewish Scriptures (Old Testament), some scholars think it was not important to the economy of Israel. It is possible that the fishing industry was more prosperous in the time of Jesus than it had been earlier, since when Jesus called James and John to be his disciples, they left the family fishing busi-

In Jesus' time carpenters prepared lumber for shipbuilders and architects, made their own tools, and provided ironsmiths with wooden handles for farm implements like axes, plows, and sickles. Carpenters built furniture and even structural elements of houses, like doors and window frames.

ness to their father and the "hired workers" (Mark 1.19-20). For more, see the mini-article called "Fish and Fishing," p. 165.

Special Skills and Crafts

As the Israelites became more settled in and near cities, they became involved in many other types of work. Some men and women became skilled workers, or artisans, who worked on various crafts, very often at home. Many times parents taught their children these skills so they could also use them to make a living. Skilled workers were highly respected, since people needed their skills and products to live comfortably. After the time of the exile (around 538 B.C.), artisans in the same type of craft began to form into professional groups. Such groups of people in the same business were still present in New Testament times (see Acts 19.24-27). Those who worked on special crafts were builders, stonemasons (stonecutters), carpenters, woodcarvers, boatbuilders, and silversmiths, glass workers, potters, leather workers, weavers, and fullers, who worked with cleaning and texturing old and new cloth).

The Bible tells us that Jesus grew up helping his father Joseph, who was a carpenter (Matt 13.55). And the apostle Paul apparently made a living at the craft of tentmaking (Acts 18.3). Some crafts like baking, cooking, and sewing were done in the everyday work of keeping a household,

Cloth Making. *Cloth was made from both plant and animal fibers. Fibers from the flax plant (top left) were spun into the fine thread used to weave linen, a luxury fabric often used for priests' robes. Wool shorn from sheep (top right) was the most commonly used animal fiber. It was used to make ordinary, everyday kinds of fabric. After wool was spun into yarn (left), the yarn could be dyed (center) before being woven into fabric on a loom. Stripes and other patterns could be created by using different colored yarns.*

but some people used these skills to create businesses as well.

Servants and Slaves

Many people, free and slave, provided personal services as laborers. These servants included household servants, employed by royalty and other wealthy people. Such servants might work as cooks, maids, grounds keepers, tutors, or in helping to care for children. Loyal household workers were highly valued. A royal servant called a cupbearer (Gen 40.11; Neh 1.11) brought food and drink to a ruler. Others served as midwives (Gen 35.16-18), doctors (2 Chr 16.12; Mark 5.25,26), nurses (usually a woman who fed another woman's baby), money-changers (Matt 21.12), innkeepers (Luke 2.7; 10.35), and prostitutes (Gen 38.14-18; Josh 2.1).

Often the Bible is not always clear when describing the work of servants, because the word "servant" may mean either a slave or a person hired to do some task. Slavery in many forms was fairly common in Bible times. Some people sold themselves into slavery to pay back a debt, or because they were desperately poor and that was the only way they could get food and shelter. Many slaves in Bible times were prisoners of war. Most slaves performed household work rather than field work or manual labor. There are some rules regarding slavery in the Bible, including ones that put a limit on the customs for slavery and recommended when a term of slavery should come to an end (Exod 21.2-6; Lev 25.10,38-41). There was also some expectation that slaves would be treated fairly and without cruelty (Deut 23.15-16). For more, see the mini-article called "Slaves and Servants in the Time of Jesus," p. 69.

Military and Government Work

A number of jobs were related to maintaining governments and kingdoms. At the top of the social structure were kings, queens and emperors, diplomats and ambassadors, senators and governors (Acts 13.7). Within the palace there were deputies, counselors, interpreters (Gen 42.23), and messengers (Num 20.14; 1 Kgs 20.5; 2 Chr 32.31). The interests of the leaders and the nation were protected by armies which were made up of military officers (Matt 8.9; Acts 21.32), soldiers, and armor-bearers (Judg 9.54; 1 Sam 14.6). To maintain the government, additional workers were needed, such as tax collectors (Luke 19.1-2), keepers of records and secretaries (2 Sam 8.16,17), and lawyers (Acts 24.1; Titus 3.13). Some rulers hired musicians (1 Sam 16.14-23) and others paid for advice from astrologers or fortune-tellers (Isa 19.3).

The Jewish people in Jesus' day were ruled by the Roman government, which appointed a Roman governor (or procurator) to oversee the collection of taxes and keep order in the land (Matt 27.2; Acts 24.1). On the local level, the Romans allowed a council of religious and business leaders to handle certain problems and concerns, especially those related to maintaining the temple and worship (Acts 22.5).

Special Servants of God

For years, the temple in Jerusalem was the center of the religious life of the people of Israel. It took many people to see that its important work was carried out properly. According to the Law of Moses, the members of the tribe of Levi were to work as priests, serving all the people of God. Since the Levites were not given their own land, they were allowed to keep a portion of the sacrifices that the Israelite people offered to God (Josh 13.14). A high priest was in charge of the temple, and supported by chief priests, gatekeepers (1 Chr 9.17-32), temple workers (Ezra 2.43-54), and guards (1 Chr 9.17-32). For more, see the mini-article called "Israel's Priests," p. 171.

Most of Israel's neighbors had their own temples and religious practices. These employed temple priests and various kinds of workers as well, and some even used women to serve as "sacred prostitutes." All religions supported many artisans, such as architects, builders, goldsmiths, silversmiths, and sculptors, who used their skills to build and decorate temples and shrines (1 Kgs 5.13-18).

Although the sacred tent and the temple were the center of religious life for the people of Israel, many of the Kings of Israel and Judah also employed prophets (1 Chr 21.9; 2 Chr 19.1,2) who helped them make decisions based on God's will, and who warned them of the consequences of their actions. Other prophets worked independently as preachers (1 Sam 9.6-21). By the time of Jesus, a growing number of teachers known as scribes and Pharisees earned money as teachers of the Law.

Other Occupations

Unskilled workers were often poor and did difficult jobs like mining, cutting rocks, digging wells, building roads, cleaning streets, training and driving camels, loading and unloading goods along trade routes, working as a crew member or rower on a boat, and tending and harvesting crops. Still others worked as dancers, musicians, and even as professional mourners. Some of these mourners were paid to cry and wail during funeral processions (Jer 9.17; Matt 9.23); others played sad music on flutes, beat their chests with their hands, and wore rough clothing called sackcloth (Gen 37.34). Merchants and traders bought and sold all sorts of items, carrying them from town to town to offer for sale in outdoor market places. Some wealthy merchants owned ships or large numbers of camels, which they used to transport goods across long distances.

Wages and Pay

The Bible does speak of people being paid for certain kinds of work (Gen 29.15; Mic 3.11; Matt 20.1-15; Luke 3.14), but it is difficult to determine just how much people were paid early in Israel's history. Most likely they received goods or food for the work they did. During the time of the kings, some people were paid in weighed pieces of gold or silver. Later, around 600 B.C., the Persian Empire began making coins, which were sometimes used to pay workers By the time of Jesus, various kinds of coins were commonly used to pay for goods and the services of workers. The story Jesus told in Matthew 20.1-16 describes vineyard workers being paid the amount of one day's wage, which was one denarius. How much that one coin could buy is not clear, so it is hard to determine what a person's wage would have been when compared to a worker's salary today.

The Bible is a book of faith, telling the story of how God acted in history to protect and save humankind. Miracles are an important part of that story. God's actions in miracles on behalf of the faithful are contrasted with the situation of those who looked to other gods and relied on magic, reading the stars, or calling on the spirits of the dead. Throughout the Bible, the miracles of God are extraordinary acts. These miracles are often unexplainable by the expectations, common at the time, of how nature works. Many of these miracles can be described in the categories shown on the chart below.

The people praised God for these miracles, including God's amazing actions in Israel's history (Deut 7.19; 11.1-4; 34.10-12). The writers of the PSALMS and the later teachers of the Law of Moses saw God working in these miracles to preserve and reward the Israelite people, and to keep them living in God's ways (Ps 105; 107; 136; see also Neh 9).

Throughout the Bible, miracles are presented as signs that point to a larger meaning. This is evident, for example, in the descriptions of the Israelites' experiences in the desert of Sinai, which show God's special purpose for the people. Not only do they survive their ordeal, but they are brought into the land God promised to them so that they can worship the LORD (Deut 4.23-34; 6.21-25; 26.5-11; Josh 24.17). Miracles also helped the Israelites believe God's promises because the Israelites could see them being fulfilled. Even a Babylonian king came to believe that Israel's God had miraculous power after he saw how God preserved the three faithful young Israelite men in the fiery furnace (Dan 3).

HOW GOD USES MIRACLES

TYPE OF MIRACLE	SCRIPTURE PASSAGES
God's power revealed to the people	Gen 15.17; Exod 3.1-6; Josh 3.14-17; 1 Kgs 18.16-39; Luke 8.22-25; John 2.1-12; John 6.16-21; Acts 2
God helps women unable to have children	Gen 17.1-21; Judg 13; 1 Sam 1; Luke 1.5-25
God's power used to judge evildoers and rebellious people	Gen 6–9; 19.23-29; Exod 7.14—12.30; 2 Sam 12.1-23; 1 Kgs 18.1-40; Jer 18; Acts 5.1-11
God helps Israel in battle	Josh 5.13—6.27; 10.1-15; Judg 6.33—8.3; 1 Sam 17.41-54
God saves or delivers people from trouble	Exod 14; Dan 3,6; Acts 12.6-12; 16.16-34
God provides food and other blessings	Exod 16.1—17.7; 2 Kgs 4.1-7; Luke 5.1-11; John 6.5-15; 21.1-14
God heals and restores health	Num 21. 4-9; 2 Kgs 5.1-19; Mark 5.21-43; Luke 18.35-43; Acts 3.1-10
God's purposes and glory revealed in a vision	Isa 6; Ezek 1; Zech 1.7—5.11; Acts 9.1-19; 10.1-48
God overcomes death	2 Kgs 4.18-37; Matt 28.1-7; Luke 7.11-17; John 11.1-44; Acts 9.36-43
God chooses servants and gives them special gifts	Gen 41; Exod 4.1-12; Judg 6.11-24; 1 Sam 3.1-18; Dan 2; Luke 1.26-38; Acts 2.1-13; 1 Cor 12.1-11

Jesus' Miracles Show God's Love and Power

The New Testament reports Jesus' many miracles (see the chart below). Yet, when Jesus' opponents tried to test him by making him perform a miracle to prove that God was with him, Jesus refused (Matt 16.1-4; Mark 8.11,12; John 4.48; 6.26-34). Also, Jesus sometimes warned people not to tell anyone about his miracles (Mark 1.44; 5.43), possibly because non-believers would have thought Jesus was just a magician. Often, it seemed that Jesus' miracles only worked for people who believed (Mark 2.5-12; 5.34). His miracles were not for showing off. Instead, they demonstrated God's love for the people (Luke 4.18-21) and announced the presence of the Kingdom of God.

Miracles in the Early Church

At the time of the early church, public miracles helped people recognize that God was at work (Acts 2.19-22, 43; 4.30; 5.12,13; 8.13). At the same time, some people wrongly thought that the ability to heal and do miracles was a result of magical powers. In Acts 8.9-24 a magician named Simon claimed to be converted to Christianity, but he still had to learn that God's power was a gift, and not some magic power that could be bought. The apostle Paul claimed that God helped him perform miracles to confirm the good news about Jesus and Paul's own role as an apostle (2 Cor 12.12). He also told of Jesus' miracles to help people believe (Rom 15.15-19).

Magic, Sorcery, and Witchcraft

In the ancient world, the belief in magic, sorcery, and witchcraft were common. The people of Israel claimed that the miracles performed by their prophets and leaders were different from these things because they were based on God's power.

SOME WELL-KNOWN MIRACLES OF JESUS

MIRACLE	SCRIPTURE PASSAGE
Turns water into wine in Cana	John 2.1-11
Orders the wind and waves to be quiet	Mark 4.35-41
Walks on water on Lake Galilee	Matthew 14.22-33
With five loaves and two fishes, feeds a crowd of more than 5,000 people	Matthew 14.13-21
Raises his friend Lazarus to life	John 11.17-44
Raises a dead girl to life	Matthew 9.18-26
Gives sight to a man born blind	John 9.1-41
Cures the woman who had been bleeding for twelve years	Matthew 9.20-22
Cures a man of evil spirits and sends the spirits into a herd of pigs	Mark 5.1-20
Heals ten men with leprosy	Luke 17.11-19
Heals a crippled man in Capernaum	Mark 2.1-12
Heals a man who was deaf and could hardly talk	Mark 7.31-37
Heals the high priest's servant after the man's ear is cut off	Luke 22.49-52

The writers of the Scriptures often contrasted these "true" miracles with unusual acts done by the prophets and priests of other peoples and religions. For example, Joseph used God's help to interpret the dreams of the king of Egypt after the king's own magicians and wise men could not (Gen 41.1-36). Later, when the Egyptian king's magicians turned their walking sticks into snakes, Moses and his brother Aaron used God's power to do the same thing, and their snake ate the snakes created by the Egyptians (Exod 7.8-13). This showed the superiority of the God of Israel. In another case, Elijah showed that the power of Israel's God was greater than that of the god Baal when God helped Elijah win a contest against the prophets of Baal (1 Kgs 18.16-40). For more about Elijah see the mini-article called "Elijah," p. 162.

Witchcraft was forbidden by the Law of Moses (Lev 19.26), because relying on spirits or powers other than God showed a lack of faith and trust in the one true God. Disobeying the command against witchcraft could lead to harsh punishment (Exod 22.18; Deut 18.10-13). When King Saul, Israel's first king, was afraid of the approaching Philistine army, he did not pray to God for help. Instead, he broke the law forbidding witchcraft and asked a woman from Endor who talked to spirits to call on Samuel, who died some time before (1 Sam 28.4-20). In another example, when the people of the northern kingdom (Israel) disobeyed God by worshipping the stars and using magic, or by worshipping idols like Asherah and Baal, God became so furious with them that he allowed them to be defeated by the Assyrians and carried away as prisoners (2 Kgs 17.16-18). Later, King Manasseh of the southern kingdom (Judah) sinned against God by worshipping the stars and planets, by practicing magic and witchcraft, and by asking fortune tellers for advice. Apparently, the advice he received included offering his own child as a sacrifice (2 Kgs 21.4-7). For Manasseh's

terrible sins, the whole nation suffered God's judgment and punishment (2 Kgs 21.8-16). In another example, King Balak of Moab hired Balaam to put a curse on the Israelites, but Balaam would not do it (Num 22–24). His explanation to Balak contained this statement: "No magic charms can work against them—just look what God has done for his people" (Num 23.23).

Parts of the New Testament make clear that sorcery and fortune telling were caused by evil spirits. In one case, a slave girl lost her power to tell fortunes after Paul ordered an evil spirit to leave her. This angered her owners because she could no longer make money for them by telling fortunes (Acts 16.16-19). In GALATIANS, Paul includes witchcraft on the list of "shameful deeds" done by those who obey their own selfish desires instead of obeying God's Spirit (Gal 5.20). And in REVELATION, a beast fooled people into believing in the beast who opposed God by doing magical miracles, such as making an idol speak as if it were alive (Rev 13.11-15).

Medicine and Healing

What does the Bible reveal about healers in the ancient world? In one part of the Old Testament, it says that King Asa's death may have been from depending only on human healers, and not asking for God's help (2 Chr 16.12,13). Also, the prophet Jeremiah questions whether medicine or doctors can truly provide healing (Jer 8:22). After all, God is seen as the main healer in the Old Testament (Exod 15.26; Ps 41.1-4; Jer 17.14; Hos 6.1). In fact, often the priests were seen as healers on God's behalf (Lev 13.1-3; 14.1-20). That is why Hannah went to the temple to pray for God's help once she realized that she could not have children (1 Sam 1.1-18). (In ancient times, this was seen as sickness in a woman.)

Some parts of the Bible reflect the belief that disease and sickness are caused by failing to live according to God's Law (Deut 28.21-23, 27-29, 34,35), while health and well-being were seen as the reward for trusting God (Exod 15.26; Deut 7.12-15;). Other parts of the Bible question this belief (Job 2, 42.7; Eccl 8.10-13, 9.2; John 9.1-7). People with certain diseases were set apart from the rest of God's people because they were considered unclean (Lev 13; Num 12.9-14). While this was done primarily for religious reasons, those who had these diseases were not allowed to worship or be among their friends and neighbors until they were cured and had gone through a ritual cleansing ceremony (Lev 14).

Jesus knew these laws about sickness and being cleansed, but he also showed himself to be a great healer. Many of Jesus' miracles included healing people considered unclean (see the chart on the previous page). He encouraged the ten men he healed of leprosy to show themselves to the priests, probably so they could go through the ritual cleansing and be welcomed back into the community of God's people (Luke 17.1-16). Another time, Jesus' power healed a woman who had spent all her money and had gone to many doctors without finding a cure (Mark 5.25-34). Jesus offered his healing also to those who were not part of the Jewish people (Luke 4.23-29), just as the prophets before him had done (1 Kgs 17.1-24; 2 Kings 5.14). This was surely amazing to many people, and was a way of showing that God's love is for everyone.

Around the time of Jesus, Greeks and Romans went to the shrines of a god of healing, hoping to be cured of their ailments. The early stages of modern medicine began in these shrines, but some of the cures developed there, like eating the liver of a fox or drinking juice from an iris plant, had no connection with the cause of the diseases.

The Bible tends to teach trust in God and prayer and fasting as the way to be healed from illness, rather than trusting in human doctors or healers. The Bible is not always against doctors and medicine though, and biblical authors were not aware of modern scientific techniques. After all, Luke, a companion of the apostle Paul, was said to be a physician (Col 4.14). Also, modern medicine can be seen in light of the biblical command to love one's neighbor (Lev 19.18; Luke 10.25-37). In fact, Jesus instructed his followers to go heal the sick (Luke 10.9). The Bible also stresses the value and dignity of human life, teaching that all human beings are created by God and in God's likeness (Gen 1.26,27). This belief has probably influenced the practice and ethics of modern medicine as well.

In conclusion, the Bible's accounts of miracles, magic, and medicine are all stories about God's power and love. They are not scientific explanations of supernatural events, but a faithful witness to the all-powerful nature of God, the Creator.

Healing was an important part of Jesus' ministry on earth. The apostle Paul listed healing as one of the gifts the Spirit gives the church so that God's people can take care of one another (1 Cor 12.9) and grow stronger in their faith.

Both the faith of Israel and the faith of the early Christians developed in cultural contexts rich in other religious traditions. The people of Israel encountered religions with many similar beliefs and rituals in Palestine and Egypt. Christianity came into being as one among many religions and philosophies spread around the Mediterranean world by merchants and soldiers.

The People of Israel and Canaanite Religions

The people of Israel believed in one God. This belief is known as "monotheism." Many of the other religions in the ancient Mediterranean world recognized a number of different gods. When the Israelite people entered Canaan well over one thousand years before Jesus was born, they came into contact with the various gods of their neighbors. The Law of Moses commanded God's people to remain loyal to the one true God, *Yahweh,* who had led them out of slavery in Egypt and into the Promised Land of Canaan (Exod 20.1-5). Once they settled there, they were often tempted to follow the other gods, and often did.

The Gods of Israel's Neighbors. Among the Canaanites, one of the most common names for god was El. The Canaanites did not believe that El was the only god, but they did believe that El was the one who ruled over all the other gods. They believed El was the creator of the universe and the kind, compassionate father of the whole human race. El was worshiped in Palestine before the Israelites took over the land. In the Jewish Scriptures, "El" also frequently refers to the God of Israel. Some examples of the use of this name are found in the Old Testament.

Some of the enemies of El were known as Yamm (the sea), Mot (death) and Leviathan (the sea monster). See Psalm 104.26 and Isaiah 27.1.

Another name for a god in the ancient Near East was Baal, which means "master," "husband," and "lord." Baal was worshiped by the Canaanites as a god of fertility who ensured good and abundant crops. Baal was also connected to storms that came into Syria and Palestine from the sea in the winter and early spring. Since rain was essential for the growth of crops, people believed that the storms that came from the sea were powerful gods. Some ancient people believed that parts of nature itself were filled with god-like spirits, so they worshiped things like trees, rivers, fountains, and caves.

Some people in the ancient world believed goddesses provided fertility for crops and flocks and helped human beings to have children. The Canaanite goddess Asherah, who was also known as Astarte, was pictured as the mother of the gods. She was identified as the wife of El. Manasseh, a king of Judah, had a carved image of Asherah placed in the temple of the LORD in Jerusalem (2 Kgs 21.4-7). The term Asherah was also used for sacred poles that were put up in the temple as symbols of fertility (1 Kgs 14.23; 16.33).

NAMES OF GOD		
NAME	PLACE USED	SCRIPTURE PASSAGES
El Elyon (God Most High)	Jerusalem	Gen 14.18-20
El Olam (God of Eternity)	Beersheba	Gen 21.33
El Berith (God of the Covenant)	Shechem	Judg 9.46
El Shaddai (God All-Powerful or God of the Mountains)	Bethel	Gen 17.1; 35.9-11; Exod 6.3

The goddess Anat was also a fertility goddess. She was famous for performing acts of violence against those who opposed her. An important city in Israel, Anathoth, was named for her (Josh 21.9-19; Jer 1.1; 11.21). This means that she was probably worshiped in this town at an earlier time. Even during the time when Nehemiah (about 445 B.C.) was helping restore Israel to the land and reminding the people to practice God's law after the exile in Babylon, the city's name remained Anathoth (Neh 7.26-38; 11.32).

The Philistine people who lived in the narrow strip of land between Judah and the Mediterranean Sea often battled with Israel. Their chief god was Dagon (1 Sam 5.1-5). The people of Moab, another of Israel's enemies when the Israelites were settling in Canaan, worshiped the god named Chemosh.

When the people of Israel worshiped other gods, God punished them. Ahab, the king of Israel, married Jezebel, the daughter of the king Ethbaal of Sidon. Part of Jezebel's name, *Zebul*, was a form of Baal's name. Ahab went against the Law of Moses when he built a temple with an altar to worship Baal in his capital city, Samaria (1 Kgs 16.31,32), and when he allowed Jezebel to encourage him to support hundreds of prophets of Asherah (1 Kgs 18.19). Many of the people of Israel were led to worship *Yahweh,* Israel's God, as well as Baal and Asherah. This worship broke the commandment God had given to Moses: "Do not worship any god except me." Because of their sins, God allowed Israel's neighbors to defeat them and carry many of the people into exile (2 Kgs 17).

Other Religions Outside of Palestine. In the ancient world, many cities or city-states had their own gods. Often people would build altars and places of worship (shrines) where they could bring sacrifices for their gods. These sacrifices were intended to please the gods in the hope that they would then protect the people of the city and give them good crops. In ancient Babylonia, for example, each city built temples to its protector gods.

Astrology, the belief that the sun and the stars control human life, came out of Babylonia and had a great influence throughout the Greek and Roman empires. The people of Israel rejected this belief in the influence of the stars as contrary to monotheism. They believed that God created the sun, moon, and stars (Gen 1.14-19; Ps 8.3; 147.4). Since these heavenly bodies are created, they cannot be gods.

In Egypt the cults of Isis, Osiris, and Serapis were popular. In Syria, Israel's northern neighbor, people worshiped the great sky-god named Hadad, and helped spread the belief in astrology, common in Babylonia, to the Greeks. From Persia, a nation that conquered the Babylonians and ruled Palestine before the Greeks invaded the land, came the cult of Mazdaism. This was connected to the religion taught by Zoroaster, a teacher whose ideas would later influence Gnostic beliefs (see below). The most important of the cults popular in Asia Minor was the cult of Cybele, also known as the Great Mother. The Greeks identified Cybele with Rhea, the mother of the Greek gods, and with Artemis, who is mentioned in the Bible as the goddess of the Ephesians (Acts 19.21-41).

The Christian Church in the Greek World

Greek Religions. In the centuries before Jesus was born, the number of religions, cults, and forms of philosophy in the Mediterranean world had grown rapidly. The letters of the New Testament provide glimpses of how various religions, philosophies, and cult teachings opposed Christian followers. (For examples, see 1 Cor 8; 10; Gal 1.6-9; 1 John 2.26,27; Rev 2.2-6,14-16,20-25).

The greatest religious influences and new philosophies came from the ancient Greeks. When Alexander the Great and his heirs took over Syria and Palestine after 330 B.C., they gave new names to the local gods and goddesses and introduced new deities.

There was the Greek god of time, Chronos, and Zeus, the chief of the Greek gods. The Greeks also worshipped goddesses, such as Artemis, goddess of the hunt, and the Egyptian goddess Isis. Isis is not mentioned in the New Testament, but it is known that many people in the Mediterranean world at this time believed in her as the one who made crops and flocks fertile every year. Belief in Isis was spread by merchants and soldiers and became a very important religion. The worship of Isis competed with the spread of Christianity in the first three centuries A.D. Asklepios, the god of healing, was also popular at this time. The desire of Christians to show the superiority of Jesus over this god may have influenced the way some of the miracle stories about Jesus' power to heal were shaped by the writers of the New Testament.

Various "mystery cults" were popular throughout the Greek world as well. Mystery cults had secret beliefs, so becoming a member usually required going through initiation ceremonies or practicing specific kinds of rites or sacraments. Participants in these cults believed that the ceremonies brought a person into the very life of the gods. The most popular Greek mystery cults were the cults of Demeter and Dionysus. Demeter was the goddess of grain and of the tamed or cultured aspects of nature. Dionysus was the god of wine and of the wild, untamed aspects of nature. The spirit of Dionysus was said to be in the animal (and possibly human) flesh that was eaten as part of the cult rituals. Members who participated in the rite believed they were consuming part of Dionysus when they ate. To many peo-

The Egyptian fertility goddess Isis holding her son Horus. Although this goddess is never mentioned in the Bible, she was worshiped throughout the Greek and Roman world in the time of Jesus and his apostles.

ple at this time, Christians also seemed to be a mystery cult, because when they celebrated the Lord's Supper, Christians ate the bread and drank the wine that Jesus described as his body and blood (Mark 14.22-24). Dionysus was also believed to make new birth possible for his followers. These beliefs would have seemed similar to the Christians' claim that Jesus had the power to renew the life of his people (John 3.1-21).

Other religions in the first century were based on fate, fortune, astrology, and magic. Some people believed that the supreme god was Tyche ("Fortune"), who ruled the lives of human beings. If someone became rich, it was because of Fortune; if that person suddenly lost his or her wealth, that was because of Fortune, too. Similarly, some people believed in a ruler known as "Fate." Fate was thought to determine everything that would happen in the universe, including the actions of all people. Good things and bad things alike were caused by Fate, and human beings were simply thought to be the means Fate used to carry out present and future events already determined.

This type of thinking opened the way for the religions based on astrology. In astrology, it was believed that the movement of the sun, moon, and planets determined a person's life. In Greece, astrology was combined with science in order to develop "horoscopes" (maps of the positions of planets) for predicting the future of individuals. Those who did not like the idea that their lives were controlled by the planets or by fate turned to magic. They wore charms or amulets and recited spells in order to hold off the power of evil. The prevalence of this belief can be seen in ACTS where some people even believed that handkerchiefs and aprons that touched the apostle Paul had the power to heal diseases and drive out evil spirits (Acts 19.11,12).

Greek Philosophies. In Greece during the third and fourth centuries before Christ, the Greek philosophers Socrates, Plato, and Aristotle were concerned with how people could live a virtuous life that was in harmony with their city, their culture, and the natural world. Disciples of these great teachers would later form a number of schools of philosophy. By the time of the early Christian church, the teachings of these schools had spread throughout the Mediterranean world. Plato and Aristotle especially had a profound effect on later Christian writers and thinkers.

Socrates of Athens lived from about 469 to 399 B.C. The Greek philosophers who lived before Socrates were concerned with trying to discover what the world was made of, but Socrates believed that philosophy could also tell people how to live a good life. To do this, Socrates developed two forms of gathering and presenting information, called induction (to suggest general conclusions from specific examples) and definition (to try to clearly describe what is meant by the general quality of a thing), and a method of using logic in discussions called "dialectic," which involved asking and answering questions. Because of his interest in virtue, Socrates is usually considered the founder of ethics.

Originally worshiped as a goddess of fertility and successful childbearing, Fortuna was believed to control both good and bad luck. She is often represented holding a cornucopia and a steering oar.

Plato, a student of Socrates, lived from about 428 to 348 B.C. and started a school called the "Academy," which continued for more than nine hundred years. Plato's teachings, written in his *Dialogues,* have been among the most influential in the history of Western Civilization. Plato believed that Reason (in Greek, called *logos*) was the nature of the universe, controlling things from within. When he thought about how the world was constantly changing, Plato looked for things that do not change, which are represented in the things that do change. He called these "Forms" or "Ideas." Plato thought that when we call things by a general name, such as Beauty or Courage, we do so because there is a permanent Idea or Form of Beauty or Courage underlying each individual example of it. He believed that these Ideas or Forms, which are the meanings behind physical laws and material things, are what is truly real. Plato also believed that the human soul was immortal, and that the soul is superior to the body. According to Plato, it is the soul that makes us what we are, and that the highest responsibility of people is to "tend the soul," so that it is acceptable to the gods.

Aristotle lived from about 384 to 322 B.C. and was a student of Plato at the "Academy." When Plato died, Aristotle left Athens and became a teacher of Alexander the Great. When Aristotle returned to Athens, he began a school called the "Lyceum," where he taught that the knowledge of a thing requires an understanding of what caused it. Unlike Plato, he believed that form caused matter to move, and that the only pure form was God, who was the cause and goal of all motion. Aristotle's teachings, recorded by his students, cover many fields, including ethics and logic, the natural sciences, politics, physics, and poetry.

Cynics were followers of the Greek philosophical school founded by Antisthenes, a student of Socrates who lived from about 444 to 370 B.C. The most famous Cynic philosopher was Diogenes of Sinope (a town on the shore of the Black Sea). Diogenes believed that happiness came from following virtue for its own sake, and by living a life free from grasping after material possessions and pleasures. It is not clear why the Cynic school (from the Greek word *kyon* meaning "dog") was given its name. It may be a reference to their harshly critical style, in response to what they thought was a corrupt society. Or it may refer to the "Cynosarges," a school where the followers met to discuss philosophy. Cynic philosophers were not tied to one place and their wandering style was copied by some early Christian apostles. This is evidenced when Paul preached at the Aeropagus in Athens, and his audience thought he was a wandering philosopher (Acts 17.16-34).

Stoicism was founded by Zeno of Citium (a town in Cyprus), who lived from around 336 to 261 B.C. The name "stoicism" comes from the Greek word *stoa*. Zeno and his students used to meet regularly at a pillared porch, the *Stoa Poikile,* on the north side of the marketplace in Athens (see the illustration). The Stoics thought that the whole universe was a divine being, and that the gods were simply various names of the one cosmic God. They believed that virtue was living

Porch-like structures called "Stoas" were gathering places for people in the Greek and Roman worlds. One group of philosophers came to be known as the Stoics because they met in the Stoa in Athens.

in harmony with the rational force of nature. To find peace of mind, the Stoics said, people should learn what is in their power and what isn't, and should concern themselves only with the things in their power. The Stoics concluded that people had the power to live in harmony with the cosmic God, which they called virtue. They believed that people should live according to virtue (the rational force of all nature) and be indifferent (the Greek word *apatheia*) to all things—like wealth, pleasure, good or bad fortune—that might prevent them from living a virtuous life. (In English today, the word "stoic" has come to mean patient, disciplined, or self-restrained.) Like all Stoics who would come after him, Zeno preached the equality of the sexes and was strongly opposed to slavery. Stoics had many beliefs in common with early Christians. Most significantly, however, they did not believe in the divinity of Christ, his resurrection, or the judgment of the world. Stoic influences can be found in the writings of the Jewish teacher Philo of Alexandria (who lived from around 25 B.C. to A.D. 50), and even in the writings of the apostle Paul in the New Testament (for example, 1 Cor 7.32-35).

Epicureanism was founded in Athens by Epicurus, who lived from about 342 to 270 B.C. The main goal of life for Epicureans was to find true happiness. They believed true happiness was gained by encouraging serenity (the Greek word "ataraxia") and by avoiding pain. They did not believe that fate or destiny ruled their lives; instead, they believed in free will. Since they did not believe that the gods influenced a person's life, they were considered by some to be atheists. For them, true pleasure came from living nobly and justly and with a healthy lifestyle.

They believed intellectual pleasure was superior to bodily pleasure. The Epicureans valued friendship as a way for people to support each other in the search for happiness. They believed death was the end of existence, but that it was not to be feared because it brought peace and an end to pain. Epicureanism was probably most popular among the upper classes of the Roman Empire.

Gnostics is a term historians have given to a number of religious groups in the second and third centuries A.D. *Gnosis* is the Greek word for knowledge, and Gnostics believed they possessed a special or secret knowledge. Many sects who have been identified as Gnostics believed that the world was ruled by evil forces (called "archons"). Among these evil forces, they included the God of the Old Testament. Archons held humanity captive in a state of ignorance and suffering. Gnostics believed that Jesus was a godlike being (rather than a living person) who had been sent to restore people's knowledge of their origin in the true God. People, they said, were made of body, soul, and spirit. People who lived only the life of the body could not be saved. Christians might achieve a lower form of salvation through their faith, but real salvation came through a superior knowledge *(gnosis)* of the life of the spirit and soul, which is the divine element in human beings. In the early centuries after Christ, Gnosticism was a serious challenge, leading to the rise of elitist sects within Christianity. Gnostics were a very diverse group of sects, but some of their general characteristics have been described by historians.

Emperor Worship. The Jews and early Christians faced the problem of emperor worship in the centuries just before and after Jesus was born. Beginning in the fourth century B.C., Alexander the Great (356-323 B.C.), the Macedonian king who conquered much of the Near East, claimed that he was divine. Rulers who took over after he died made similar claims. They demanded that all their subjects honor them as gods. One of these rulers, Antiochus IV Epiphanes put up a statue of Zeus in the Jerusalem temple. This set off the Maccabean revolt of 168-165 B.C., in which the Jewish people reclaimed the temple and gained their freedom for a brief period of time.

Roman emperors, whose armies conquered Palestine in 63 B.C., also claimed that they were gods. The Roman emperor Gaius Caligula (ruled A.D. 37-41) wanted to put up a statue of himself in the temple, but he died before he could make this happen. Around the end of the first century, the emperor Domitian ordered people to address him as "Lord and God." REVELATION pictures a prostitute and a horrible beast which likely symbolized the Roman Empire's attempt to destroy God's people and their worship of "the Lamb" (Christ), and to force Christians to honor the emperor as divine instead (Rev 17).

The Bible and the Beliefs of the Ancient World

As Jews and Christians moved away from Jerusalem after the destruction of the temple in A.D. 70 and settled in other parts of the Roman Empire, they encountered the various religions and philosophies described in this article, and many others as well. Many of these systems of belief were not compatible with the monotheism of Judaism and Christianity. Sometimes, however, they adopted or adapted some of the teachings from these other systems of thought in response to the situations they faced. In light of these situations, both the Jewish Scriptures (Old Testament) and the New Testament contain direct and indirect references to these other forms of belief. It is, therefore, important to become aware of these other beliefs in order to understand the Bible more fully.

The list of the descendants of Noah's sons comes to an end (Gen 11.26) with Abram ("exalted father"). He later became known as Abraham ("father of many"). God told Abram (Gen 12.1-3) to move from his home in Ur of the Chaldees (in southern Mesopotamia) to the land of Canaan (see the map on p. 200). God promised that his family would become "a great nation" with a special relationship to God. And all nations would be blessed because of Abraham and his wife Sarah and their descendants (Gen 12.1-3; 15.1-21). So Abraham went with Sarah and his nephew Lot. After passing through places that would be important in the later history of Israel (Shechem and Bethel; Gal 12.4-9) and after a long stay in Egypt, they settled in the land of Canaan. Lot settled east of the Jordan River, and Abraham settled to the west, where he lived by the sacred trees of Mamre near Hebron (Gen 13).

God promised Abraham that he would have many descendants, even though he had no son (Gen 15). Finally, when Abraham was ninety-nine, Sarah bore him a son. This son was named Isaac, meaning "laughter" or "laughed," because Sarah laughed at the idea that she would have a child in her old age (Gen 18.9-15). Abraham trusted God's promise (Gen 17.1-27), and the child was born. Isaac was circumcised as a sign of Abraham's special relationship with God (Gen 21.1-7). Abraham's trust in God continued even when God told him to kill Isaac as a sacrifice. But God spared Isaac and once again promised Abraham that his numerous descendants would be a blessing to all the nations of the earth (Gen 22.1-19).

In the New Testament, Abraham is frequently given as an example of human trust in the promises of God (Acts 7.2-50; Rom 4.1-25; Gal 3.1-29; Heb 6.13,14; 7.1-10; 11.8).

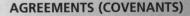

The Bible often speaks of agreements, pacts, alliances, or treaties between individuals or groups of equal or unequal standing. Often these agreements were designed to make clear the relationship that existed between them. In Hebrew, people were said to "cut a covenant" with each other. This may refer to the practice of cutting a sacrificial animal in half and then walking between the two parts as a way to pledge loyalty to the agreement (Gen 15.7-21; Jer 34.18,19). In Genesis 21.22-34 Abraham and Abimelech agreed that the well at Beersheba belonged to Abraham; Solomon and Hiram made a peace treaty that included trade agreements (1 Kgs 5.1-12); marriage was an agreement made between husband and wife that included obligations with God serving as a witness (Mal 2.14).

Agreements were usually completed with some act, such as eating a meal together (Gen 26.26-31), giving gifts (1 Sam 18.3,4), setting up a stone or a pile of rocks as a reminder (Gen 31.43-55), giving someone a sandal (Ruth 4.7,8), or even a simple handshake (2 Kgs 10.15). Agreements were designed to establish loyalty and faithfulness, and breaking an agreement was thought to be a very serious matter.

This way of thinking about relationships guided Israel's faith from the beginning. The most important agreements were those that God made with his people. Some of these include God's agreements with Noah (Gen 6.18), Abraham (Gen 12.1-7; 15.4-21; 17.1-16), Phineas (Num 25.10-15), and the tribes of Israel under Joshua (Josh 24.25). God promised to establish David's family as kings forever (2 Sam 7.12-16; 2 Chr 13.5; see also 1 Kgs 8.22-26; 2 Chr 6.12-15). This promise became the basis of Israel's hope for the Messiah that Christians see fulfilled in Jesus.

The most significant agreement took place on Mount Sinai. There God reminded the people of Israel that he had chosen them and was giving them commandments and laws that would guide their worship and life together. For their part, Israel promised to obey the LORD's laws and worship only the LORD. This agreement was sealed when Moses sprinkled blood on the people and on an altar he had set up for that purpose (Exod 24). The history of Israel was closely connected with this agreement. If the people obeyed this agreement and continued to be faithful to God, they would receive the blessings God had promised in earlier agreements. But if they disobeyed God's Law and worshiped other gods, they would be punished (Deut 4.1,2,39,40; 7.12-15; 8.19,20).

The prophet Jeremiah spoke of a "new agreement," one the LORD would write on the hearts and minds of the people (Jer 31.31-37). Christians see Jesus' words at the Last Supper (Matt 26.28) as the fulfillment of this prophecy. See also Hebrews 10.16 and the mini-article called "God's Saving Love (Salvation)," p. 85.

The word "angel" in English is based on the Greek word *angelos*, which means "messenger." Most often in the Bible, this is exactly what angels do—bring messages from God to people. Sometimes angels deliver messages or give orders in a personal meeting (Gen 16.7-12; Num 22.22-35; Luke 1.11-20,26-38). At other times they bring messages to people in their dreams (Gen 31.10-13; Matt 1.20,21). Angels often are present in visions. Angels may guide human beings to a vision and they may interpret the meaning of vision (Zech 1.7-17; 5.5-11; Acts 10.3-23; Rev 10.1-11).

But angels are more than messengers. They carry out God's will by acting as God's agents. They protect God's people (Exod 14.19; 23.23; Ps 34.7; Dan 6.22) or punish them when they have sinned against God (1 Sam 24.11-17). God's angels also punish the enemies of God's people or punish other evil forces (Exod 12.23,29,30; Isa 37.36; Matt 13.49,50; Rev 14.14-20; 20.1-3). Angels are said to be part of a council that surrounds God in heaven (Job 1.6; Zech 3.7). Angels came to help Jesus after his time of being tested by the devil in the wilderness (Matt 4.11), and one set Jesus free from the tomb after Jesus died on the cross and was buried (Matt 28.2).

Angels are often pictured in art as beings in long robes with wings. But in the Bible they appear in many forms. Moses saw an angel in a burning bush (Exod 3.2). Jacob saw angels going up and down a ladder between heaven and earth (Gen 28.12) and probably wrestled with the Lord's angel (Hos 12.4). Two of the three "men" who ate with Abraham and told him that he would have a son probably were angels (Gen 18.1-10). The being who appeared in the fiery furnace to protect Daniel's friends was said to "look like a god," and may have been an angel (Dan 3.21-25). The winged guardians (seraphim) of the most holy place in the temple (Isa 6.1-7) may have been some kind of angelic beings. The angel who helped Peter escape from prison appeared in a flash of light and somehow made Peter invisible to the prison guards (Acts 12.6-10).

Some angels in the Bible have names. DANIEL mentions Gabriel (Dan 9.21), who also later appears to Mary (Luke 1.26-28), and Michael, who is called one of God's strongest guardian angels (Dan 10.13). It is possible that Satan may have been part of God's council of angels (Job 1.6; Zech 3.1). In the New Testament period, angels became known more and more as spiritual beings who helped God battle against and defeat Satan and his helpers, the demons. See also the mini-article called "Satan," p. 185.

"Circumcision" was the ceremony of cutting off the foreskin of a male's penis. This was a common rite among many people in the ancient Near East, though the reasons why are not clear. It may be that the blood of a circumcision was thought to have protective power, as when Zipporah circumcised her son to protect Moses from death (Exod 4.24-26).

Circumcision is first mentioned in the Bible in connection with God's promise to make Abraham's descendants a great nation and to give them a land they could call their own. In return, Abraham and his descendants were to obey God. To show that they were keeping their promise to God, every male descendant of Abraham was to be circumcised (Gen 17.1-14). Even non-Israelite men who wanted to be part of the Israelite people were to be circumcised (Gen 34.21-24). Circumcision became a requirement of the Law of Moses (Lev 12.3). The New Testament reports that both John the Baptist and Jesus were circumcised eight days after being born (Luke 1.59; 2.21).

The prophet Jeremiah warned that the outward practice of circumcision alone was not a true sign of being one of God's people, since other nations also practiced circumcision. The important thing was to worship God. His strong words to the people of Judah were, "Your bodies are circumcised, but your hearts are unchanged" (Jer 9.25,26). Later, he described a final and permanent renewal of the agreement with God that would be written on the people's "hearts and minds" (Jer 31.31-34). The writer of HEBREWS in the New Testament used Jeremiah's words to back up his message that the first agreement based on God's Law has been replaced by a new agreement brought by Christ (Heb 8.1-13).

The practice of circumcision caused arguments and division among early Christians. Some Jewish Christians who had lived according to the Law of Moses felt that they and any Gentile (non-Jewish) follower of Christ should obey all the Jewish laws and practice all its rituals, including circumcision (Acts 11.1, 2; 21.17-24). Others, especially the apostle Paul, challenged the belief that Gentiles had to be circumcised in order to be acceptable to God. Paul had been circumcised and was a strict follower of the Law of Moses (Phil 3.2-6). But he came to believe that Gentile men could be acceptable to God and become part of God's true people, even if they were not circumcised. Paul argued that being circumcised is worthwhile only if a person can obey the whole Law of Moses. If someone does not obey the whole Law, circumcision cannot make that person "a real Jew." Like Jeremiah, he believed true circumcision is something that happens in the heart (Rom 2.25-29). People are acceptable to God, not by doing everything the Law requires, but because they have faith (Rom 3.28; Phil 3.7-9).

Paul also criticized people he called "troublemakers," Jews who insisted that Gentile believers must practice the Jewish rites, such as circumcision (Gal 1.6-9; 6.12-14; Phil 3.2). Paul said it was wrong for them to argue that being circumcised was the way to "complete" what God's Spirit started (Gal 3.1-3). In the end, Paul said simply, "It doesn't matter if you are circumcised or not. All that matters is that you are a new person" (Gal 6.15).

Crucifixion was a common way to punish criminals and to publicly humiliate them in the ancient world. In Jesus' day, the Romans used crucifixion to put criminals to death. A person was tied with cords or nailed to a wooden cross that was shaped like a T or like a plus sign (+). Usually the worst criminals, slaves who had done wrong, and those who had led revolts were crucified.

After a criminal was sentenced to die on the cross, he had to carry his cross to the place where he would die. Sometimes he carried only the crosspiece. Before being put on the cross he would be beaten and stripped of his clothes. Then he would be fastened on the cross with his arms stretched out. This painful position made it difficult for the condemned person to breathe, and eventually he would die from suffocation. Sometimes the victims lived for as long as a week before dying.

Those who broke the major laws of Jewish society and religion were often put to death by stoning. A group of people would force the accused person to lie down and then push him off a ledge. Then people would throw huge stones down on him, which would crush him to death and cover up his body.

If Jesus had been guilty of breaking an important Jewish law he could have been stoned to death. Instead, he was accused of starting a revolt against the Roman government by allowing himself to be called "King of the Jews." A sign with this title was placed on the cross over Jesus' head when he was crucified (Matt 27.37).

God overcame the death of Jesus by bringing him back to life after he died on the cross. That's why the cross became the major symbol for God's power to forgive sins and give new life to people (1 Cor 1.18-24).

David ruled from about 1010 to 970 B.C. David was a military hero (1 Sam 17.41-54; 18.6,7), but he also was remembered as a musician and poet (1 Sam 16.14-23; 2 Sam 22.1-51; 2 Chr 29.30). The temple was not built until the reign of David's son, Solomon, but David is given credit for making the preparations for music to be played and psalms to be sung as part of worship in the temple (1 Chr 6.31,32; 16.4-36; 25.1,2).

David may have written some of the psalms, but many were written after David's time. The psalms that contain David's name in their title probably were collected in memory of David. The titles of Psalm 3 and twelve other psalms mention events in David's life. These titles were added by the collectors of the psalms and are included in brackets in the CEV. The intent was not to mislead readers but rather to invite readers to see in David and his life an example of how a psalm might apply to their own lives.

For instance, the title of Psalm 3 refers to the rebellion of David's son, Absalom.

God promised David that his family would rule forever (2 Sam 7). A long line of his family members did rule until 586 B.C., when Jerusalem was destroyed and the people of Judah were taken into exile. At that time it seemed to the Israelites that God's promise to David had been broken. Even so, the hope for a good ruler like David did not disappear. Many years later, Jesus' followers would view him as a king in David's family line (Matt 1.1; Luke 1.27,32). Jesus was given the same titles used for King David and the kings that followed him. One of those titles was "chosen one." Another title was "Son of God" (Ps 2.2,7; Mark 1.1). As God's representatives on earth, David and all of Israel's kings were to use their authority to work for "peace and justice" by defending "the poor" (Ps 72.3,4). Compare this to the work Jesus said he had come to do (Luke 4.16-18).

DAY OF THE LORD

The "Day of the LORD" refers to a future time when the LORD will act in history to punish his enemies and to save those who have been faithful. In the Old Testament, the day of the LORD (or simply, "the day") is described most often in the books of the prophets. It usually refers to some future historical event, rather than to a final judgment when God's enemies receive eternal punishment and God's faithful people receive eternal life. This idea of a final judgment day is more common in the New Testament (see below).

The oldest passage in the Bible that mentions the LORD's day of judgment is found in AMOS (Amos 5.18-20). This and other passages from the prophets describe the day of the LORD as a dark day of disaster when the LORD will punish the wicked. The "wicked" may be other nations (Isa 13.1-6; Amos 1.3—2.3; Obad 15), the people from Israel and Judah (Ezek 7.2-13; Joel 1.15), or the people of the earth in general (Isa 2.12-21; Zeph 1.14-18). Punishment connected with the day of the LORD can take the form of an invasion by an enemy nation (Isa 10.5-12; Hos 10.10-14) or natural disasters such as swarms of locusts (Joel 1.4-7; Amos 7.1,2), earthquakes and darkness (Joel 2.10; Amos 8.9), and famine (Ezek 5.13-16).

The day of the LORD also is described as a time when God will restore the people of Israel and Judah and save those who have been faithful. This time of restoration follows a time of punishment. For example, the prophets Isaiah, Jeremiah, and Ezekiel each warned the people that their exile in Babylon was punishment for being unfaithful to the LORD. But the LORD would forgive them and lead them back to Jerusalem, where they could once again be a "light" among the other nations (Isa 40.1-11; 49.8-12; Jer 23.7,8; Ezek 37.15-23; see also Amos 9.11-15). Often this time of restoration is described as time of peace when the people would once again be ruled by a chosen ruler (messiah) from the family of David (Isa 11.1-9; Jer 23.5,6).

A few Old Testament passages hint that God's saving love and judgment affect more than events in this life. For example, the prophet Daniel speaks of a time when the dead will rise from death. At this time, some people will receive eternal life and others will receive eternal shame (Dan 12.1-3). See also Job 19.25-27 and Isa 26.19. These passages and later passages that come from writings dating to the period between the Testaments (first and second century B.C.) laid the foundation for the many New Testament passages that describe a coming day of judgment.

The Gospels refer to a day of judgment (Matt 10.15; 12.36; Luke 21.34,35), and Jesus describes a time of coming judgment that sounds a great deal like the disastrous day of the LORD described above (Mark 13). But his words introduce the idea that the coming time of disaster is a warning that the end of time is near and soon the Son of Man will return and gather his chosen ones (Mark 13.24-27). One of Jesus' parables describes a coming time of judgment that is meant to encourage people to help their neighbors in this lifetime (Matt 25.31-46).

When the apostle Paul speaks of the coming day of the Lord he connects it to the return of Christ (1 Cor 1.8; 5.5; Phil 1.6-11; 2.16; 1 Thes 5.2). REVELATION describes the future day when God will finally defeat the forces of evil as "the day of God's great victory" (Rev 16.14). Death itself will be thrown into the lake of fire along with all those whose names are not written in the book of life (Rev 20.14,15). Then God will create a new heaven and new earth (Rev 21.1-7). Some New Testament passages suggest that people face judgment immediately after they die (Luke 16.19-24; 23.39-43).

Elijah was a prophet who lived in Israel in from around 899 to 850 B.C. This was after the Israelite kingdom of David and Solomon had divided into northern (Israel) and southern (Judah) kingdoms. In Elijah's day, many people in the northern kingdom were worshiping foreign gods such as Baal and Asherah. The worship of these gods was encouraged by Israel's King Ahab and his Phoenician queen, Jezebel (1 Kgs 16.30-33; 21.25-29). At this time, Elijah seems to have been the only prophet who had the courage to challenge the influence of powerful people.

Elijah challenged the priests of Baal to see whose god was stronger (1 Kgs 16.29—19.18). And he confronted Ahab and Jezebel because they killed a man named Naboth just so they could take his land and vineyard (1 Kgs 21). After this, he challenged Ahab's son, Amaziah, when Amaziah turned to the god "Baalzebub" for guidance instead of turning to the LORD (2 Kgs 1.1-16). And finally, Elijah challenged the false worship and cruel behavior of Jehoram, king of the southern kingdom, Judah (2 Chr 21.12-15).

Elijah was also known for his miracles. He predicted a drought (1 Kgs 17.1); provided food that would not run out (1 Kgs 17.14); raised a dead boy back to life (1 Kgs 17.17-24); and called for fire to come from heaven (1 Kgs 18.36-38; 2 Kgs 1.12).

According to 2 Kings 2.11, Elijah did not die but was taken to heaven in a "strong wind" (or whirlwind). This story probably led to the belief that Elijah would return one day (Mal 4.5). Many centuries later, some people believed that John the Baptist was Elijah (Matt 11.14; 17.10-13; Luke 1.17). Others thought Jesus was Elijah (Matt 16.14; Luke 9.8; John 1.21). See also Mark 9.11-13.

In ancient times, the people of Israel based their hope for life beyond death on the lives of their descendants. It was considered a tragedy when a man died without having a son to carry on the family line. Most people expected that their bodies would rot and turn to dust after they died (Eccl 12.7; Ps 104.29; Job 7.9,10). Some believed that the souls of the dead went to a special place, but these souls had no thoughts or feelings there (Eccl 9.10; Isa 38.10). The Bible reports that a few people did not die but were taken up to be with God (Gen 5.21-24; 2 Kgs 2.1-14).

The idea of people being raised from death appears in the book of the prophet Daniel, who said that both good and bad people would be raised from death to new life. The good would experience eternal life, while the bad would have eternal shame (Dan 12.1-3). Some psalms express confidence that God would not send faithful people to the world of the dead, but would save them from death (Ps 16.10,11; 49.13-15; Isa 26.19).

The people of Israel were taken into exile in Babylon around 586 B.C. Later, the Persians defeated Babylon and let the people of Israel begin to return home (538 B.C.). Some Israelites were influenced by Persians who believed that God's enemy, Satan, would be defeated and that the souls and bodies of faithful people who had died would be brought back to life. During the four centuries before the birth of Christ, the Jewish people were also influenced by some Greek thinkers who believed that the physical human body had no lasting value and would rot away, but the invisible soul or spirit would live forever. The apostle Paul told the church in Corinth that the physical bodies of Christ's followers will die, but when God raises them to new life, their bodies will change into "spiritual bodies" (1 Cor 15.35-54). This is different from the belief that only the soul would live on after the body decayed. Paul says that the whole person—both soul and body—will be new and experience life after death (eternal life).

Jesus called himself "the one who raises the dead to life" (John 11.25,26) and promised that all who believe in him will have eternal life (John 3.16). One group of religious Jews called Sadducees questioned Jesus' teachings about life after death (see the note at Luke 20.27). Jesus told them that when God's people rise from death they will not marry but will be like angels in heaven (Mark 12.18-27). Jesus was also asked which people would be part of God's future kingdom. See his answer in Luke 14.15-24.

Early Christians believed that God's people would be raised to new life because God raised Jesus from death to new life (Acts 2.22-24,29-32; 1 Cor 15.20-28; 1 Thes 4.13-17). Revelation 21 describes the New Jerusalem, where God will live among people on earth and where God will feed and protect his followers forever (Ezek 37.26,27; Matt 1.23; 2 Cor 4.16—5.5).

Fire is important in the Bible in at least four different ways:

(1) *Fire is one sign that God is present.* Examples of this in the Jewish Scriptures (Old Testament) are the burning bush from which God spoke to Moses (Exod 3.2); the column of fire that led Israel through the desert at night (Exod 13.21,22); and God's appearance to Moses and the people on Mount Sinai (Exod 19.18; 24.17,18; Deut 4.11,35,36). In the New Testament, the coming of the Holy Spirit on the day of Pentecost (Acts 2.1-4) is compared with "fiery tongues moving in all directions." And when John sees Jesus in Revelation 1.14,15 his eyes look like "flames of fire" and his feet glow "like bronze being heated in a furnace." The prophets of Israel expected God to appear surrounded by fire (Isa 4.5), to appear in fire (Isa 66.15), or to be seated on a throne surrounded by fire (Dan 7.9,10).

(2) *Fire was important in the worship of God in Israel's temple.* The flame that burned on the altar was a reminder that God was always present there (Lev 6.12,13). Fire was used to burn incense or to make offerings (Lev 6.14,15). The author of HEBREWS quotes Psalm 104.4, describing God and God's servants in terms of fire (Heb 1.7).

(3) *God would use fire to punish wicked people.* This was true at Sodom and Gomorrah (Gen 19.24,25) and when God punished the clan that stole items from the destroyed city of Jericho (Josh 7.15). Fire is a symbol of God's anger (Ps 79.5; 89.46), and God will use it to punish sin and evil in the future (Deut 32.22; Isa 50.10,11; 66.15,16; Amos 7.4). The evil powers will be destroyed by fire at the end of the age (Dan 7.11; Mal 4.1). Jesus says that the fire of judgment will fall on the earth and its wicked people (Matt 3.11,12; 13.37-42; Luke 17.29,30). God's final judgment of the evil world includes punishment by fire (2 Pet 3.7). This is pictured in detail in REVELATION (Rev 8.7; 9.18; 11.5; 14.9,10; 19.20; 20.9-15).

(4) *God will use fire to purify his people.* Often such purifying (or testing) is experienced by facing life's trials (Ps 66.12; Isa 43.2; 1 Pet 1.7). And God's judgment in the future will also purify God's people by fire (Zech 13.9; 1 Cor 3.12-15).

In Jesus' time, fishing took place mostly on Lake Galilee, because the Jewish people could not use many of the harbors along the coast of the Mediterranean Sea, since these harbors were often controlled by unfriendly neighbors. The most common fish in the Lake of Galilee were carp and catfish. The Law of Moses allowed people to eat any fish with fins and scales, but since catfish lack scales (as do eels and sharks) they were not to be eaten (Lev 11.9-12). Fish were also probably brought from Tyre and Sidon, where they were dried or salted.

The creation story tells that God ordered the waters of the earth to bring forth fish along with all other kinds of sea plants and animals (Gen 1.20-22). God gave human beings control over the creation, including fish (Gen 1.28; Ps 8.6-8), but people are forbidden to make or worship an image of any created thing, including fish (Deut 4.15-18). When God renews the creation, the salty Dead Sea will become fresh water and will be filled with fish (Ezek 47.7-10).

Fishing was also an important source of jobs and income in Galilee, and several of Jesus' followers were fishermen. Jesus told them that they were going to bring in people instead of fish (Mark 1.16,17; Matt 4.18,19). When Jesus fed the hungry crowd that followed him out of town, the food he provided was bread and fish (Mark 6.30-44; Matt 14.14-21; Luke 9.10-17). Jesus used fishing to show his disciples the amazing results they could expect from having faith in him and sharing the good news with others. The net the apostles threw into the lake became so full of fish they could not pull it into their boat (John 21.4-12).

Among early Christians, the fish was a favorite image for Jesus, because the Greek word for fish (*ichthus*) consists of the first letters of the Greek words that tell who Jesus is:

I hsous	Jesus
Ch ristos	Christ
Th eou	of God
U ios	the Son
S wthr	Savior

The English word *gentile* comes from the Latin word for "people." In the Bible, Gentiles are all the peoples who are not Jews. The descendants of Noah and his family spread out over the world and became divided into many different nations or peoples (Gen 10). God divided these nations by giving them different languages, because they had acted in evil ways (Gen 11). But then God chose Abraham and Sarah and told them that he would use them and their descendants to bring God's blessing to "all the families of the earth" (Gen 12.1-3). Later, Israel's king Solomon urged the people to be kind and open toward those of other nations, so that they would come to honor the LORD God (1 Kgs 8.41-43).

The prophets of Israel kept telling the people that God was eager to have other nations honor him (Jer 4.2) and that they wanted to know the God of Israel (Isa 42.1-4; 51.4-5). If the people of God were obedient, they would be a model and witness to all the nations of the world (Isa 61). The story of Jonah shows how God reached out with mercy to a nation that was Israel's enemy. God will one day be the single ruler over all nations, and they will join to honor God (Ps 47.8,9; 86.8,9). In the kingdom that God will establish, "people of every nation and race would serve him" (Dan 7.14).

In the New Testament Simeon blesses the child Jesus, and says that he will be a "light to the nations" (Luke 2.29-32). Jesus reaches out to heal people who are not Jewish, like the man with the demon in the Greek city of Gerasa (Mark 5), the deaf man in the region of Tyre and Sidon (Mark 7.31-37), and the young servant of a Roman officer (Matt 8.5-13). The apostles decide that anyone from any nation who worships God and does right is acceptable to God (Acts 10.35). Paul says that both Jews and Gentiles who trust what God has done through Jesus are accepted into the life of his new people (Gal 2.11-16). The author of REVELATION celebrates the fact that Jesus was willing to die for the sins of the *whole* world and makes it possible for people from every tribe and nation, language and race to share in the kingdom of God (Rev 5.6-10). They can share the privilege that only Israel's priests were previously allowed to enjoy—they can enter into God's presence.

The ancient Hebrews spoke of heaven as a great ocean in the sky. A dome was said to cover the earth and kept back the heavenly ocean (Gen 1.6, 7). Rain was said to fall on earth when God opened windows in the heavenly ceiling (Gen 7.11,12; Isa 24.18; Mal 3.10). Because this heavenly dome was so heavy, it had to be held up by pillars (Job 26.11).

God lives and rules in heaven (1 Kgs 8.30; Isa 66.1; Matt 5.34). Heaven is also where God's court meets (Gen 1.26; 3.22; Job 1.6; 2.1; 15.7,8). Some of Israel's prophets had visions of God in heaven (1 Kgs 22.19), and the prophet Elijah was taken up to heaven in a strong wind (2 Kgs 2.1-12). The apostle Paul also spoke of being taken up into a "third heaven," where he heard wonderful things (2 Cor 12.1-4). A man named John had a vision of heaven that revealed secrets about the future (Rev 4.1—22.17).

The Old Testament does not describe heaven as a place where God's faithful will live with God after they die. In fact, it was only in the fifth or sixth century B.C. that some Israelite people began to believe in eternal life after death. The prophet Daniel had a vision of the people whose names were written in *The Book*. These people were to rise from death and be given eternal life (Dan 12.1-3). But even this vision does not say that those who are raised from death will live in heaven.

The New Testament also describes heaven as the place where God lives and rules. The angels who announced the birth of Jesus praise God in heaven (Luke 2.14). When Jesus was baptized, God's voice came from heaven and called Jesus "my own dear Son" (Luke 3.22). Jesus described God as a Father in heaven (Matt 6.1,9; 18.4; John 6.32). Jesus himself came from heaven (John 6.38-42) and returned there after death (Luke 25.50, 51). And he will come back from heaven in the future (Matt 24.30,31; 1 Thes 4.16).

When Jesus spoke of the kingdom of heaven (Matt 4.17; 5.3; 13.44-47) he usually meant where God's will and purposes were done, rather than God's home. The promise of life after death is common in the New Testament (see the mini-article called "Eternal Life," p. 163). Jesus told his disciples that he will go to his Father's house to prepare a place for them (John 14.1-3). The apostle Paul said that those who are raised from death will have new bodies like those who are in heaven (1 Cor 15.45-54). Paul also said that those who have faith in Christ are "citizens of heaven." Christ will make their poor earthly bodies like his own glorious body (Phil 3.20,21). Other New Testament books say that heaven and earth will be destroyed or replaced and made new (2 Pet 3.10-13; Rev 21.1—22.5). See also the mini-article called "Paradise," p. 181.

In English Bibles, three different words are translated as "hell": the Hebrew words *Gehinnom* and *Sheol*, and the Greek word *Hades*. The Hebrew word *Gehinnom*, means "Valley of Hinnom." This narrow valley is located south and west of Jerusalem and runs into the Kidron Valley. During the time of Israel's kings, this valley became the site of a worship place known as *Topheth*, which in Aramaic means "fireplace." Some Israelites and their kings disobeyed God and worshiped the god Molech at this place. This worship of Molech included sacrificing children by throwing them into the fire and burning them to death (Lev 18.21; 20.2-5; Jer 32.35). For this terrible sin, the prophet Jeremiah said that this place would one day be known as Slaughter Valley (Jer 7.31,32; 19.6).

In the two hundred years before Jesus was born, some Jewish teachers said that the place where wicked people go when they die is like the burning Valley of Hinnom. The Greek word used to describe this place is *Gehenna*. Because the word *Gehenna* (hell) is always used in the New Testament to describe a place of fiery death and punishment, it has a different meaning than the Hebrew *Sheol* or the Greek *Hades*. These words refer to the dark place where all the dead go (Job 30.23; Ezek 31.16-18; Acts 2.27), or where the dead wait for God's final judgment (Rev 20.13). *Sheol* (*Hades*) is a place somewhere under the earth that is totally silent and where no one knows or feels anything (Job 10.21,22; Ps 88.12; 94.17). Punishment and torture are not connected with *Sheol*.

In the New Testament, hell (*Gehenna*) is the place of judgment where God sends evildoers to face fiery torture and everlasting punishment (Matt 5.22; Luke 16.23,24; Rev 20.14,15). It is pictured as a flaming furnace (Matt 13.42,50), a fire that never goes out (Mark 9.43,44), a fiery lake (Rev 20.14,15), and an everlasting fire prepared for the devil and his angels (Matt 25.41). Jesus warned people that they might end up in hell for committing certain sins (Matt 23.13-15,29-33; Mark 9.45-48; Luke 12.5), and the book of JAMES warns that the human tongue can be used to speak evil, setting a person's entire life on fire with flames that come from hell (Jas 3.6).

The Holy Spirit is God's presence at work in the world. The Jewish Scriptures (Old Testament) declare that the Spirit of God was at work in the creation of the world (Gen 1.2), giving life to plants, animals, and humans (Ps 104.27-30). The leaders of Israel were given power and direction by the Spirit, including Moses and the seventy-two leaders chosen to help him (Num 11.24-30), Gideon (Judg 6.34), and Kings Saul and David (1 Sam 10.6-13; 11.6; 16.13; 2 Sam 23.1-4). Earlier prophets like Elijah and Elisha (2 Kgs 2.9-15, where the CEV translates "spirit" as "power") and later ones like Isaiah and Ezekiel (Isa 61.1; Ezek 2.2; 3.12-27) were guided by the Spirit of God and given messages for the people.

The LORD promised to give his Spirit and message to his people so that they would become eager to obey God's law and teachings (Isa 59.21; Ezek 36.24-29). The prophet Isaiah reminded the people that it was by the Spirit that God guided the history of Israel from the beginning (Isa 63.10-14). If God's people disobey the Spirit, they will be punished (Isa 63.10), but when they follow the Spirit, their lives and hearts will be transformed and purified (Ezek 36.26,27). And ultimately, their hope for the future is that God's Spirit will renew them and their relationship with God (Isa 44.3-5; Ezek 11.19,20), and send them a new ruler filled with wisdom and justice (Isa 11.2-5).

For the writers of the New Testament, Jesus is seen as the one who fulfills the vision that inspired the prophets. LUKE reports that an angel told Mary that the Holy Spirit would come down to her, and God's power would come over her and that her child, Jesus, would be called the holy Son of God (Luke 1.35). Jesus' relationship with God is again emphasized at his baptism when "the Holy Spirit came down upon him in the form of a dove" (Luke 3.22). At the beginning of his ministry Jesus read a passage from ISAIAH to people gath-ered on the Sabbath and declared that the Lord's Spirit had come to him and had chosen him to tell the good news to the poor (Luke 4.16-19). Although Jesus' enemies accused him of having an unclean spirit (Mark 3.28-30), Jesus claimed that it was by God's Spirit, not by the devil, that he was able to drive out demons (Matt 12.28). The writer of MATTHEW also claimed that Jesus was the "chosen servant" Isaiah said would be given the Spirit of God and bring justice to the nations (Matt 12.15-21; see also Isa 42.1-4).

In JOHN, Jesus tells his disciples he will send the Holy Spirit to help them; to teach them everything and remind them of what Jesus had already taught them; to show them what is true; and to guide them in the full truth (John 14.15-17; 25,26; 15.26; 16.4-15).

After Jesus died and was raised to life he spent forty days with his apostles. He told them that they would be baptized by the Holy Spirit (Acts 1.3-5) and that the Spirit would give them the power to take the good news about Jesus "everywhere in the world" (Acts 1.8). Then, on the day of Pentecost, the Spirit came to the apostles who were gathered in Jerusalem (Acts 2.1-12). ACTS goes on to tell of the many ways the Holy Spirit guided and strengthened the apostles as they took the good news about Jesus to other lands and people (for example, see Acts 4.8,31; 6.3-5; 8.29; 13.2-9; 20.22-18).

For Paul, it is the Spirit who sets free God's new people and who changes their lives so that they can have peace and be obedient to God (Rom 8.1-17). The Spirit gives them the ability to understand God's will, to live together in love, to see what the future will bring, and to carry out the different kinds of work that need to be done in the churches (1 Cor 12–14). The Spirit produces within them the love and the lifestyle that God wants for his people (Rom 4.9-13; Gal 5.22,23).

ISRAEL

The name "Israel" is used in several different, but interrelated, ways in the Bible. The following summary describes these different uses.

The Name. The Hebrew word for "Israel" means "one who wrestles with God" or "May God join in the struggle!" The second meaning implies "May God defeat the forces that oppose God and the people of God." The name "Israel" was given to Jacob, the son of Isaac and Rebekah and grandson of Abraham and Sarah, after Jacob wrestled with someone who seemed to be a human but later turned out to be God (Gen 32.22-32). Later, Israel's twelve tribes were named for the sons of Jacob (Israel) and for two of his grandsons (see Gen 48,49).

The People. After the time of Jacob, it likely took many years before those who belonged to the separate tribes became known as "the people of Israel." Exactly when that happened is not easy to say. The earliest historical evidence of the people known as Israel comes from an Egyptian stone carving known as the Merneptah Stele, which dates from about 1230 B.C. There "Israel" is the name of a foreign people. Not long before this time Moses had led God's people, the descendants of Jacob, out of Egypt to the land God promised to give them (Canaan; see Exod 3.7,8,16,17). When the twelve tribes were settling in the land of Canaan (to be known later as Israel), they were only loosely linked together (Judg 5).

The Nation (Land). About 1000 B.C. the people from the separate tribes began to come together under their first king, Saul (1 Sam 9,10). But it was King David who brought all the tribes together in one unified nation under one ruler (2 Sam 5.1-5). Jerusalem became the nation's capital and the central place for the people to worship God. David's son, King Solomon, built a temple in Jerusalem where all Israel could come together to worship the LORD (2 Sam 7; 1 Kgs 6; 8.2). Under Solomon, the territory known as Israel stretched from the Gulf of Aqaba and the northern boundaries of Egypt in the south to Kadesh and the Euphrates River in northern Syria.

After Solomon died (924 B.C.), the ten northern tribes broke away from the two southern tribes known as Judah. These northern tribes built their own temple in the north at Samaria, and called themselves "Israel" (2 Sam 19.41; 1 Kgs 12). In 722 B.C. the Assyrians invaded from the north and deported the people of the northern kingdom (Israel), sending them into various regions in the Assyrian Kingdom. The people in the southern kingdom (Judah) were not captured by the Assyrians, but in 586 B.C. Judah were defeated by the Babylonians and many of its people sent to live throughout Babylonia. This period in the history of Israel is known as "the exile." During the time before and after the exile, "Israel" was often used by the prophets as the name for all God's people (Isa 43; Ezek 36; Hos 4,5).

God's Holy People. After the time of the Babylonian exile, the Israelites who returned to Judah were governed by the Persians and, later, by the Greeks. At this time the people of Israel, regardless of where they lived, came to be known as "Jews," a term derived from the Greco-Latin term "Judea," meaning Judah. Because they lived in so many different places the Jewish people did not base their identity so much on the geographic area they controlled or on political power, but on their commitment to following God's Law. This desire to obey God is what set them apart from other nations. At the time of Jesus, the people of Israel were ruled by the Romans but continued to follow the traditions, ceremonies, and festivals that made them God's holy people.

The people of Israel were holy, or "set apart for God," and they were to obey God's commandments. In Exodus 19.5 God tells Moses to tell the Israelites, "You will be my holy nation and serve me as priests." The prophet Isaiah repeated this promise and challenge. He said to the people who mourned in Jerusalem, "They themselves will be priests and servants of the LORD our God" (Isa 61.6).

Even though all the people were like priests, God commanded that special priests be selected from the tribe of Levi (Num 1.49-51; 3.5-13) to serve first in the sacred tent, and then later in the temple that would be built in Jerusalem. These priests are described according to their duties: (1) the Levites, who did basic work in preparing sacrifices and cleaning the holy place; (2) the priests, who offered the sacrifices and performed various ritual acts; and (3) the high priest, who was in charge of the holy place, and who was the only one who could go into the inner part of the temple (most holy place), where God was believed to live (Exod 28.29).

The priests wore special robes (Exod 28.4-39), a golden crown with the words, "Holy to the Lord," and a breastplate marked with the names of the twelve tribes of Israel. Israel's priests had two main purposes: (1) to keep contact with God in the holy place of worship (the tent, and later the temple); and (2) to help the people become pure.

The Jewish people returned to Jerusalem from exile in Babylon beginning in 538 B.C. Soon after, the prophets told the people to rebuild the temple that the Babylonians had destroyed in 586 B.C. and once again worship God there (Hag 1.1,12,14; Zech 3.6,7; 4.14). In the second century B.C., the Syrian king, Antiochus IV, put a statue of a foreign god in the temple and tried to force Jews to offer sacrifices to it. The Jewish people were greatly offended by this and revolted until once again proper worship of God in the temple was restored.

Some of the priests helped lead the revolt that set up an independent Jewish nation. This nation existed from 165 to 63 B.C., when the Romans invaded and took over Palestine. Israel's priests then began to cooperate with the Romans, who let King Herod build a great new temple in Jerusalem. Israel's priesthood came to an end in A.D. 70 when the temple was destroyed by the Roman army during another Jewish rebellion. The temple has never been rebuilt.

Until this final destruction of the temple, it was the job of the priests to offer sacrifices to thank God and to gain God's forgiveness for the sins of the people. The New Testament says that Jesus offered himself on the cross (Mark 10.45) and that God sent Jesus as a sacrifice in order to set people free from their sins (Rom 3.25,26). In HEBREWS Jesus is seen as the great high priest, whose death on the cross was the full and final sacrifice for the sins of the world (Heb 4.14—5.7; 10.1-18).

Jerusalem, in the hill country eighteen miles west of the north end of the Dead Sea, began as a small settlement around 3500 B.C. It grew around the Gihon Spring, one of only two sources of water in the area around what would later be called the "temple mount." The city is mentioned in ancient Egyptian writings and might have once been called Salem (Gen 14.18).

When David became king of Israel, he captured the walled city of Jerusalem around 1000 B.C. from the Jebusites (Gen 10.6-20; 2 Sam 5–6) and made it Israel's new capital. This decision helped to unify the country, since this neutral city was located between the feuding northern and southern tribes of Israel. The city grew under David's son, King Solomon, who extended the city to the north and built his palace and a temple to the LORD on the eastern hill. King Hezekiah (ruled 727-688 B.C.) further enlarged the city to include the western hill. In 586 B.C., when Judah's most important citizens were taken off to Babylonia as prisoners, much of Jerusalem was left in ruins. Under the Jewish Maccabean kings (140-63 B.C.) it became prominent once again. By the time of Herod's rule (40-4 B.C.) Jerusalem covered more than 200 acres and had a population of forty thousand.

Solomon's temple, which the Babylonians destroyed in 586 B.C., was rebuilt on a smaller scale by Nehemiah after the Persians allowed the Jews to return to their land, then known as Judea (445 B.C.). When Alexander the Great (356-323 B.C.) conquered the Near East, the influence of Greek culture began to spread throughout the world. The Syrian (Seleucid) rulers who took over control of Palestine after Alexander's death had been influenced by the Greeks, and so began to turn Jerusalem into a typical Greek-style city. In 168 B.C., Antiochus IV of Syria made the temple a shrine to the Greek god Zeus. He also built a fortress just north of the temple so that his troops could keep an eye on the city and surrounding area. When the Jewish family known as the Maccabees came to power around 140 B.C., they made the western hill their seat of government. See the map on p. 203.

The Romans took over Judea in 63 B.C., but it wasn't until 37 B.C. that Herod was able to capture Jerusalem. He expanded the city by enlarging the temple area on the eastern hill. He built a huge stone platform for the temple and its courtyards that covered more than one and a half million square feet. He lived in a palace on the western hill, surrounded by his wealthy supporters. Massive towers protected the palace, and a bridge crossed the valley between two hills. Another huge tower was built north of the temple area. A grand staircase led south from the temple mount to the older, poorer part of the city below. The northern city wall connected the tower overlooking the temple with Herod's palace. All of these structures would still have been in place in Jesus' day. See the map on p. 198.

During the first Jewish revolt against the Romans (A.D. 66-70), the temple and much of the city were destroyed. After the second revolt (A.D. 130-135), the Romans built a new temple to their god Jupiter on the temple mount. They renamed the city Aelia Capitolina, and would not allow the Jews into the city in an effort to prevent any new uprisings. Since then, many different groups have controlled Jerusalem, including Byzantine Christians, Islamic rulers, Latin Christians, and Ottoman Turks. Today it is the capital of the Jewish state of Israel, as well as a holy city for Jews, Christians, and Muslims around the world.

JESUS' TWELVE DISCIPLES

The twelve disciples of Jesus are listed in three of the four Gospels. See how the disciples named in MARK and LUKE compare to the list in MATTHEW.

MATTHEW 10.2-4	MARK 3.14-19	LUKE 6.13,16
Simon (Peter)	Simon (Peter)	Simon (Peter)
Andrew, Peter's brother	Andrew	Andrew, Peter's brother
James, son of Zebedee	James, son of Zebedee (Boanerges)	James
John, son of Zebedee	John, son of Zebedee (Boanerges)	John
Philip	Philip	Philip
Bartholomew	Bartholomew	Bartholomew
Thomas	Thomas	Thomas
Matthew, the tax collector	Matthew	Matthew
James, son of Alphaeus	James, son of Alphaeus	James, son of Alphaeus
Thaddaeus	Thaddaeus	Jude, son of James
Simon, the Eager One	Simon, the Eager One	Simon, the Eager One
Judas Iscariot	Judas Iscariot	Judas Iscariot

John is sometimes called the last "Old Testament prophet" because of the warnings he brought about God's judgment and because he announced the coming of God's "Chosen One" (Messiah). LUKE reports that John was born to an old couple named Elizabeth and Zechariah, who had learned from the angel Gabriel that God was going to give them a son. This son would have special work to do in preparing the way for God's Messiah (see Luke 1.13-17,57-66). In the Gospels, John is described as a prophet who preached in the desert and warned people that they should get ready for the new thing God was going to do (Matt 3.1-12; Mark 1.4-8; Luke 3.1-20). John wore clothes made of camel hair (see 2 Kgs 1.8), and he ate grasshoppers and wild honey (see Lev 11.20-23). He told the people of Israel that they could not count on being accepted by God simply because they were descendants of Abraham. They had to realize how they were disobeying God and how they could get ready to accept the new powerful messenger God was going to send to live among them (Luke 3.16).

John baptized people who were sorry for their sins and many people thought he was the Messiah (Luke 3.15). But John told everyone that the Messiah would be more powerful than he was (Matt 3.11,12; Luke 3.16,17). Jesus compared John with Elijah, the prophet who many believed would come back before God judged the world (Matt 11.14), and he said that John's work was to prepare people for the coming of God's kingdom (Luke 7.27; Matt 11.10). Herod Antipas, a son of Herod the Great and brother of Archelaus (see Matt 2.19-22), ordered that John the Baptist be killed (see Matt 14.1-12; Mark 6.14-29).

The Hebrew word that the CEV usually translates "Law" is "torah." It means "teaching" or "instruction." Because the instruction that God gave Moses at Mount Sinai (Exod 20.1—Num 10.10) is so important, it became known as "the Law." The Law was never meant to be just a set of rules to be obeyed in order to earn God's favor. God had already set the people free from slavery in Egypt when he gave them the Law. Its purpose was to help the people stay in God's favor and to remain free.

Actually, the five books GENESIS through DEUTERONOMY also became known as *The Torah* or the Law. They tell the story of God's love for and activity on behalf of Israel and the world. The instruction that God gave to Moses cannot fully be understood apart from the story of God's love for the world.

Beyond what God gave Moses at Mount Sinai, more rules are found in DEUTERONOMY, which means "second law." God's giving of a "second law" suggests that the Law is not set for all time. It grows and changes. After the exile, Jewish scribes and rabbis were responsible for interpreting the Law, including the task of helping it change and grow to meet new situations. Jesus continued to do this. (See, for example, Matt 5.21-39.) Jesus changed certain rules of the Law not "to do away with them, but to give them their full meaning" (Matt 5.17). Jesus summarizes the full meaning of the Law as loving God and loving one's neighbor (Matt 22.37-40; compare Deut 6.4; Lev 19.18).

The apostle Paul also continued to interpret the Law, helping it to change and grow. Like Jesus, Paul summarizes the full meaning of the Law as love (Rom 13.9). Paul also said that all people are welcome in God's kingdom, regardless of what they eat, what day they worship on, or whether they are circumcised. This goes against many of the rules found in GENESIS to DEUTERONOMY. But Paul said that people are saved by God's love shown in Jesus, not by following any set of rules (Rom 10.4; Gal 5.1-6). According to Paul, the Law is useful because it points out our sin (Rom 3.20; Gal 3.19) and because it shows what is holy and good (Rom 7.12).

Certain psalms (Ps 1; 19; 119) celebrate the Law as the means for people to stay in God's favor and receive God's blessings. Happiness and true life come from listening to and obeying God's instruction, rather than trying to please oneself (Ps 1.1,2; 19.7,8; 119.1,92,174).

The Hebrew word "Messiah" means "anointed one," and is usually translated in the CEV as "chosen one." Anointing is the practice of pouring oil on the head of a person who is chosen to serve God and God's people. For example, priests were anointed (1 Chr 29.22); prophets were sometimes anointed (Isa 61.1,3); and Cyrus, a Persian king, was even called an "anointed one" (CEV "chosen one") when God chose him to help the people return to Judea from their exile in Babylon (Isa 45.1).

In the Jewish Scriptures, it is the king who is most often called an "anointed one" (1 Sam 10.1; 16.1,13). Several psalms about the king make it clear that as God's "chosen one" (Ps 2.2) or "son" (Ps 2.7), the king is responsible for establishing God's justice and peace on earth. This means rescuing victims of injustice, "especially the poor" (see Ps 9.8,9).

God's agreement with King David was that one of his descendants would always be king (Ps 89.4). But when Jerusalem was destroyed and the exile began in 586 B.C., the kingdom of David and his descendants was ended (see Ps 89.38-45). After the exile, some people looked for the restoring of the kingship of David's line. Others suggested that all of God's people were now responsible for doing what the kings had done.

This matter was still being discussed hundreds of years later when the early Christians expressed their belief that Jesus was God's "chosen one." The early Christians saw in Jesus a "chosen one" who rescued the poor and established peace by inviting all people into God's kingdom. The author of MARK uses the two titles for the king from Psalm 2 and applies them to Jesus: "Christ" (which is Greek for "anointed one") and "Son of God" (Mark 1.1; see Ps 2.2,7). MATTHEW identifies Jesus as a descendant of David and so places him in David's royal line (Matt 1.1). Jesus became known as "Jesus Messiah" (or Jesus Christ; Mark 8.29; 14.61,62), and confessing Jesus to be the Messiah set early Christians apart from their Jewish contemporaries (John 9.22-23; 1 John 2.22).

People came to Jerusalem at the time of the yearly celebration of Passover and for other religious holidays. Part of the celebration and worship involved sacrificing animals and making offerings of grain to God. Different sacrifices required different types of animals (for example, see Lev 3.1-13; 14.10, 21; Num 28.16-25), so many sellers set up animal pens and cages in the outer court of the temple, which was called the court of the Gentiles. This court was the only part of the temple that Gentiles (non-Jewish people) were allowed to enter, so moneychangers often set up money tables where out-of-town Jewish visitors could change their money into the special kind of money used at the temple.

The people used this money to pay the annual temple tax.

Sometimes, the sellers overcharged people, and the moneychangers did not give a fair amount of money back to people in return for the foreign money they had exchanged. Jesus accused these sellers and moneychangers of being robbers. He was also making the point that Amos the prophet had made eight centuries earlier: Offering sacrifices was not as important as worshiping God and being fair to people (see Amos 5.21-24). The chief priests and other temple officials, as well as their families, made money from the activity of selling and buying at the temple, so they didn't like it when Jesus attacked this system.

Moses was born in Egypt to Hebrew parents but later was adopted by the Egyptian king's daughter (Exod 2.1-10). Growing up in Egypt, Moses saw how cruelly the Egyptians treated the Hebrew people. One day Moses killed an Egyptian guard and escaped to the land of Midian, where the LORD told him to go back to Egypt to free the Hebrew people from slavery (Exod 3.1—4.17). He did return to Egypt and warned Egypt's king that the LORD would send disasters on Egypt unless the king let the Hebrew people go free. Eventually, Moses led the people out of Egypt and through the Red Sea (Exod 5–15).

Moses was a great leader and a miracle-worker (Exod 15.22-25), but he had many other roles as well. He was the great "law-giver," chosen by the LORD to receive the Ten Commandments and other laws that were to guide the lives and worship of the Israelite people. These laws are described in detail in the books of EXODUS (20–40), LEVITICUS, NUMBERS, and DEUTERONOMY. Moses is also described as a prophet (Deut 34.10; 12.7), who preached God's words of judgment and promise to the people (Deut 7.12-15).

Though Moses is not called a "priest," the LORD gave to him the directions for building Israel's sacred tent and the rules that were to govern Israel's worship and sacrifices. He also prayed to the LORD on behalf of the whole people (Num 14.11-20) and went to the sacred tent to meet the LORD (Exod 33.7-11).

Moses also decided legal cases, and he appointed judges to help him make decisions on the basis of God's laws (Exod 18.13-26). Moses acted as a military leader when Israel had to battle unfriendly people on their way to the promised land of Canaan (Num 21.21-35).

The LORD did not allow Moses to lead the people of Israel into the promised land (Num 20.12; Deut 3.23-29), but Moses was able to look across the Jordan Valley from Mt. Nebo and see the land that was to become the land of Israel (Deut 32.48-52).

The New Testament primarily refers to Moses' role as "law-giver" (Matt 19.7; John 1.17; 2 Cor 3.7-14), but he is also described as an example of faith (Heb 3.2; 11.23-28) and as a prophet (Acts 3.22,23).

Of the many words used to name God in the Bible, the following are especially important. The most common is the general noun *Elohim*, usually translated as "God" when it refers to the God of Israel, or "gods" when it refers to other gods. This name is related to *El*, the Semitic word for god that appears in many ancient languages. *El* is frequently used with other terms, creating various names such as: *El Shaddai* (God All-Powerful), *El Elyon* (God Most High), *El Olam* (Eternal God), and *El Berith* (God of the Agreement).

The most important word for God in the Old Testament is *Yahweh*. In English Bibles it usually appears as "the LORD." But this is not a translation. *Yahweh* is God's personal name that God made known to Moses by the burning bush (Exod 3.13-15).

Unlike the other names for God, "The LORD All-Powerful" is a title. In 1 Samuel 1.3 it is the name used in the worship of God at Shiloh. It is commonly used in the books of the prophets. Literally, the Hebrew phrase means "The LORD of Hosts," though it is unclear whether the "hosts" are the armies of Israel, or the sun, moon, and stars, or the angels and heavenly forces that are ready to obey God.

NUMBERS IN THE BIBLE

Certain numbers had special meanings in the ancient world and to the writers of the Bible. This chart gives some key examples. Keep in mind, however, that sometimes these numbers represent actual quantities and are not intended to be understood symbolically.

ONE	**Monotheism, uniqueness, and unity.** "The LORD our God is the only true God!" *Deut 6.4* "We have only one LORD, one faith, and one baptism." *Eph 4*
THREE	**Completeness or totality. Many ancient religions considered three a divine number.** Three men who visited Abraham at Mamre *Gen 18.1-15* Three annual pilgrimage festivals (Thin Bread, Harvest, Shelters) *Exod 23.14-19* Number of days and nights Jonah was inside the big fish *Jonah 1.17* Number of days between Jesus' death and resurrection *Mark 8.31; 1 Cor 15.4*
FOUR	**Totality of the created world. Most cultures speak of four winds or directions, and divide the year into four seasons.** Number of rivers flowing out of the garden of Eden *Gen 2.10* Four living creatures of Ezekiel's vision *Ezek 1.4-28 (see also Rev 4.1-8)* Four horses and riders of John's vision *Rev 6.1-8*
SEVEN	**Completeness and perfection. Like three it was considered a sacred number to many cultures in the ancient world.** Number of days in the week based on Creation story *Gen 1.1—2.3* The "seventh" day is a holy day of rest (Sabbath) *Exod 20.8-11* The Israelites were to let the land rest every "seventh" year (sabbatical year) *Exod 23.10,11* Every fiftieth year (7 X 7 + 1) the Israelites were to celebrate a Year of Celebration (Jubilee) to mark a time of freedom and forgiveness *Lev 25.8-55* Temple furnishings and decorations were often arranged in seven parts *1 Kgs 7.17; Ezek 40.22, 26* Number of times blood is to be sprinkled during sacrificial ceremonies *Lev 4.6,17; 14.7; Num 19.4* Number of several items mentioned in REVELATION (lampstands, stars, churches, seals, trumpets, bowls) *Rev 6–11; 15; 16* Number of times Jesus said to forgive (seventy-seven or seven times seventy) *Matt 18.21,22*
TEN	**Because ten is the sum of three and seven it sometimes represents complete perfection.** The number of times "God said" is repeated in the Hebrew text of the Creation story *Gen 1.1-31* The Ten Commandments *Exod 20.1-17; Deut 5.1-22*
TWELVE	**Also a number of completeness and perfection.** Number of Jacob's sons, and the number of tribes of Israel *Gen 35.23-26; 49. 1-28* Number of gates to Jerusalem in Ezekiel's vision *Ezek 48.30 (see also Rev 21.11-21)* Number of Jesus' apostles *Matt 10.1-4; Mark 3.13-19; Luke 6.12-16; see also Acts 1.12-26*
FORTY	**A long, but limited period of time.** Number of days it rained during the Great Flood *Gen 7.4,17,18* Number of days Moses stayed on Mount Sinai *Exod 24.17,18* Number of years the Israelites wandered in the desert *Num 14.33, 34; Deut 2.7; 29.4-6* Number of days Jesus went without eating in the desert *Matt 4.2; Mark 1.12,13; Luke 4.2* Number of years David and other favored kings ruled *2 Sam 5.4; 1 Kgs 11.41, 42; 2 Chr 24.1*

The Hebrew word for "paradise" was borrowed from a Persian word which means a wooded park where everything is peaceful and beautiful. The people of Israel began to use this borrowed word some time after their return from their exile in Babylon. In Nehemiah 2.8, it is used for the king's forest, and in Song of Songs 4.13 and Ecclesiastes 2.5 it is a well-watered orchard or garden. Some of Israel's prophets had begun to say that the faithful who died would live again after dying (Dan 12.2,3; Isa 26.19), and the term "paradise" eventually was used as the place where they would live after death. For some, "paradise" was thought of as being on the earth or in heaven. For others, it was a new Garden of Eden where the tree of life (see Gen 2.9) would grow forever. Still others believed paradise was where the faithful who had died would wait for the day of judgment.

A similar understanding of paradise can be found in various places in the New Testament. Jesus, for instance, promised the man who was crucified beside him that he would be with him in paradise that day (Luke 23.39-43). Another reference by Jesus to paradise can be inferred from the parable he told about a poor man, Lazarus, and a rich man. When the poor man in this story dies he is described as being taken to a place of honor next to Abraham (Luke 16.19-22).

Paul teaches in 2 Corinthians 12.1-4 that when God was giving him a special message, he was taken up to heaven. Paul was not sad at the prospect of dying, since he would return to be with Christ (Phil 1.23). In REVELATION, paradise is where the tree of life is (2.7; 22.1-5), and where God's people will be gathered when the powers of evil have been defeated, and God's rule has taken over the whole of the creation. In this new paradise, God's people will share in the fruits of the tree of life (Rev 22.14). See also the mini-article called "Heaven," p. 167.

PONTIUS PILATE

Pontius Pilate was governor (prefect) of Judea from A.D. 26 to 36, during the time that Tiberius was the Roman emperor (A.D. 14-37) and Herod Antipas was governor (tetrarch) of Galilee (4 B.C. to A.D. 39). The Roman historian, Tacitus, tells in his *Annals* that Jesus was put to death by Pilate during the reign of Tiberius. An Egyptian Jewish scholar and leader told a later emperor (Gaius, A.D. 37-41) that Pilate had made the Jerusalem Jews angry by displaying metal shields that pictured the emperor as though he were a god at his palace in Jerusalem (next to the temple). Josephus, the Jewish historian, tells about the strong Jewish objection that was raised when Pilate brought into Jerusalem fancy poles that pictured the emperor as a god, and when he took funds from the temple treasury to pay for an aqueduct he was building to bring water into Jerusalem.

In the New Testament, Pilate is mentioned several times (Acts 3.13; 4.27; 13.28; and 1 Tim 6.13), but he is most important in the Gospel accounts of Jesus' trial and execution (see Mark 15.1-15; Matt 27.1-26). When the crowd demanded that Jesus be crucified, Pilate washed his hands in public to show he did not intend to take the blame for Jesus' death. Luke brings Herod Antipas into the story as the one who advises Pilate not to put Jesus to death. Still, Pilate gives in to the demands of the crowd (Luke 23.1-25).

If Jesus had been put to death for breaking the Jewish law, his execution would have been done under Jewish authority by crushing him to death with stones. This was the form of punishment commanded in the Law of Moses and that was used to kill the church's "first martyr" Stephen (Acts 7.54-60; Deut 13.9,10; 21.18-20). But Pilate had him put to death by the Roman method of execution called crucifixion. And the sign he had put over Jesus' cross said that Jesus wanted to be the political ruler of the Jews (Matt 27.37; Mark 15.38; John 19.19).

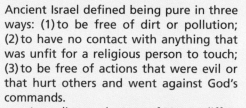

Ancient Israel defined being pure in three ways: (1) to be free of dirt or pollution; (2) to have no contact with anything that was unfit for a religious person to touch; (3) to be free of actions that were evil or that hurt others and went against God's commands.

According to the Law of Moses, different things could be clean or unclean (pure or impure). People could become unclean if they had certain kinds of diseases, when they touched a dead body, or when they ate certain kinds of food like pork or certain kinds of fish. The Law told the people what to avoid so they wouldn't become unclean (see especially Lev 11–18). It also told them how they could become clean again by waiting for a period of time and then being washed and making the right kind of sacrifice.

God's priests also showed the people how to take care of who or what was unclean. Other people who lived in the ancient Near East believed that evil powers or spirits lived in certain kinds of animals and plants. Such beliefs may have had some influence on what the Israelites thought was unclean. Some of the nations that lived around them thought other animals, such as pigs, were holy or sacred. The Law of Moses told the Israelites not to eat or touch such animals.

Ordinary human experiences like sexual relations (1 Sam 21.4; Exod 19.4-15), birth (Lev 12), and death (Num 6.6) were believed to involve impure powers or forces. So, for example, anyone who made contact with a dead body was impure and had to be made clean.

Once a year on the Great Day of Forgiveness all of the people were made pure. On this day, an animal was killed and its blood was sprinkled in the Most Holy Place of the tabernacle or temple. This was an offering to God as a sacrifice for the sins of the people. Another animal (a scapegoat) was driven out into the desert and carried Israel's sins away (see Lev 16; 23.26-32; Num 29.7-11). See the charts called "Jewish Calendar and Festivals," p. 114.

The early Christians understood that the sacrifice that made the people pure and clean was the death of Jesus Christ (Mark 10.45). Jesus' blood was poured out for the forgiveness of sins (Matt 26.28), and it cleanses his people from all sin (1 John 1.7). The death of Jesus, they affirmed, makes it possible for his followers to be with God, and it makes their hearts and minds pure (Heb 10.19-22).

When people in ancient Israel died and were buried, it was believed that their souls went down and stayed in the dark underworld called "Sheol" or "Hades." Later, when the people of Judah were in exile in Babylon about 600 years before Jesus was born, some prophets announced the idea of someone coming back to life after being dead. This was an important belief that helped God's people look forward to the future with hope (Isa 26.19; Ezek 37). The prophet Daniel declared that the people of God will be raised from the dead. The wicked will be punished, but those who have obeyed God will awaken to everlasting life (Dan 12.2,3).

Other cultures in the ancient world had similar, but not identical, ideas about what happens to people after they die. Many Greeks, for instance, believed in the immortality of the soul, meaning that the soul would continue to exist even after the body died. But resurrection as it is often described in the New Testament is different because a person's whole being, including the body, is raised to life.

The disciples who saw Jesus after he had risen from death believed that God had accepted Jesus' death as a sacrifice for human sins. Mark reports that the disciples are told they would see Jesus (Mark 16.8), but the other Gospels report that the disciples actually did see him (Matt 28; Luke 24; John 20,21). Paul describes how he met Christ risen from the dead, just as Peter and many others had (1 Cor 15.3-8). Adam's disobedience was the model for all human beings until Christ came. Now all God's people can be sure of life beyond the grave, since Christ continued to obey God even when it led to his being put to death (Phil 2.8). So, he was raised from death (Phil 2.10) and became the first of a whole new family of God (1 Cor 15.20-24) who would be raised from death.

Even though Jesus had told his followers that God would raise him from the dead, they did not believe him until he met them as the risen Christ and Lord. They were given his promise that they would always live with him (John 14.19,20) and that they would be accepted by God (Eph 2.5,6). The new family of God (Col 1.18) has confidence that sin and death will be completely overcome and that even now they are being changed by God and given new life (2 Cor 3.18; Phil 3.21). The climax will come when Christ comes back again as the one who defeats death and the powers of evil (1 Cor 15.23,24; 1 Thes 4.14). Christ's people will join with him in ruling over a brand new creation (Rev 20.4).

In the Old Testament, Satan (the "Accuser") is described as: (1) a trouble-maker who causes King David to count the people of Israel, a secret that was supposed to be known only to God (1 Chr 21.1,2,16,17); (2) the one who is allowed to cause suffering for Job (Job 1.6—2.7); and (3) the one who accuses God's chosen servant, Joshua the high priest (Zech 3.1, 2). The snake who convinces Adam and Eve to eat the fruit that God warned them not to eat (Gen 3) is sometimes called Satan, but this name is not used in that story.

In 538 B.C., the Persians defeated the Babylonians and allowed the Jewish people who had been living in exile in Babylon to return to their own land. During this time and for another two hundred years or so, the people of Israel were greatly influenced by Persian culture, government, and religion. The Persian religion told of a being who was God's chief opponent (Satan), and who had creatures like the angels who helped him work out his evil schemes. It is possible that JOB was written during this "Persian" period, or even later.

In the Greek translation of the Jewish Bible, this enemy of God was called the Devil, from the word *diabolos*, which means "accuser." During the two hundred years before Jesus was born, Satan (the devil) became known more and more as the force of evil that opposed God. In the Bible, the battle between God and Satan is fought in human history and will end when God defeats the powers of evil.

In Jesus' time, the powers of evil were known as the Kingdom of Satan. The New Testament describes Jesus as the one who came to turn people "from darkness to light and from the power of Satan to God" (Acts 26.18). The Gospels describe how Jesus struggled against Satan's temptations (Mark 1.12,13; Luke 4.1-13) and drove out Satan's demons who harmed human beings (Mark 1.21-28,32-39; 5.1-13; 7.24-30). Some people accused Jesus of working for Beelzebub, another name for Satan (Mark 3.22-26). But Jesus said that his power to defeat Satan came from God and that his victory over Satan was an example of God's kingdom at work (Luke 11.18-20).

The apostle Paul believed that Satan tried to keep him from preaching the Good News about Jesus (2 Cor 12.7; 1 Thes 2.18). He also said that Satan sometimes makes himself look like an "angel of light" in order to trick God's followers (2 Cor 11.14,15). But Paul was sure that God would crush Satan (Rom 16.20). Revelation 20 describes the final battle between God and Satan, which will end with the devil being thrown into a lake of fire (Rev 20.10).

SCROLLS

In ancient times, writing was done on scrolls made of leather or papyrus. The papyrus plant, which grew in Egypt, provided the material for scrolls as early as 3000 B.C. Making scrolls involved a series of steps: (1) Strips were cut from the center of the papyrus plant's stalk, (2) soaked in water to soften them, (3) and laid in crisscrossed rows. (4) The sheets were pounded with a mallet to break down the fibers and force them to join together and then (5) rubbed smooth with shells. When the sheets were dry, they could be written on. Black ink made from carbon soot mixed with water and tree sap was applied with pens made from reeds. Errors in writing could be erased with water.

Papyrus scrolls are rare because moisture causes them to decay. Most surviving papyrus scrolls were discovered in dry, desert-like climates.

Leather scrolls were also used, and they eventually replaced papyrus as the preferred writing material. Leather scrolls were made from sheep, goat, or calf skins that had been scraped to remove the hair, stretched, and dried on a frame. Writing was done on the side where the hair had been removed. Texts written on leather could not be erased. Separate leather sheets were stitched together to make a long scroll. The Scroll of Isaiah, found at Qumran by the Dead Sea, measures twenty-four feet long. It is made of seventeen sheets of sheepskin joined by linen thread.

Sin is pictured in GENESIS as beginning with Adam and Eve, who disobeyed God by eating fruit from the tree of the knowledge of good and evil (Gen 3.9). The Jewish Scriptures, which Christians call the Old Testament, describe sin in a number of ways:

1. Sin is breaking the Law of Moses and failing to live as God intended (Exod 20.20; 32.31-34), or turning one's back on God to follow other gods (Ezek 44.10).

2. Sin is defying God or rebelling against God (Jer 2.22-24,29-37), with the result that a right relationship with God is broken.

3. Sins are acts of violence against others (Gen 6.10-12), or ways of secretly hurting or harming others (Ps 64.1-6).

4. Sin occurs when the people do not follow the Law of Moses by failing to offer correct sacrifices. This makes them unfit to come into God's presence (Lev 4–5; Num 5.1-4).

5. Sinful people are proud of the wrongs they have done (Isa 2.12). The prophets understood this pride to come out of an evil human heart (Jer 17.9-11).

6. Sin is not living up to or reflecting God's glory. Humans are to reflect God's glory, since they were created in God's image (Gen 1.27; Ps 8.3-8). Sinful people do not live by the Law or love others as God desires. This is why Paul says in Rom 3.23 that, "All of us have sinned and fallen short of God's glory."

7. The sin of one person can have consequences for many others. For example, when the head of a family did wrong, all members were considered guilty (Josh 7; Deut 22.21,22). God was expected to punish the wicked, and the final punishment was to be death (Gen 2.17; Exod 21.15-17; Lev 24.10-17).

In contrast to this understanding, the New Testament brings a new message. All people are descendants of Adam and are inheritors of sin that leads to death. But Jesus brings new life because he brings forgiveness. This new life includes being raised to life from the dead (1 Cor 15.22,23). God used Jesus' death to take away the power of sin (Rom 3.9) by having Jesus suffer the guilt for the sins of everyone (1 Cor 15.3; 2 Cor 5.21). He was sacrificed in order to forgive sins (Rom 3.25,26; Heb 2.17; 9.25-28). Jesus paid the penalty for our sins, and God has a new agreement with people, which includes eternal life (Rom 6.23). Instead of continuing as slaves to sin, God's new people are now slaves to God (Rom 6.20-22).

Solomon, the tenth son of David and the second son of Bathsheba, became the third king of Israel in 970 B.C. and reigned for forty years. Though his path to the throne was marked by the murder of his political rivals (1 Kgs 2.25,34,46), Solomon's kingship was regarded as Israel's "Golden Age." It was a time of peace, prosperity, and great cultural achievements. The name "Solomon" in Hebrew means "peaceful." Only one military campaign is recorded during his time (2 Chr 8.3). The long period of peace during Solomon's reign caused great unity in Israel and loyalty to the throne. It also provided the time and wealth needed for Solomon's most important project, the construction of the Jerusalem temple. It was built from the materials generously provided by David (1 Chr 22) and, like the sacred tent before it, the temple symbolized God's continuing presence with his people.

Solomon earned large amounts of tax money by controlling major trade routes than went through Israel (1 Kgs 9.26-28; 10.14,15). Even so, he was always in debt because of his many other building projects (1 Kgs 7.1-12). His financial problems forced him to give up territory (1 Kgs 9.11,12), to charge the people heavy taxes, and to make many people work in his projects without pay (1 Kgs 4.1-6). Unrest grew throughout the empire. While the taxes continued to be paid during his lifetime (1 Kgs 4.21), many places, such as the countries of Edom and Damascus, became increasingly independent (1 Kgs 11.14,23-25).

More serious was Solomon's spiritual failure, which was due, in part, to the influence of his many non-Israelite wives, who worshiped foreign gods (1 Kgs 11.1-9). God was prompted to say, "You did what you wanted and not what I told you to do. Now I'm going to take your kingdom from you and give it to one of your officials" (1 Kgs 11.11). When Solomon died, his son Reheboam became king. He could not keep the northern tribes from breaking away and forming their own nation. The descendants of David and Solomon continued to rule over the two southernmost tribes, which became known as the nation of Judah. That way, David would always have a descendant ruling in Jerusalem (1 Kgs 11.12,13,34-36).

Many passages in the Jewish Scriptures, which Christians call the Old Testament, describe the people of Israel as God's son or child (Exod 4.22,23; Jer 31.19,20; Hos 11.1), but the title "son of God" is given to an unnamed king of Israel (Ps 2.7). God said that King David is "my first-born son, and he will be the ruler of all kings on earth" (Ps 89.27). David is also told that one of his children would be God's son (2 Sam 7.14). The later prophets spoke of the faithful members of the people of Israel as God's children (Isa 43.6; Hos 1.10).

Only in later Jewish writings is the Messiah spoken of as Son of God (*Enoch* 105.2; *2 Esdras* 7.28,29). For more about these books, which are included in some Bibles, see the article called "What Books Belong in the Bible?" p. 7.

In the Gospels, Jesus is the only true Son of God, as is declared by the voice from heaven at his baptism (Mark 1.11). The religious leaders who wanted to have him put to death asked him if he was the Son of God, and he said that he was (Mark 14.61, 62). The devil recognizes Jesus as the Son of God (Luke 4.1-12), and the demons that he brought under control do so as well (Mark 3.11; 5.7).

Most important is the direct claim of Jesus in Luke 10.21,22 to be the Son of God who has been given God's wisdom, which he shares with those who trust him as one sent by God. Before Jesus was born, he was identified by the angel as the Son of God (Luke 1.32-35). Matthew 2.15 quotes Hosea 11.1, which speaks of God bringing his Son back from Egypt. Paul wrote that Jesus is by human birth the son of David, but he is now the Son of God, because God raised him from the dead (Rom 1.3,4). John wrote that Jesus is the Son of God (1.12-14) who was sent by God into the world to save his people from their sins (3.16,17). He does God's work in the world (10.34-36) and is one with God (17.1,22).

In the Jewish Scriptures, (Old Testament) the expression "Son of Man" often refers simply to a human being. This is clear from EZEKIEL where the LORD's prophet is called "son of man" nearly one hundred times. In this way, the LORD reminded Ezekiel that he was a mere human being, and that he must accept God's power and purpose in the world.

The prophet Daniel also uses the expression, but with a slightly different meaning. He says he saw what "looked like a son of man coming with the clouds of heaven" (Dan 7.13). Here "son of man" refers to a savior—the person God will choose to rule over all the world and its people. Like this son of man, Jesus comes as God's chosen one (Messiah).

In the Gospels, Jesus speaks of himself as the Son of Man. Sometimes he uses the term to express his humanity (Matt 8.20) or to emphasize his role as the one who will suffer and die to forgive sins (Mark 8.31; 9.31; 10.45). But this expression is used as well when referring to Jesus' future glory, when God's people will be gathered together and God's kingdom (rule) will be set up (Mark 8.38—9.1). People will see the Son of Man sitting at the right side of God All-Powerful (Mark 14.62). Also, he will be seen returning to earth with great power and authority (Matt 24.30). Because of these passages from the Gospels, some scholars think Jesus was using the expression in the same way Daniel was.

People are called to decide and publicly acknowledge who the Son of Man is (Mark 8.27; Matt 16.13). Those who believe that he was sent by God to renew God's people and to bring all creation under God's control will be part of God's family. They will also be rewarded for what they have done (Matt 16.27, 28).

See also the mini-articles called "Son of God," p. 189 and "Messiah (Chosen One)," p. 176.

Synagogue comes directly from a Greek word that means "gathering." In the Bible, a synagogue is any group of people who meet together for worship. Just when the synagogue meetings began is not certain, but they may have begun after the Babylonians defeated Judah and took many of the Jewish people away in 586 B.C. While in Babylonia, the people could not worship or offer sacrifices to God at the temple in Jerusalem, so they were forced to find different ways to worship.

Later, the Jewish people began moving to other parts of the world, especially to Egypt, Greece, and areas known today as Turkey and southern Russia. They also began meeting together for worship, study, and to keep their group identity. These meetings were called synagogues. In their own land, Jews continued to have these meetings even when Seleucid kings tried to force them to worship Greek gods. One of these kings, Antiochus IV Epiphanes, who ruled Palestine from 175-164 B.C., claimed that he himself was a god, just as Alexander the Great had done years before him. Jewish priests from the family known as the Maccabees led a revolt against the Greek leader. They gained freedom for the Jews and ruled the land, but the actions of the Mac-cabean leaders later caused divisions among their own people. Some of the people were not content just to go to the temple for worship. They met in homes and public rooms to study the Scriptures and find the real meaning of their lives as God's people.

This was the situation during the lifetime of Jesus (Mark 1.21; 6.2) and the apostles (Acts 1.12-14; 9.2-20; 13.5). The places where Jews met outside their own land became known as "places of prayer" (Acts 16.16). After the Roman military forces destroyed the Jerusalem temple in A.D. 70, the temple's priests no longer had a place to lead the people in worship of God. With the loss of the temple, synagogues became the most important feature of Jewish worship and community experience throughout the Mediterranean world. The Jewish people continued to meet in homes or public halls, as was the case when Paul was in Ephesus (Acts 19.8-10). It wasn't until the second and third centuries A.D. that houses were re-modeled or new meeting places were built to serve as formal settings for worshiping God. These meeting places were also called synagogues. The remains of many have been found in various parts of the land of Israel and throughout the countries that border the Mediterranean Sea.

Typical Residence in Palestine in the Time of Jesus. Most people in Jesus' day lived in simple one-room houses that sometimes included an area where animals were kept and fed. Roofs were flat and made of layers of branches packed with mud. Because the roofs were used for some kinds of gardening and as a place to sleep when it was hot, a first century house often had a set of stairs leading to the roof. It was probably easy for the friends of the crippled man to make a hole in the roof of the house where Jesus was teaching, and lower their friend inside, so he could be healed. (See Luke 5.17-26.)

In the Middle East wine is made from grapes that are picked late in the summer and then spread out on the ground for a while before they are pressed to get out the juice. The annual Festival of Shelters, which celebrated Israel's journey through the desert on their way to the promised land, took place in the early fall. It was at this time that grapes were gathered (Deut 16.13-15). Pits or vats were dug out of the rock or out of rocky ground. The pits were joined together in pairs, so that when the grapes were pressed in the upper pit, the juice would flow down into the lower pit. Workers squeezed the juice out of the grapes by walking back and forth on them in the pit (Isa 16.10). The juice was collected from the lower pit in clay jars or in bags made from animal skins. These containers had to have an opening to let out the gas that was created as the wine fermented (Job 32.19). Skins that had become old and stiff would often burst when new wine was stored in them (Matt 9.17).

Palestine and Syria produced large quantities of excellent wine. Even before the people of Israel settled in Canaan they knew the land was fertile. When Moses sent spies to inspect the land, they brought back a bunch of grapes so large it had to be carried on a pole (Num 13.21-27). Other reports of the things produced in Canaan often mention grain, olive oil, and wine (Gen 27.28; Deut 7.13; 18.4; 2 Kgs 18.32; Jer 31.12).

Since water was scarce in Palestine, people drank wine at both ordinary meals and banquets, and especially at wedding feasts (John 2.1-12). Wine was also used as medicine (Luke 10.34; 1 Tim 5.23). Jewish people visiting the temple brought wine with them (1 Sam 1.24) and drank it when they celebrated Passover.

Because wine and winemaking were so familiar to people in Israel and Judah, the Prophets could refer to them when trying to explain God's attitude toward the people. Joel, for instance, compares God's coming judgment of the wicked with the stomping of grapes (Joel 3.13). He also says wine is one of the good things God will give the people to bless them (Joel 3.19).

In the New Testament, wine is the symbol of Jesus' blood, which was poured out when he died in order to save people from their sins (Mark 14.23-25). Jesus compared the new life he brings to new wine put in fresh wine skins (Matt 9.17). And the writer of REVELATION uses the image of grapes being crushed in a pit to describe how God will judge the wicked (Rev 14.19,20).

According to Proverbs, "all wisdom comes from the Lord, and so do common sense and understanding. God gives helpful advice to everyone who obeys him" (Prov 2.6,7). These verses summarize two important understandings of wisdom found in the Jewish Scriptures, which Christians call Old Testament. First, true wisdom comes from God, and second, God's wisdom is based on the Law that God gave to Moses and the people at Mount Sinai (Exod 19–34). This wisdom based on God's law was what parents were to teach their children (Deut 5.16; 6.4-9).

The prophet Jeremiah warned that the people should not brag about their own wisdom or strength or wealth, but boast only that they worship God (Jer 9.23,24). Jeremiah goes on to say that the wisdom God used to create the world will win out over the schemes of those who rely on their own wisdom and follow other gods (Jer 10.1-15).

Over the centuries God gave special wisdom to certain people. Chief among these was Solomon, who asked God for wisdom (1 Kgs 3.1-15; 10.1-10). Solomon's wisdom included legal wisdom, understanding of how people should treat one another, and knowledge about animals and plants. Many wise sayings in Proverbs, have traditionally been said to have been written by Solomon (Prov 1.1).

The book of Job mixes wise sayings about human behavior and God's will for his people with a story of the man who remained faithful to God in spite of difficulties and sufferings. Ecclesiastes also includes many wisdom sayings, as do the wisdom writings included in the Old Testament Deuterocanon/Apocrypha (see the article called "What Books Belong in the Bible," p. 7). These writings, used by some Jews and Christians, are the Wisdom of Solomon, which was written in Greek and uses Greek philosophical terms, and Sirach (also called Ecclesiasticus), which views the Law of Moses as the symbol and basis of all wisdom. In the book of Baruch wisdom is identified wholly with the Law of Moses as God's special gift to Israel (Bar 3.27—4.4).

In the New Testament, Jesus is described as one whose wisdom is greater than that of Solomon (Matt 12.42). His wisdom is described as being so great that the people in his own hometown could not understand where he got it (Matt 13.54; Mark 6.2). The writer of Colossians says that Jesus is the key to God's mystery . . . and "wisdom and knowledge are hidden away in him" (Col 2.3). Paul contrasted human wisdom, which is often foolishness, with the wisdom of God (1 Cor 1.18—2.16). God's mysterious wisdom is that God sent Jesus to die on a cross to forgive sins and to save those who believed this message about Jesus. To those who don't believe, this message seems foolish. People who think this way are using the world's wisdom and not the wisdom God gives.

Growth of the Roman Empire, 27 B.C to A.D. 180

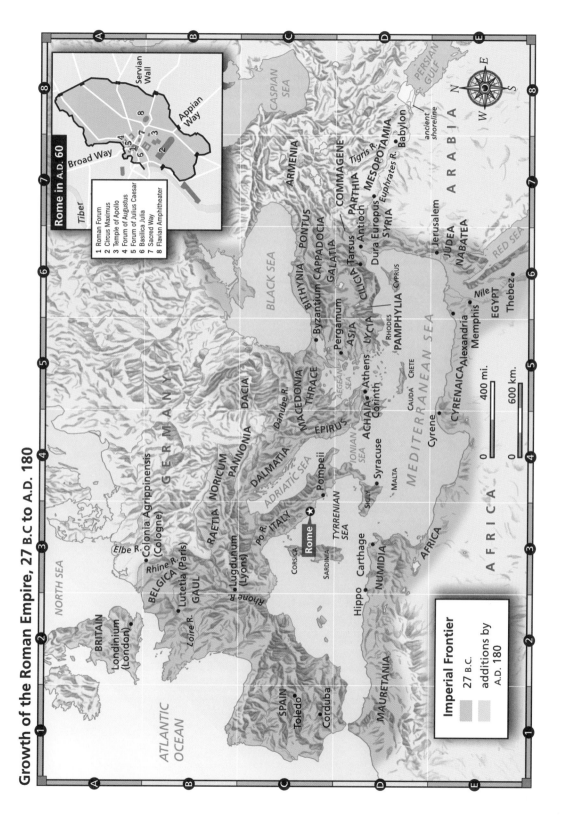

Rome in A.D. 60

1 Roman Forum
2 Circus Maximus
3 Temple of Apollo
4 Forum of Augustus
5 Forum of Julius Caesar
6 Basilica Julia
7 Sacred Way
8 Flavian Amphitheater

Tiber
Servian Wall
Appian Way
Broad Way

N E
W S

Imperial Frontier
27 B.C.
additions by A.D. 180

CASPIAN SEA
PERSIAN GULF
ancient shoreline
ARMENIA
COMMAGENE
Tigris R.
Babylon
PARTHIA
MESOPOTAMIA
Euphrates R.
ARABIA
Antioch
Dura Europos
SYRIA
Jerusalem
JUDEA
NABATEA
RED SEA
PONTUS
BITHYNIA
CAPPADOCIA
GALATIA
Tarsus
CILICIA
BLACK SEA
Byzantium
Pergamum
ASIA
LYCIA
RHODES
PAMPHYLIA
CYPRUS
Nile
Alexandria
Memphis
EGYPT
Thebez
CYRENAICA
Cyrene
MEDITERRANEAN SEA
AEGEAN SEA
Athens
ACHAIA
Corinth
CRETE
CAUDA
Syracuse
SICILY
MALTA
AFRICA
IONIAN SEA
THRACE
MACEDONIA
EPIRUS
DACIA
Danube R.
PANNONIA
NORICUM
DALMATIA
ADRIATIC SEA
Pompeii
RAETIA
Po R.
ITALY
Rome
TYRRHENIAN SEA
CORSICA
SARDINIA
Carthage
Hippo
NUMIDIA
AFRICA
GERMANY
Colonia Agrippinensis (Cologne)
Elbe R.
Rhine R.
BELGICA
Lutetia (Paris)
Lugdunum (Lyons)
GAUL
Loire R.
Rhone R.
NORTH SEA
BRITAIN
Londinium (London)
ATLANTIC OCEAN
SPAIN
Toledo
Corduba
MAURETANIA

0   400 mi.
0   600 km.

Palestine Under the Herods, 4 B.C to A.D. 44

HEROD'S KINGDOM

- Archelaus (4 B.C.-A.D. 6)
- Herod Antipas (4 B.C.-A.D. 39)
- Philip (4 B.C.-A.D. 34)
- Governor of Syria
- - - - Border of Herod the Great's Kingdom (4 B.C.)
- ═══ Roads
- ○ Decapolis city

Abila

ABILENE

Sidon

PHOENICIA

LEBANON MTS.

ITURAEA

SYRIA

Mt. Hermon

Damascus

Zarephath

Leontes R.

Tyre

Yarmuk R.

Caesarea Philippi

BATANEA

Hazor

Capernaum

AURANITIS

Ptolemais (Acco)

Lake Galilee

Raphana

Mt. Carmel

GALILEE

Hippos

Sepphoris

Tiberias

Dion

MEDITERRANEAN SEA

Nazareth

Mt. Tabor

Abila

Dor

Gadara

DECAPOLIS

Rabbah-Ammon

Scythopolis

Caravan Route

Caesarea

SAMARIA

Pella

Samaria

Gerasa

Sychar

Jabbok R.

King's Highway

Joppa

PEREA

Jordan R.

Philadelphia

Ephraim

Lydda

Jericho

Jabneel (Jamnia)

Jerusalem

Ashdod (Azotus)

Qumran

Bethlehem

Ascalon

JUDEA

Hebron

Gaza

Dead Sea

Arnon R.

IDUMEA

Raphia

Beersheba

NABATEA

modern shoreline

Zered R.

N
W E
S

0   30 mi.

0   40 km.

Palestine in the Time of Jesus, A.D. 6 to 30

Jesus in Galilee

Chorazin
Capernaum
Cana
Magadan
Lake Galilee
Tiberias
Hippos
Nazareth
Mt. Tabor
Yarmuk R.
Nain
Gadara
Jordan R.
Mt. Moreh

Sidon
Abila
ABILENE
PHOENICIA
LEBANON MTS.
SYRIA
Zarephath
Damascus
Mt. Hermon
ITURAEA
Tyre
Leontes R.
Caesarea Philippi
BATANEA
Ptolemais (Acco)
Capernaum
Area of Detail
Raphana
Mt. Carmel
GALILEE
Lake Galilee
Hippos
AURANITIS
Tiberias
Dion
MEDITERRANEAN SEA
Nazareth
Yarmuk R.
Gadara
Abila
Dor
Mt. Tabor
DECAPOLIS
Caesarea
SAMARIA
Scythopolis
Pella
Salim
Aenon
Samaria
Mt. Ebal
Gerasa
Mt. Gerizim
Sychar
Jabbok R.
Joppa
PEREA
Arimathea?
Lydda
Ephraim
Jabneel (Jamnia)
Philadelphia
Jericho
Emmaus
Jerusalem
Bethany
Ashdod (Azotus)
Bethlehem
Qumran
Ascalon
JUDEA
Hebron
Gaza
Dead Sea
Arnon R.
IDUMEA
Raphia
Beersheba
NABATEA
modern shoreline
0   30 mi.
0   40 km.
Zered R.

N
W   E
S

Jerusalem in the Time of Jesus, Around A.D. 30

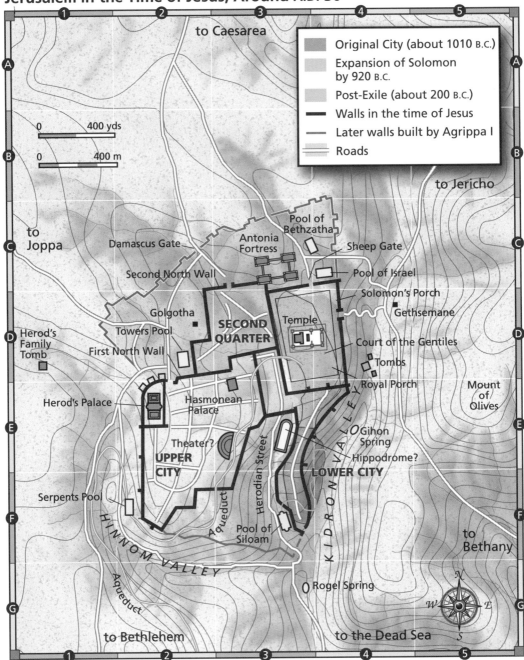

to Caesarea

Original City (about 1010 B.C.)

Expansion of Solomon by 920 B.C.

Post-Exile (about 200 B.C.)

Walls in the time of Jesus

Later walls built by Agrippa I

Roads

to Jericho

400 yds

400 m

to Joppa

Damascus Gate

Pool of Bethzatha

Antonia Fortress

Sheep Gate

Second North Wall

Pool of Israel

Solomon's Porch

Golgotha

Temple

Gethsemane

SECOND QUARTER

Towers Pool

Court of the Gentiles

Herod's Family Tomb

First North Wall

Tombs

Royal Porch

Mount of Olives

Herod's Palace

Hasmonean Palace

Theater?

Gihon Spring

UPPER CITY

Hippodrome?

Herodian Street

LOWER CITY

Serpents Pool

KIDRON VALLEY

HINNOM VALLEY

Aqueduct

Pool of Siloam

to Bethany

Aqueduct

Rogel Spring

N

W E

S

to Bethlehem

to the Dead Sea

World of the New Testament, Around A.D. 50

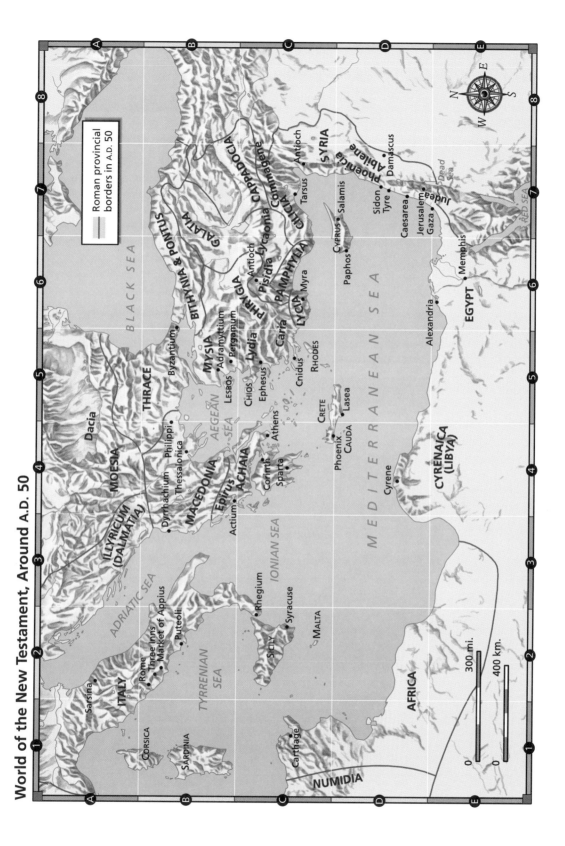

Roman provincial borders in A.D. 50

The Ancient Near East, 1800 to 1400 B.C.

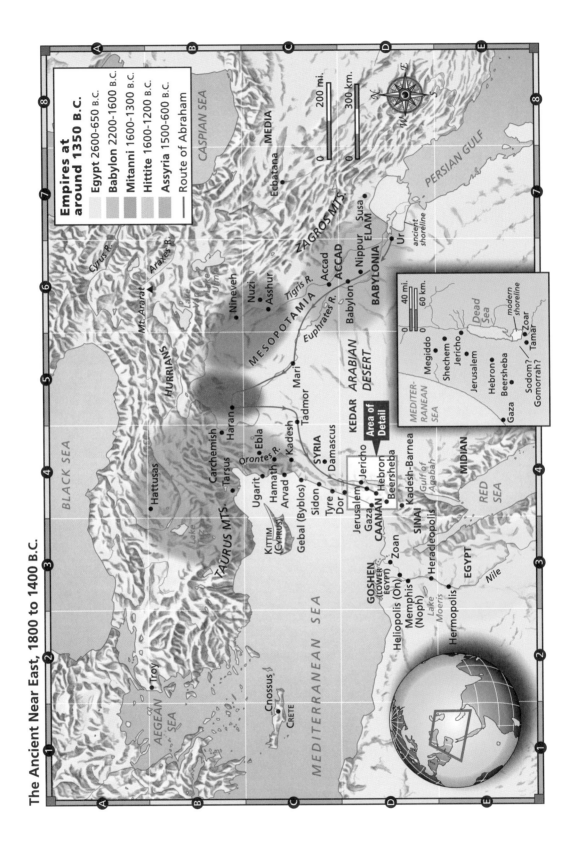

Empires at around 1350 B.C.

- Egypt 2600-650 B.C.
- Babylon 2200-1600 B.C.
- Mitanni 1600-1300 B.C.
- Hittite 1600-1200 B.C.
- Assyria 1500-600 B.C.
- Route of Abraham

200 mi.

300 km.

CASPIAN SEA

MEDIA

Ecbatana

Cyrus R.

Araxes R.

Mt. Ararat

Lake Urmia

ZAGROS MTS.

Susa
ELAM
Nippur

Accad
ACCAD

Babylon
BABYLONIA

Ur
ancient shoreline

PERSIAN GULF

Nineveh
Nuzi
Asshur

Tigris R.

MESOPOTAMIA

Euphrates R.

HURRIANS

Mari

Tadmor

KEDAR

ARABIAN DESERT

Lake Van

Carchemish
Haran

Ebla
Kadesh
Orontes R.
Hamath
Arvad

SYRIA
Damascus

Jericho
Hebron
Beersheba

Area of Detail

Tarsus

TAURUS MTS.

Ugarit

Gebal (Byblos)

KITTIM (CYPRUS)

Sidon
Tyre
Dor

Jerusalem
Gaza
CANAAN

Kadesh-Barnea

Gulf of Aqabah

MIDIAN

SINAI

RED SEA

Hattusas

BLACK SEA

Lake Tuz

Troy

Cnossus
CRETE

AEGEAN SEA

MEDITERRANEAN SEA

GOSHEN (LOWER EGYPT)

Zoan

Heliopolis (On)
Memphis (Noph)

Heracleopolis

Lake Moeris

Hermopolis

EGYPT

Nile

Area of Detail inset

40 mi.

60 km.

Dead Sea

modern shoreline

MEDITER-RANEAN SEA

Megiddo
Shechem
Jericho
Jerusalem
Hebron
Beersheba
Gaza

Sodom?
Gomorrah?

Zoar
Tamar

Egypt and Sinai, 1400 to 1200 B.C.

Legend:
- Traditional route of the Exodus
- Major trade routes

MEDITERRANEAN SEA

Lake Galilee

Jordan

Jericho
Mt. Nebo
Jerusalem
Hebron
Dibon
Gaza
DEAD SEA
Arad
Ar of Moab
Beersheba
Hormah
Zalmonah
MOAB

NILE DELTA

Lake Sirbonis
Baal-Zephon?

ZIN DESERT
Tophel
Baal-Zephon?
Rameses?
Etham
Migdol?
Egyptian Gorge
Kadesh-Barnea
EDOM
GOSHEN
Succoth
SHUR DESERT
Pithom?
Jotbathah
Bitter Lakes
SINAI
PENINSULA
ARABAH
Heliopolis (On)
Pi-Hahiroth?
Memphis (Noph)
EGYPT
Lake Moeris
PARAN DESERT
Marah
Ezion-Geber
(Elath)
Elim
SIN DESERT
Heracleopolis
Hazeroth
MIDIAN
Mt. Sinai
(Horeb)
(Gulf of Suez)
(Gulf of Aqabah)

0   100 mi.

0   150 km.

N
W   E
S

Akhetaton(Tell el-Amarna)

RED SEA

United Israelite Kingdom,
Israel in the Time of Kings Saul, David and Solomon, 1000 to 924 B.C.

Israelite Kingdom under King Saul

Lands conquered by King David

Kadesh

Orontes R.

SIDONIANS

LEBANON MTS.

BETH-REHOB

ARAMEANS
(SYRIA)

Gebal

*MEDITERRANEAN
SEA*

Sidon

Damascus

Tyre

Abel • Dan (Laish)

Hazor

MAACAH

Cabul

BASHAN

Yarmuk R. • Ashtaroth

Dor • Megiddo

GESHUR • Edrei

Taanach

Jezreel

• Ramoth

Jordan R.

Jabesh

Shechem

Jabbok R.

Gath-Rimmon

Zarethan

EASTERN
DESERT

Joppa •

Beth-
Horon

• Jazer

Gezer

Bethel

• Rabbah

Ashdod • Ekron

Jericho

AMMONITES

Ashkelon

Jerusalem

• Heshbon

Gaza

• Gath?

Dead Sea

• Medeba

PHILISTINES

Debir

Hebron

• Dibon

Gerar

Ziklag?

Arnon R. • Aroer

Beersheba

*modern
shoreline*

MOABITES

N

Egyptian Gorge

• Kir-Heres

W   E

AMALEKITES

Zered R.

S

Tamar

Kadesh-Barnea •

• Bozrah

SOUTHERN
DESERT

EDOMITES

ASIA

0   50 mi.

• Sela

Area of
Detail

0   75 km.

AFRICA

RED SEA • Ezion-Geber

*INDIAN
OCEAN*

Jerusalem in Old Testament Times,
The Growth of David's City, 960 to 44 B.C.

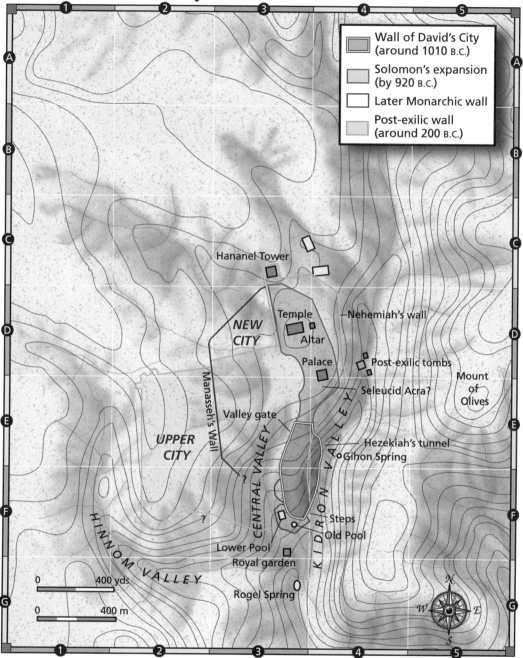

Wall of David's City
(around 1010 B.C.)

Solomon's expansion
(by 920 B.C.)

Later Monarchic wall

Post-exilic wall
(around 200 B.C.)

Hananel Tower

NEW
CITY

Temple

—Nehemiah's wall

Altar

Palace

Post-exilic tombs

Mount
of
Olives

Seleucid Acra?

Manasseh's Wall

Valley gate

UPPER
CITY

Hezekiah's tunnel

Gihon Spring

?

CENTRAL VALLEY

KIDRON VALLEY

?

Steps

Old Pool

Lower Pool

Royal garden

HINNOM VALLEY

0   400 yds

0   400 m

Rogel Spring

N
W   E
S

The Kingdoms of Israel and Judah, 924 to 722 B.C.

MEDITERRANEAN SEA

PHOENICIA

LEBANON MTS.

ARAM (SYRIA)

Sidon

Zarephath

Damascus

Mt. Hermon

Tyre

Leontes R.

Kedesh

Hazor

GALILEE

BASHAN

Lake Galilee

Mt. Carmel

Shunem

Yarmuk R.

Edrei

Megiddo

Jezreel

Ramoth

Mt. Gilboa

ISRAEL

GILEAD

Samaria

Shechem

Succoth

Penuel

Mahanaim

Jabbok R.

AMMON

Shiloh

Joppa

Rabbah

Bethel

Geba

Gilgal

Ekron

Jericho

Jerusalem

Jordan R.

Ashdod (Azotus)

Libnah

Heshbon

Ashkelon

Bethlehem

PHILISTIA

Gath?

Lachish

Hebron

Gaza

JUDAH

Dead Sea

Arnon R.

Besor Gorge

Gath?

Beersheba

modern shoreline

Kir-Hareseth

MOAB

0   30 mi.

EDOM

Zered R.

0   40 km.

N
W   E
S

Assyrian and Babylonian Kingdoms, 9th to 6th Centuries B.C.

Assyrian Kingdom about 824 B.C.

Assyrian Kingdom about 640 B.C.

Babylonian Kingdom about 550 B.C.

BLACK SEA

CASPIAN SEA

Cyrus R.

Abydos

MESHECH · Gordion

Sardis

URARTU

TUBAL · ARMENIA

Araxes R.

PHRYGIA · KUE

Miletus

LYCIA

Tarsus

Haran · Gozan

Arpad

Aleppo · Carchemish

ASSYRIA

Nineveh

CILICIA

CRETE · RHODES

CYPRUS · Arvad

Tadmor · Tiphsah

Asshur

Ecbatana

Sidon

Tyre

Damascus

KEDAR

Euphrates R.

Tigris R.

MEDIA

MEDITERRANEAN SEA

Hamath · Kedesh

Sippar

Samaria

Gaza

AMMON

Babylon

BABYLONIA

Susa

Jerusalem

MOAB

Erech

ELAM

Tahpanhes

Athribis

JUDAH

EDOM

Heliopolis

SINAI · Sela

ARABIAN DESERT

Ur

ancient shoreline

EGYPT · Memphis

Ezion-Geber

ARABIA

PERSIAN GULF

Hermopolis

LIBYAN DESERT

Siut

Nile

RED SEA

Abydos

Thebez

Syene

Major Powers 670-550 B.C.

Kingdom of Lydia 670-546 B.C.

Kingdom of the Medes 612-550 B.C.

Babylonian Kingdom 550 B.C.

MEDITERRANEAN SEA

Kingdom of Egypt 663-525 B.C.

N W E S

| 0 | | 400 mi. |
| 0 | | 600 km. |

Persian Kingdom, 550 to 330 B.C.

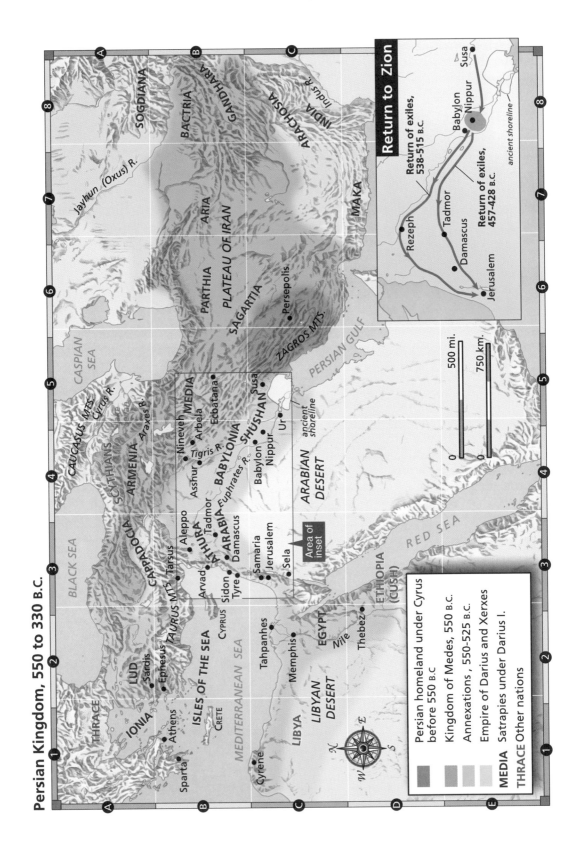

Return to Zion

Susa

Babylon
Nippur

Return of exiles,
538-515 B.C.

Tadmor

Damascus

Rezeph

Return of exiles,
457-428 B.C.

Jerusalem

ancient shoreline

SOGDIANA
BACTRIA
GANDHARA
ARACHOSIA
INDIA
Indus R.
MAKA

Jayhun (Oxus) R.

ARIA

PLATEAU OF IRAN

PARTHIA

SAGARTIA

Persepolis

ZAGROS MTS.

PERSIAN GULF

CASPIAN SEA

Cyrus R.
Araxes R.
CAUCASUS MTS.

ARMENIA
SCYTHIANS

MEDIA
Nineveh
Arbela
Ecbatana
Asshur
Tigris R.
BABYLONIA
SHUSHAN
Susa
Euphrates R.
Babylon
Nippur
Ur
ancient shoreline

ARABIAN DESERT

CAPPADOCIA
TAURUS MTS.
Tarsus
Aleppo
ATHURA
Tadmor
ARABIA
Arvad
Damascus
Sidon
Tyre
Samaria
Jerusalem
Sela

Area of inset

BLACK SEA

LUD
Sardis
Ephesus
IONIA
THRACE
Athens
Sparta
ISLES OF THE SEA
CRETE
CYPRUS
MEDITERRANEAN SEA

RED SEA

ETHIOPIA (CUSH)

Tahpanhes
Memphis
EGYPT
Nile
Thebez

LIBYAN DESERT

LIBYA

Cyrene

500 mi.

750 km.

0

0

Legend

Persian homeland under Cyrus before 550 B.C

Kingdom of Medes, 550 B.C.

Annexations , 550-525 B.C.

Empire of Darius and Xerxes

MEDIA   Satrapies under Darius I.

THRACE Other nations

Palestine in the Time of the Maccabees, 175 to 63 B.C.

Legend:
- Judea, 166 B.C.
- Conquests, 134 B.C.
- Total Maccabean conquests, 76 B.C.
- Major roads
- ○ Free city state

MEDITERRANEAN SEA

PHOENICIA
SYRIA
LEBANON MTS.

Sidon
Damascus
Mt. Hermon
Leontes R.
Tyre
Kedesh
Hazor
Seleucia
Baskama
Ptolemais (Acco)
Karnaim
GALILEE
Lake Galilee
Yarmuk R.
Mt. Carmel
Mt. Tabor
Gadara
Dor
Edrei
Beth-Shan (Scythopolis)
Ephron
GILEAD
SAMARIA
Gerasa
Apollonia
Samaria
Jabbok R.
AMMON
Joppa
King's Highway
Coastal Highway
Great Trunk Road
Jordan R.
Lydda
Ephraim
Berea
Philadelphia (Rabbah)
Modein
Mizpah
Tyrus
Jabneel (Jamnia)
Gezer
Beth-Horon
Ashdod (Azotus)
Emmaus
Jericho
Ekron
Jerusalem
Heshbon
JUDEA
Ashkelon
Beth Zechariah
Bethbasi
Medeba
PHILISTIA
Marisa
Hebron
Gaza
Beth-Zur
Dead Sea
NABATEA
IDUMEA
Masada
Arnon R.
Raphia
Beersheba
modern shoreline
Zered R.

0 30 mi.

0 40 km.

N W E S

Paul's First and Second Journeys

THRACE

BLACK SEA

MACEDONIA

Philippi

Apollonia
Thessalonica
Neapolis

Byzantium

BITHYNIA

Berea

SAMOTHRACE

MYSIA

ASIA

GALATIA

AEGEAN SEA

Troas

Pergamum
Thyatira

CAPPADOCIA

ACHAIA

Smyrna
Sardis

PHRYGIA

Antioch
Iconium

LYDIA

Corinth
Cenchreae
Athens

Ephesus
Colossae

Lystra

Tarsus

Miletus

Sparta

Perga
Attalia

PAMPHYLIA

Derbe

CILICIA

Seleucia

Cnidus

LYCIA

Antioch

Rhodes
RHODES

Patara Myra

CRETE

SYRIA

Phoenix

Salamis

CAUDA
Lasea
Fair Havens

CYPRUS

Paphos

MEDITERRANEAN SEA

Sidon
Tyre

PHOENICIA
ABILENE

Caesarea

Alexandria

Jerusalem

CYRENAICA

JUDEA

EGYPT

—— Paul's first journey
—— Paul's second journey
Roman provincial
boundaries

0   200 mi.

0   300 km.

RED
SEA

Paul's Third Journey and His Journey to Rome

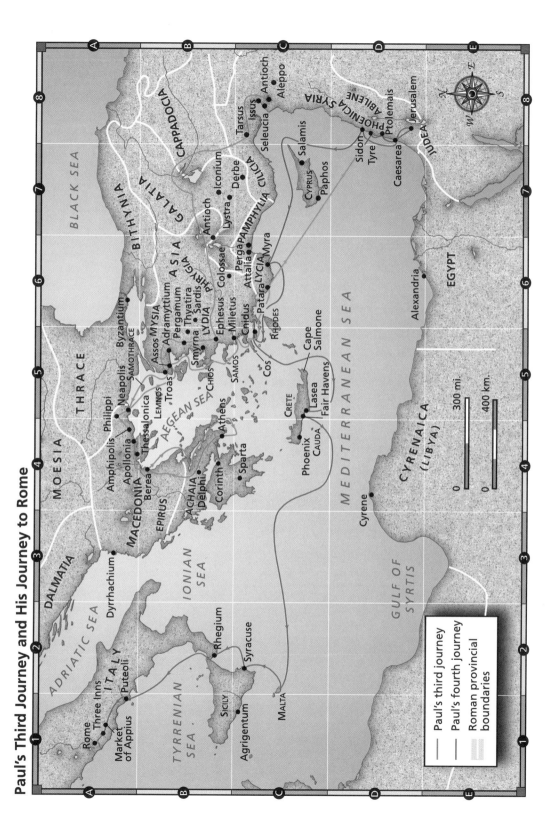

Legend:
- Paul's third journey
- Paul's fourth journey
- Roman provincial boundaries

Division of Canaan, 1200 to 1030 B.C.

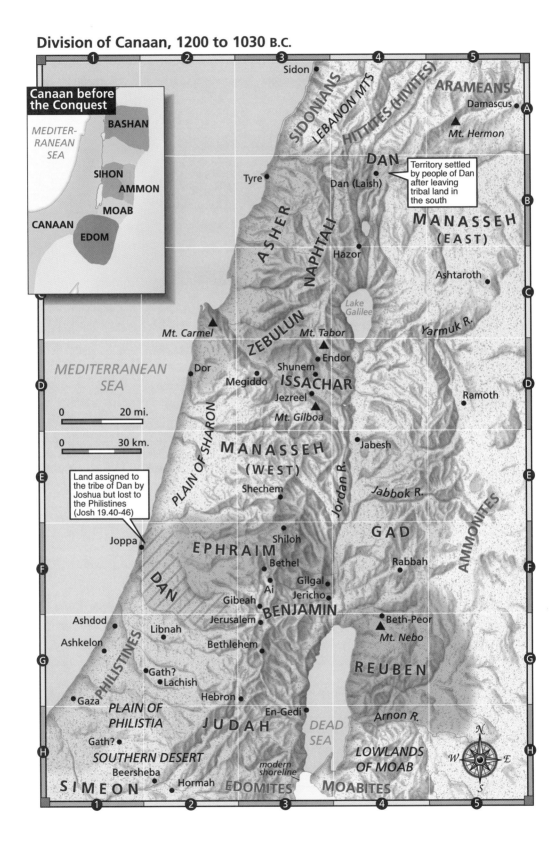

Canaan before the Conquest

MEDITER-
RANEAN
SEA

BASHAN

SIHON

AMMON

MOAB

CANAAN

EDOM

Sidon

SIDONIANS

LEBANON MTS

HITTITES (HIVITES)

ARAMEANS

Damascus

Mt. Hermon

DAN

Tyre

Dan (Laish)

Territory settled
by people of Dan
after leaving
tribal land in
the south

MANASSEH
(EAST)

ASHER

NAPHTALI

Hazor

Ashtaroth

Lake
Galilee

MEDITERRANEAN
SEA

Mt. Carmel

ZEBULUN

Mt. Tabor

Yarmuk R.

Dor

Shunem

Endor

Megiddo

ISSACHAR

Ramoth

Jezreel

Mt. Gilboa

0   20 mi.

0   30 km.

PLAIN OF SHARON

MANASSEH
(WEST)

Jabesh

Shechem

Jordan R.

Jabbok R.

Land assigned to
the tribe of Dan by
Joshua but lost to
the Philistines
(Josh 19.40-46)

GAD

AMMONITES

Joppa

Shiloh

EPHRAIM

Bethel

Rabbah

DAN

Ai

Gilgal

Gibeah

Jericho

Jerusalem

BENJAMIN

Beth-Peor

Mt. Nebo

Ashdod

Libnah

Bethlehem

REUBEN

Ashkelon

PHILISTINES

Gath?

Lachish

Gaza

Hebron

PLAIN OF
PHILISTIA

En-Gedi

Arnon R.

JUDAH

DEAD
SEA

LOWLANDS
OF MOAB

Gath?

N

SOUTHERN DESERT

W   E

Beersheba

modern
shoreline

S

SIMEON

Hormah

EDOMITES

MOABITES

210 • Maps

CREDITS

3, 4 Illustrations by Hal Just, © ABS. **5** *left* Ben Zvi Institute, Jerusalem. *center* The Scheide Library, Princeton, New Jersey. *right* Reproduced by courtesy of the Director and University Librarian, the John Rylands University Library of Manchester. **11** Corbis-Bettmann. **14** *Le Nouveau Testament,* 1664, Antoine Cellier, Charenton, France. From the collection of the American Bible Society. **15** Datafoto and Christian History Institute. **16** *New Testament: A Pictorial Archive from Nineteenth Century Sources,* edited by Don Rice, © 1986 by Dover Publications, Inc. **18** Engraving in John Foxe's *Acts and Monuments of Martyrs,* 1684 edition: image in public domain. From the collection of the American Bible Society **28** Giraudon/Art Resource, NY. **30** © David Harris, Jerusalem. **31** Erich Lessing/Art Resource, NY. **32, 35** Illustrations by Hal Just, © ABS. **37** Giraudon/Art Resource, NY. **39** Illustration by Hal Just, © ABS. **41** *center* Map by Joe LeMonier, © ABS. *top center* Illustration by Theresa Heidel, © ABS. *top right* © Sonia Halliday Photographs, photo by Jane Taylor. *bottom right, center* Illustrations by Theresa Heidel, © ABS. *far left* © Gil Yarom, Israel. *near left* Photographer: Shalom Zisso, The Israel Department of Antiquities, The Yigal Allon Museum. **42** Scala/Art Resource, NY. **44** Illustration by Hal Just, © ABS. **55** Illustration by Theresa Heidel, © ABS. **59** Illustration by Hal Just, © ABS. *top left photo inset* Collection of the Israel Antiquities Authority, courtesy of the G. Barkay, Ketef Hinnom Expedition. *top right photo inset* Photograph by Bencini Raffaello, Florence, Italy, © American Bible Society Archives. **62** Vincent Van Gogh, Stichting Kröller-Müller Museum. **67** Illustration by Theresa Heidel, © ABS. **70** Erich Lessing/Art Resource, NY. **75** Illustration by Gregor Goethals, © ABS. **76** Scala/Art Resource, NY. **79** Vanni/Art Resource, NY. **81** Photo copyright Julia Hedgecoe, from *Stories in Stone: The Medieval Roof Carvings of Norwich Cathedral,* Herbert Press, A & C Black, London; Thames & Hudson, N. Y. **95** Illustration by Hal Just, © ABS. *photo inset* The Jewish Museum, NY/Art Resource, NY. **98** By permission of the British Library, OR. 481, f. 104v. **99** Illustration by Hal Just, © ABS. **101** National Museum of American Art, Washington DC/Art Resource, NY. **103** *top* Schmidt-Rottluff, Karl, Way to Emmaus, 1918, Philadelphia Museum of Art: Given by Dr. George J. Roth. *right* Map by Collin Kellogg, © ABS. **112** Illustration by Laszlo Kubinyi, © ABS. **114, 115** Illustrations of scroll, stone tablets, ram's horn, candlesticks by Steve Morrell, © ABS. Illustration of barley by Gregor Goethals, © ABS. Illustration of loaves of bread by Theresa Heidel, © ABS. Illustration of priest with scapegoat by Hal Just, © ABS. Illustration of shelter by Kate McKeon, © ABS. **116** Scala/Art Resource, NY. **118** *top* © David Harris, Jerusalem. *bottom* Erich Lessing/Art Resource, NY. **121** Erich Lessing/Art Resource, NY. **122** Map by Collin Kellogg, © ABS. **124** The Granger Collection, New York. **125** Map by Collin Kellogg, © ABS. **126** Erich Lessing/Art Resource, NY. **127** *center* © John C. Trever. *bottom left* © The Israel Museum, Jerusalem. Photo: David Harris. *bottom right* © Jeff Greenberg/Visuals Unlimited. **130** Grec 139 f. 136v The Penitence of David, with David and Nathan, from a psalter, 10th century/Bibliothèque nationale de France/Bridgeman Art Library. **131** Woodcut print by Sally Barton Elliott, 1973. **133** Erich Lessing/Art Resource, NY. **135** © North Wind Picture Archives. **138, 139, 140** Illustrations by Hal Just, © ABS. **141** Illustration by Hal Just, © ABS. *top left photo inset* © Joyce Photographics, The National Audubon Society Collection/Photo Researchers, NY. *top right photo inset* © 1997 Richard T. Nowitz. **147** Erich Lessing/Art Resource, NY. **150** Statuette of the goddess Isis and the child Horus, Egyptian, Late Period (c. 664-332 BC) Louvre, Paris, France/Peter Willi/Bridgeman Art Library. **151** Erich Lessing/Art Resource, NY. **152** Vanni/Art Resource, NY. **195-210** Maps by Joe LeMonier, © ABS.